INDIAN LEGENDS FROM THE NORTHERN ROCKIES

THE CIVILIZATION OF THE AMERICAN INDIAN SERIES

INDIAN LEGENDS FROM THE NORTHERN ROCKIES

✽

by Ella E. Clark

UNIVERSITY OF OKLAHOMA PRESS : NORMAN AND LONDON

BY ELLA E. CLARK

Poetry: An Interpretation of Life (New York, 1935)
Indian Legends of the Pacific Northwest (Berkeley, 1953)
Indian Legends of Canada (Toronto, 1960)
Indian Legends from the Northern Rockies (Norman, 1966)

FRONTISPIECE: Blackfoot Medicine Pipe
Courtesy American Museum of Natural History

DEDICATED TO THE INDIANS OF THE NORTHWEST

LIBRARY OF CONGRESS CATALOG CARD NUMBER: 66–13421

ISBN: 0–8061–2087–8

Indian Legends from the Northern Rockies is Volume 82 in The
Civilization of the American Indian Series.

Contents

≈≈≈

Contents

Contents

Acknowledgments

LIKE ANTHOLOGIES in any literature, this one is the product of many minds and many hands. I am especially grateful to the Northwest Indians who told me their tribal traditions directly and gave me bits of information. Their names are given above their narratives and are also listed at the end of this book. Printed and manuscript sources are given briefly in the Source Notes and in detail in the Bibliography.

To the following I again express my appreciation:

To Pat Shea, of the United States Forest Service, the Flathead Reservation, for helping me make contacts with Indian informants and for relating the Kutenai story of "Chief Cliff."

To J. A. Harrington of Boise, Idaho, for six landscape legends which, because he knew the sign language, he recorded about forty years ago.

To Bon Whealdon, near Hot Springs, Montana, for twelve traditions that he recorded from his elderly Flathead-Kalispel neighbors between 1918 and 1924. In the 1930's, he was one of three people engaged by the Federal Writers' Projects of the Works Progress Administration to record Indian traditions on the Flathead Reservation. When the project was dropped early in 1942, all but five of the sixty-eight "stories" (some were factual) recorded by Mr. Whealdon were lost. I include the fact here with the slight hope that someone may be able to locate these irreplaceable manuscripts.

To the archivists and curators who have permitted me to use the manuscripts listed at the end of the book.

To Sven Liljeblad for the Bannock creation myth.

To the editors of these scholarly journals who have permitted me to reprint traditions I have published through them, as indicated in the bibliography: *Western Folklore; Montana: The Magazine of Western History; Northwest Review;* and the *Oregon Historical Quarterly.*

To archivists and librarians in twenty-four places who have helped me locate material. The following have been especially helpful: Margaret Blaker, Bureau of American Ethnology, Smithsonian Institution, Washington, D. C.; Eugenia Langford, library of the Department of Interior, Washington; Virginia Walton and Anne McDonnell, formerly of the Historical Society of Montana, Helena; Reta Ridings, formerly with the Wyoming State Archives and Historical Department, Cheyenne; Mary Avery, Margaret Hilty, and Trude Smith, Washington State University Library, Pullman; Annette Hurst, at the Museum of Man, and several librarians in the Central Library, both in San Diego, California.

Research for this study was financed in part by a grant from the Washington State University Research Fund. Also the University granted me a leave of absence for research.

Introduction

꒦꒰꒾

I N THIS VOLUME, the general reader of any age will find selections
from the oral literature of the Indians in the northern Rocky
Mountain region of the United States. Included are myths, legends, personal narratives, and historical traditions from the tribes
whose homes in historical times have been in the present states of
Idaho, Montana, and Wyoming. Although attention is focused on
these three states, the stories and the factual introductions to them
reveal much about the life of the Indians in a larger area—from the
Cascade Range of western Washington and Oregon to almost as far
east as the Mississippi River.

To readers who do not know the Northwest, the names of the Indian tribes represented in this volume will appear strange. But to
people who live or have lived in the region, the names will be familiar
because they have become the names of towns, counties, forests, mountains, rivers, and lakes. The tribes that have lived near the northern
Rockies since white men came to the region, according to John R.
Swanton of the Bureau of American Ethnology, are the Nez Percés,
Coeur d'Alênes, Flatheads, Kalispels (or Pend d'Oreilles), Kutenais,
Shoshonis, Bannocks, Arapahos, Gros Ventres, Blackfeet, Assiniboines, and Crows. Because the Sioux frequently came into Montana
and Wyoming to make war or to hunt buffalo, four of their landscape
legends are included.

The arrangement of the stories in this volume is linguistic, each
section representing one of the six languages spoken by the Indians
of the three states.

Approximately half of these narratives have never before appeared in print. Some of them I have recorded directly from the Indians themselves. The number of these is small, however, because my visits to reservations from 1950 through 1955 for this volume and for my *Indian Legends of the Pacific Northwest* introduced me to only an occasional Indian who was able to relate a few stories, except among the Nez Percés. Usually the storyteller was an old person eager to have his information recorded. By careful questioning I was often able to get him to recall a tradition that was different from the numerous culture-hero-transformer-trickster tales already published.

A larger number of previously unpublished stories have come from manuscripts in archives and personal collections. Most of these were recorded by pioneers at a time when Indians knew many more of their tribal traditions than they did in the 1950's. Some of these tales were precious stories told to neighbor-friends among the white people who the Indians knew would not ridicule their beliefs. A few of these whites spoke the language of their Indian neighbors; at least one conversed with them in the Chinook jargon, long used by white traders and Western Indians; another could understand and use their sign language as he sat on the ground in a circle of old Indian men and asked them for stories about the landscape features in the area.

Of the previously published traditions, more than half have been gleaned from scattered sources—a story here and a story there— almost all of them recorded in the nineteenth century. Fur-traders, explorers, army officers, pioneers, missionaries, even an adventurous young surveyor and photographer at the end of the century—each recorded one or several stories that interested him. These traditions would probably have been lost if they had not been appreciated by the white people before the days of the anthropologists.

The remaining tales in this anthology I have chosen from the collections made by specialists and published for specialists by universities, museums, learned societies, and the Bureau of Ethnology of the Smithsonian Institution. Ethnologists—that is, scholars studying the culture and the life history of a people—often include folk tales as part of their study. Here, mythology and ethnology overlap.

From these varied sources, published and unpublished, I have selected narratives that I consider suited to the purposes of this book: (1) to give pleasure to general readers of all ages, (2) to inform them about Indian beliefs and customs, and (3) to contribute to an appreciation of the first Americans. My second and third purposes have led me to include a number of myths explaining the origins of tribal ceremonies and of sacred objects. Here again, mythology and ethnology overlap.

This collection should not be considered entirely representative. Apparently, most of the tales the American Indians used to tell around their winter fires concerned their own particular culture-hero-transformer-trickster. Among the Indians of the northern Rockies these stories are paralleled in tribe after tribe, whether the main character is Coyote, Old Man, or Old Man Coyote. My many years of teaching English literature to general readers and of being sensitive to their reactions have taught me that they would soon find such tales monotonous and that they would want variety in Indian literature, too. Therefore, I have not included some of the Coyote tales that I recorded directly from Indians.

For other reasons, very few of the collections of Indian tales published by ethnologists are representative, or could be, of the traditions once related around the winter fires for the entertainment and instruction of the whole family group. Probably they were not intended to be representative. "I doubt that we ever consider whether the tales are representative or not," said an anthropologist, after hearing for the first time well-educated Indians' objections to the specialists' collections they had read. "We usually just say," he continued, " 'Tell us a story.' "

College-educated Indians (not typical of their race, to be sure) from the Quinault, the Mohawk, and the Chickasaw tribes have told me or written me that they had been shocked by the caliber of many of the stories published from their own and other tribes. Such tales were never related around their firesides in their youth and, in their opinion, give an unfair impression of the literature of their people.

An anthropologist sympathetic with their point of view explained very simply, "We recorded what was available at the time we could record. Now they tell us how much they resented our questions."

Most of the scientific study of the American Indians has been done by graduate students and college faculty members, necessarily during summer vacations. Until comparatively recent years, Indians believed that they should not tell their traditional tales in the summer. And the aged custodians of treasured myths would not share them with a stranger at any season. On a Northwest reservation I visited, middle-aged Indians told me that the elders of a certain bent and crippled old man had believed that he had become bent and crippled because of his interviews with a university student: he had, in 1930, given a stranger information about his people, and he had related tribal tales in the summer. My informants of 1950 and 1952 laughed as they told me, but they all remembered that they, too, had "once believed there was a law against telling the old stories in the summertime."

By the time Indian storytellers were willing to relate treasured traditions to a white stranger in the summer, it seems likely that many of them were lost. Walter McClintock, who came into the northern Rockies as a surveyor in 1896, lived with the Blackfeet most of the time for the next fourteen years. "It required, however, a long period of cordial relations to overcome a natural prejudice of the Indians against a white man," he said in a book published in 1910. And yet he had been adopted as a son by one of the chiefs and was made an adopted member of the tribe. He "gradually gained their confidence."

While he was recording all that he could learn about the customs and traditions of the Blackfeet, the younger members of the tribe "were indifferent to their ancient customs and religion." The valuable myths about the origin of religious ceremonies and sacred objects which McClintock recorded were related by the elders when the group was snowbound. Clark Wissler and D. C. Duvall, collecting for the American Museum of Natural History just prior to 1908, believed that the Blackfeet had no taboo against telling stories in the summer; McClintock wrote that they did. Some treasured myths were related to McClintock because he was a trusted friend "who would speak the truth about the Indians."

Again and again I have read from pioneers and missionaries on both sides of the Canadian border such statements as this one written by a missionary among the Blackfeet about 1890: "I have listened to some of these legends as told, over and over again, for the past nine years, and I find that the young men are not able to relate them as accurately as the aged; besides, as the country is becoming settled with white people, they are less disposed to tell to others their native religious ideas, lest they be laughed at. . . . As the children grow up, they are forgetting these things, and the years are not far distant when the folklore of the Blackfeet will be greatly changed and many of their traditions forgotten."

Finally, let me say a few words about my style in these Indian traditions selected from a variety of sources, many of them never published before. The narratives that I recorded directly from Indians who spoke English are phrased as related, except for the correction of an occasional error in grammar. Those narratives recorded through interpreters have been changed as little as possible for smooth reading. A few published by laymen have been rewritten to achieve a simplicity appropriate to the subject matter. The near-literal translations of ethnologists—painful reading for anyone sensitive to prose rhythm or lack of rhythm—have been rewritten for smoothness and for variety in diction and sentence structure. My ideals of style have been simplicity, sincerity, a conversational or oral quality, and the variety of rhythms in everyday speech. These qualities, in my opinion, are appropriate to the folk literature of any people.

Ella E. Clark

La Jolla, California
March 16, 1966

Pronunciation of Indian Names

❦

Algonquian—ăl-gŏng′kĭ-ăn
Arapaho—ȧ-răp′ȧ-hō
Assiniboine—ȧ-sin′ȧ-boin′
Bannock—băn′ŭk
Cayuse—kī-ūs′
Cheyenne—shī-ĕn′
Chickasaw—chĭk′ȧ-sô′
Chinook—chĭ-nŏŏk′ (or nōōk′)
Chippewa—chĭp′ȧ-wä′
Coeur d'Alêne—kôr′d'lăn′
Comanche—kō-măn′chĭ
Gros Ventre—grō′vänt′
Hidatsa—hē-dät′sä
Iroquois—ĭr′ȧ-kwoi′ (or kwoiz′)
Kalispel—kăl′ĭspĕl (or spĕl′)
Kiowa—kī′ȧ-wä
Kutenai—kōō′te-nä (or kōōt′nä)
Nez Percé—nā′pĕr′sā′
  (more commonly
  Nez Perce, nĕz′pûrs′)

Ojibway—ō-jĭb′wā
Paiute—pī-ōōt′
Pawnee—pô-nē′
Pend d'Oreille—pŏn′dŭ-rā′
Piegan—pē-găn′
Quinault—kwĕ-nŭlt′ (in
  Northwest, usually kwĕ-nält′)
Sacajawea—săk′ȧ-jȧ-wē′ȧ (usual
  pronunciation in Northwest)
Sahaptian—sä-hăp′tĭ-ăn
Salish—sā′lĭsh
Salishan—sā′lĭsh-ăn
Shoshoni—shó-shō′nĕ
Sioux—sōō
Umatilla—ū′mȧ-til′ȧ
Walla Walla—wŏl′ȧ-wŏl′ȧ
Wallowa—wŏ-lou′ȧ
Washakie—wŏsh′ȧ-kē′
Yakima—yăk′ĭ-mô (in North-
  west yăk′ĭ-mȧ)

SOURCES: *The American College Dictionary* (Random House); the Merriam-Webster *Geographical Dictionary;* and the Merriam-Webster *Biographical Dictionary.*

INDIAN LEGENDS FROM THE NORTHERN ROCKIES

I. How These Indians Lived

❦

I N FORMER TIMES, the lives of the Indians of Idaho, Montana, and Wyoming followed two fairly distinct patterns, each pattern adapted to the geographical environment. The Rocky Mountains divided the two. West of the Great Divide is a broad plateau cut by deep canyons, through which numerous streams rush down from the snow-crowned mountains on either side until they join the Columbia River, the great waterway of the Northwest. Along these tributaries, once well stocked with salmon, and along the lakes that are also part of the Columbia River system lived many tribes known to anthropologists as the Plateau Indians. Their pattern of living has often been called "Plateau culture."

East of the Rocky Mountains stretch the Great Plains, formerly grasslands that supported large numbers of buffalo, antelope, deer, and elk. The tribes that once roved there are well known as the Plains Indians, and their former way of life has often been called "Plains culture." Depending chiefly upon the buffalo for their subsistence, they adjusted their lives to the animals' movements and habits; therefore, their pattern of living is also sometimes called "bison culture."

West of the Plateau Indians, on the other side of the Cascade Range, lived the Northwest Coast Indians. But the barriers between the three geographical groups were not nearly so distinct and fixed as the two mountain ranges. Partly because both the Plateau and the Northwest Coast Indians depended upon salmon for much of their food and because they met to trade along the lower Columbia, some of their customs, crafts, and folktales were similar.

3

After they acquired horses, many Plateau families went regularly to the plains to hunt buffalo. There the Plains Indians and the Plateau Indians influenced each other, as will be shown occasionally in the introductions to the different tribes and in the headnotes to certain stories. When the first explorers and fur traders reached the Plateau, they found many features of Indian life similar to those observed among Plains tribes. But many Plateau families never hunted buffalo, and so their lives continued to follow the old pattern, true even of the childhood of a few Indians living after 1960.

THE PLATEAU INDIANS

The Plateau area includes southeastern British Columbia, eastern Washington and eastern Oregon, western Montana, and much of Idaho. The Nez Percés, Coeur d'Alênes, Kalispels (or Pend d'Oreilles), and Flatheads represented in this volume are only a few of the many Plateau tribes.

Salmon was the staple food in most of this region. At special fishing places considered the common property of the tribe, the men caught salmon with spears, hooks, traps, and nets; the women smoked, dried, and stored the fish for winter use. They supplemented salmon with trout, sturgeon, deer and elk meat, small game, and vegetal foods. They had no agriculture until the first missionaries came.

Camas (a bulb of the lily family), kouse (called "biscuit root" by early white travelers), and bitterroot were the most important roots prepared for winter. Wild carrots, wild onions, both the roots and the seeds of sunflowers, and nuts from pines and other conifers were secondary vegetal foods with some Plateau tribes. Huckleberries, service berries, and chokecherries were often dried and made into cakes, both for family use and for trade. Softer berries were eaten fresh. The women and girls were very busy from spring until autumn gathering and preserving these foods for winter. In some tribes, wealth was measured by the amount of stored food a family had.

In the generations immediately preceding the annual buffalo hunt (and much later with families that did not hunt buffalo), Plateau lodges consisted of a framework of poles, usually of lodgepole pine, covered with mats which were usually made of tules (bulrushes) woven together with wild hemp. For the winter houses, excavations two or three feet deep, twenty to seventy feet long, and ten to fifteen feet wide were made, some of which were oblong, others square, and a few cone-shaped. The earth dug up from the excavation was banked around the base of the lodge after dry grass and pine needles had first been laid against the mats to prevent decay. Pine boughs were placed over the earth to keep it in place. Double or treble layers of mats were often used for protection against the cold. An opening the full length of the lodge was left at the top, for the escape of smoke. A Plateau Indian describing to me these winter lodges of her childhood said, "I have never lived in a cozier home,"—although she now has electricity in her cottage.

These were communal houses, built and lived in by four or more families. Fires were arranged down the middle of the lodge, with two families using each fire. Beds built up of dry grass, pine needles, and the inner bark of cottonwood trees, and then covered with skins and furs, were made near the mat walls. Lewis and Clark in 1805–1806 reported that all the inhabitants of one Nez Percé village lived in such a winter lodge. It was about 150 feet long, contained twenty-four fires, and about twice that number of families. But old house rings show that smaller lodges were more common.

At least some of the Plateau tribes constructed, with great care, a large and permanent long house in each of the principal villages. It was the gathering place for all the band and the place for the winter dances and feasts.

In the summer when bands moved to be near their food supplies, temporary lodges,—often simply three-sided lean-tos—were erected either on the surface of the ground or over slight excavations. After the buffalo hunts became annual affairs for entire families, skin tents only were used in traveling, and skins soon replaced mats for the winter lodges. As among the Plains Indians, the tipi covers were decorated, usually by the senior male inhabitant of the dwelling; in bright colors he painted on the buffalo skins his war honors or scenes from his dreams.

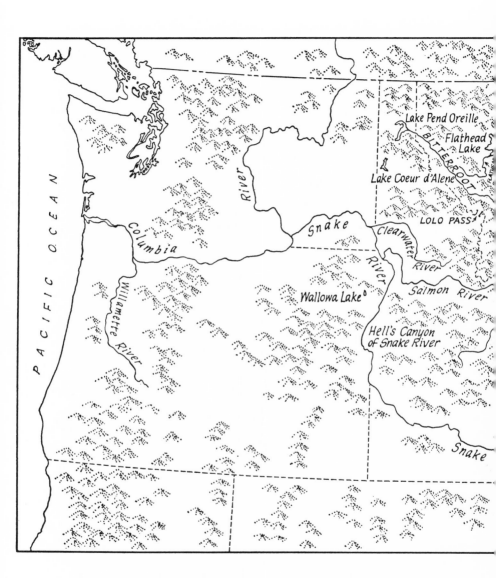

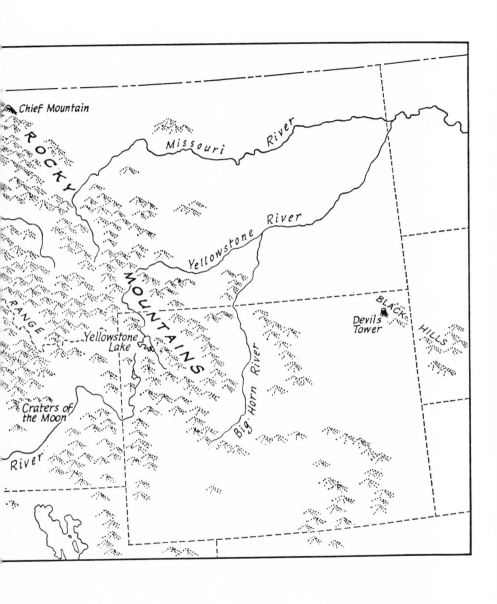

Chief Mountain

ROCKY

Missouri River

Yellowstone River

MOUNTAINS

RANGE

Yellowstone
Lake

Craters of
the Moon

River

Big Horn River

Devils
Tower

BLACK

HILLS

The clothing of the Plateau Indians in the early days was chiefly made from deerskins, the dressing of which was a highly developed craft among the women. The garments for festive occasions were made from the soft skins of mountain sheep and decorated with dyed porcupine quills or elks' teeth and, in historic times, with beads obtained from white traders. The Kutenais of the mountains, however, used no decorations except fringes; they thought that the pure white of their skin-clothing was the chief mark of beauty. The women of all the tribes, both Plateau and Plains, tanned skins for bags of various shapes and sizes. Those bags that were to contain valuables were highly ornamented, whereas rawhide bags were used for storing and carrying dried meat and salmon.

Basketry was another important craft among Plateau women. Baskets were needed for storage, for gathering berries and roots, and for boiling food. In making them, the women used rushes, cedar bark, and fine cedar roots gathered in the spring and woven in the winter. Some baskets they made into watertight vessels; some they constructed for usefulness only. Others were works of art, colorfully decorated. Nez Percé "twined wallets," woven of Indian hemp, were of such fine workmanship that other tribes often obtained them through trade. They are now known as cornhusk bags because, after the missionaries taught the Nez Percés to grow corn, the women used cornhusks in their manufacture.

Pottery among the Plateau Indians was either unknown or very crude. Stone work was limited to the making of tools and arrow points. Canoes were usually dug-outs made of logs hollowed out by fire. In the days before horses, dogs were sometimes used as pack animals.

The ceremonies and festivals of the Plateau Indians will be discussed in the introduction to the individual tribes.

THE PLAINS INDIANS

The Plains Indians, as has often been said, are the ones most likely to come to mind when the word "Indians" is read or spoken. Their vast territory extended from the Rocky Mountains eastward toward the Mississippi River, and from what is now northern Alberta south into Texas. More than twenty tribes are regularly listed as living in this area in historic times. Of these, five represented in this volume—the Assiniboines, Arapahos, Blackfeet, Crows, and Gros Ventres—are among those whose way of life is considered typical of the area as a whole. The Kutenais, the Bannocks, and the Idaho Shoshonis, as will be seen, were not distinctly Plateau or distinctly Plains people, either geographically or culturally.

The life of the typical Plains tribes depended upon the buffalo. Its flesh was their most important food. When it was fresh, they ate it boiled, roasted, or broiled over coals; they preserved it for winter use by making it into "jerked meat" or pemmican. They used buffalo skins for tipi covers, as robes for clothing and bedding, and for smaller objects such as drum heads, shields for battle, and bags or other containers of many shapes and sizes.

From the sinew they made ropes, bowstrings, snowshoe webbing, and thread for sewing. From the bones they made knives, tools, and other implements. From the horns came spoons, drinking cups, arrowheads, and powder horns. The hair they used for saddle padding, braided ropes, and woven wallets. Hoofs became rattles used in ceremonials; ribs became runners on sleds. Even the neck cord they hardened by fire and used as a moving target in a game popular with the men. A buffalo skull was a sacred object in the Sun Dance.

It is not surprising that old Chief Plenty-Coups of the Crow Indians said, "When the buffalo went away, we became a changed people. . . . Idleness that was never with us in the buffalo days has stolen much from both our minds and bodies. The buffalo was everything to us. When it went away, the hearts of my people fell to the ground, and they could not lift them up again."

These people of the northern area adapted their general pattern of living to the buffalo and the climate. In the winter, they separated into different bands and went into more or less permanent quarters, "generally along a stream, amongst the trees and brush, in spots well sheltered from the winds." On clear days hunters ventured forth, singly or in small groups, probably on snowshoes, looking for a stray buffalo or for small game. In the spring, the bands of each tribe gathered at some predetermined place and went on a big buffalo hunt, the whole cavalcade following the animals in their wandering from one grassy area to another. Summer gave the Plains Indians opportunity for social feasting and for tribal unification through council meetings, festivals, and ceremonies.

For secondary foods and for skins, individuals and small parties hunted deer, elk, antelope, and Rocky Mountain sheep. The Plains Indians seldom fished except when meat was scarce. They made much less use of vegetal foods than did the Plateau people, but they prized wild turnips and they used chokecherries to make pemmican for the winter food supply. From the Plateau Indians the Blackfoot women learned the technique of steaming camas roots in a pit in which wet willow branches had been placed over hot stones.

The clothing of the Plains Indians was made by the women from carefully dressed skins. A man's costume, as described by observers in 1830–35, consisted of a knee-length shirt, leggings reaching to the hips, moccasins of buffalo or elk leather, and a robe of buffalo skin "tanned to wondrous softness." The seams of shirts and leggings were trimmed either with fringe or with tufts of horse hair or human hair dyed in various colors; porcupine quills were sewed to the roots of the hair. The men fastened beads, shells, and feathers to the hair on their heads. Among the Crows, these ornaments indicated gradations in rank, the highest rank being indicated by the tail feathers of a golden eagle. (The long feathered headdress a white boy wears today when "playing Indian" was saved for war or other special occasions.)

A woman's costume consisted of an ankle-length dress, knee-high leggings, moccasins, and a light robe "thrown gracefully over the shoulders." Sleeves and hemlines were trimmed with a good deal of fringe; the hemlines were also often scalloped. Dresses for festivals and ceremonies were sometimes decorated with many rows of elks' teeth; others were ornamented at the neck and shoulders with dyed porcupine quills and glass beads. According to Warren A. Ferris of the American Fur Company, the decorations on these ceremonial gowns weighed from eight to ten pounds.

Dressing skins for clothing—scraping off the hair, removing fat and muscle, soaking, stretching, softening them—was a highly developed skill among the women. They sewed the dressed skins with buffalo sinew, after punching holes with bone awls. Among many women, ornamenting the ceremonial shirts, dresses, leggings, and moccasins was an art. Embroidery with dyed porcupine quills and beads was done in a variety of designs, some very simple, others as complicated as figures of mounted warriors with feather headdresses.

On their buffalo robes, rawhide containers, and lodge linings, the women usually painted geometric designs—rectangles, triangles, etc., in various combinations. On their shields the men painted sacred symbols to protect them from the arrows or bullets of the enemy. On the inner surface of their robes they depicted their experiences in horse raiding and in battle. On their tipi covers the men painted larger than life-size pictures of the animals and birds that had appeared to them in their dream-visions. Robert H. Lowie's admirable study, *Indians of the Plains,* contains many pictures of these decorated skins and hides. The chapter "Artists and Craftsmen" in John C. Ewers' book on the Blackfeet makes vivid the arduous labor and remarkable inventiveness of the women in dressing and decorating the skins.

The Plains Indians used stone for making hammers, food grinders, and the heads of war clubs. They usually made their pipes of stone and their knives of either stone or bone. Spoons, cups, and ladles were made by both men and women from the horns of buffalo and mountain sheep. The women of some tribes made bowls and cups from large burls on cottonwood trees. There was no basketry, except among the Wind River Shoshonis, and no weaving. Some of the tribes had traditions of ancient pottery vessels, but these were not practical after horses enabled families to travel farther and oftener.

Until some time in the first half of the eighteenth century, travel was by foot. Crude rafts were constructed when a deep stream had to be crossed. Dogs carried loads on their backs and were also trained to draw the travois, which was a simple vehicle made of two long poles, the front tips of which were attached to a harness on the dog's shoulders and the ends left dragging on the ground; midway was a frame in which wood, stored food, and even small children or feeble old people were carried. Later, both dogs and horses were used to pull travois.

The coming of the horse greatly affected the life of the Plains Indians, as well as that of the Plateau peoples. Its importance in hunting and transportation is obvious, and it soon became a standard of value and a medium of exchange. Wealth and prestige were measured by the number of horses a man owned. A man might purchase a ceremonial privilege with a horse or purchase a desirable bride from her father for ten horses. A wide gap developed between rich and poor.

An important feature of Plains life not found on the Plateau was the organization, mostly of men, into societies or clubs. Some were chiefly secular, some chiefly religious. In some tribes, virtually every male belonged to one of these secular societies from boyhood to old age. Each group had its own badges, songs, dances, and privileges; each had its own lodge, where members met for their social functions. At important times at least one of the societies was appointed by the chief to police the whole band or tribe—on a journey, on the communal buffalo hunt, at the tobacco-planting ceremony, or at the Sun Dance. And at all times the majority of these clubs promoted the warlike spirit characteristic of the Plains Indians. Religious organizations included men who had received the same guardian spirit in their dream-visions and, among the Crows, included the Tobacco Society, which ceremonially planted the sacred tobacco each year.

Another characteristic that distinguished the Plains Indians from the Plateau Indians was the greater number and complexity of their ceremonials. In the simplest forms the rituals of the two geographical areas were similar—and also similar to rituals in other areas. Prayers and offerings, the singing of sacred songs, ceremonial pipe-smoking, purification by means of the sweat bath before any significant event —these were alike. Important among the Plains Indians, but not dramatic, were the solemn opening of the bundles containing the sacred objects of an individual or a group and the ceremonial uncovering of a warrior's shield. Significant also were the festivals of the different societies.

Most important and most conspicuous of all the festivals was the Sun Dance, the great tribal ceremony of each of these Plains tribes of the northern Rockies and of a dozen others. It was held in the late spring or early summer, after the assembling of the scattered bands from their winter quarters. The name for this religious festival—first used to describe the Sioux ceremony, for which it was appropriate— is misleading; few tribes followed the Sioux custom of "looking at the sun" or even referred to it in their rituals.

Some tribal differences in the ceremony will be noticed in the introductions to the Blackfeet and the Crows, and in the headnotes and myths of "The Shoshoni Sun Dance," "The Origin of the Arapaho Sun Dance," and the Kutenai "Why the Indians Had No Metal Tools." The ceremonial, which commonly lasted eight days, included the secret preparations of the sacred objects to be used upon the altar or worn by the priests during the public performance, and the ritualistic construction of the Sun Dance Lodge and its dedication. The ceremonial included also the participants' singing sacred songs and performing simple dance movements to the rhythm of whistling through eagle-bone whistles.

And yet the festival was not entirely a religious occasion. There were reunions with friends in other bands, policy-making meetings of the tribal council, processional marches and outdoor dances by the military societies, and entertainment for all the spectators in the Sun Dance itself.

Banned for several years by the Department of the Interior because of the self-torture inflicted by some participants, the Sun Dance was later revived and is still held by certain tribes with a few changes in the ceremony. Traditional rites are still observed, and the whole procedure is full of symbolism. The camp circle, for example, symbolizes the horizon (which stands for the universe) or the constellation Corona Borealis (which is the camp circle of the sky spirits); the lodge represents the earth, the home of man. Every part of the ceremony has a symbolic meaning, usually held by the tribe as a sacred secret.

A young Shoshoni studying for the Christian ministry once confided to me while we watched a Sun Dance that he had had no experience more purifying or more satisfying spiritually than his participation in the Sun Dance a few years earlier.

RECREATION

The games and amusements of the Plateau and Plains Indians were similar to those of tribes in other parts of the United States. Variations, Stewart Culin found, were due to environment and therefore to materials used.

Children imitated the activities of their elders: small boys had mimic hunts and fights, girls played with dolls, both "played house" by making little tipis of sticks and gopher skins. They flew kites of bladder skins, played hide-and-seek and other games children play today, spun tops on the ice and snow, and coasted down slopes on raw buffalo hides or on sleds with runners made of buffalo ribs. "Indian children are light-hearted and cheerful, rippling with laughter and mischievous mirth," wrote an early observer. "They play sly tricks upon the dogs and one another incessantly, and are much given to singing."

Adolescents and adults played several games of ball, not touching the ball with their hands but striking it with a club or a racket or kicking it. Shinny was especially popular with women; among the Crows, men sometimes played against women. Men and boys hurled darts and javelins along ice or frozen ground to see whose would go the farthest. They played a game of "hoop and ball," by throwing a spear or an arrow at a moving target. Among the Blackfeet, this was a ring about three inches in diameter.

Dancing, although an expression of religious feeling in the Sun Dance and certain simpler festivals, at other times had other purposes. The war dance, performed not only before the men went to war but also before the whole tribe started on the buffalo hunt, was a vigorous, almost frenzied affair. And the scalp dance after a battle, held only if there were no deaths on the winning side, was an expression of tribal or intertribal rejoicing. Occasionally, men and women danced together; then they usually alternated in a circle and shuffled their feet slowly to the left, accompanied by drummers seated in the center of the moving circle. More typical, however, were the dances of the military societies where the men danced alone.

Gambling was a favorite pastime among both men and women, by day and by night, outdoors and indoors. One form of gambling using sticks as dice was so popular that it is called "the stick game." There was gambling at athletic contests and other activities also. As many observers have reported, Indians had "a passion for gambling."

Archery, swimming, wrestling, foot-racing, riding, horse racing, sham battles on horseback—all these sports were considered not only recreation but physical and military training, too. "Horse-stealing was a legitimate game among all the tribes," wrote Granville Stuart, who lived on the frontier for forty years, "and a clever horse thief ranked with a sub-chief." To slip into an enemy's camp at night and cut loose his horses was a daring deed of valor. Naturally there was horse-stealing in retaliation, and often there was fighting.

War, too, was thought of as a sport by some tribes, except when the fighting was in defense of what the warriors considered their tribal territory. Then it was serious.

STORYTELLING

Storytelling was one of the most popular pastimes in the winter for both children and adults. To arouse martial spirit among warriors, the old men frequently related their own military exploits before the departure of a war party, but narration of tribal traditions was reserved for winter evenings. "I hope I will not find a rattlesnake wrapped around my legs for telling the old stories in the summertime," a ninety-year-old Flathead said to me in 1955. She was joking, but her mother probably would not have related those Coyote tales in July.

Shoshonis believed that they would displease Coyote if they told the old traditions at any time except during the "snowy months." Blackfeet believed that Old Man would cause a person to go blind if he related stories while it was still light. A Crow Indian said that people used to be afraid to tell the old stories in the summer "because the morning star comes only in the summer." Some believed that in the summer the spirits would hear stories about themselves and would have their feelings hurt. Others believed that the animals and birds, the chief characters in most of the tales, would hear people talking about them in the summer and would have their feelings hurt.

But "it is good to tell stories in the winter time; there are long nights in the winter time." "Most old men and women can recount these stories," wrote the fur trader Edwin Denig, who lived among the Plains Indians for about twenty years and whose wife was an Assiniboine, "but there are some particularly famed for their talents in this respect, and these are compensated for their trouble by feasting, smoking, and small presents. At night, when all work is over, a kettle is put on containing some choice meat, tobacco mixed with weed is prepared, the lodge put in order, the family collected, the storyteller invited, who often prolongs his narrations the greater part of the night."

Many of the storytellers were superb actors—even some that I heard and watched in 1950. Their facial expressions, voices, and gestures almost told the tale without words as they entertained eager listeners with amusing stories, tales of adventure and war, horror stories, and myths and legends of the wondrous days of long ago. In fact, some stories were told graphically in the sign language!

Storytelling, however, was not for entertainment only. In the childhood of my principal Nez Percé informant, Otis Halfmoon, special winter lodges were made, partly underground, which were heated with hot rocks. There the most highly respected storytellers, one for the boys and one for the girls, taught the children in story form, preparing them for their lives as adults close to nature.

But most Indian teaching was done on winter evenings before the entire family or group of families living in one lodge. Fables and other narratives gave moral and ethical instruction to youth as their elders sought to develop in them the ideals of the tribe. Some myths and legends satisfied normal curiosity by explaining the origin of landscape features (the Craters of the Moon, the Badlands, etc.) and of other natural phenomena. Many stories gave information of many kinds—information about animals and birds, tribal ways of doing things, tribal history, ritualistic procedures, the origin of sacred objects, and the origin of ceremonies.

"The Indians are possessed of peculiarly retentive memories," wrote the famous trapper and guide George Belden, "and are always respectful and attentive to the narratives of their old men. A tale once told is remembered by the hearers for years, and in like manner is handed down by them to another generation."

One of the sacred duties of the elders of the tribes was to hand down the traditions to the younger generations. Thus the winter storytelling preserved the continuity of the tribe by keeping alive its history and its significant traditions. The best storytellers were highly respected by their people; they were not only entertainers, but also teachers, historians, and guardians of the sacred ceremonies.

INDIAN RELIGION

Some of the myths and personal narratives in this book will be more easily appreciated if the reader knows the chief facts about the native religion of the North American Indians. The subject is really too complex for brief treatment, but additional information will be found in the introductions to the sections and in several personal narratives. Basic is the fact that the Indians were animists; that is, they believed that there were spirits everywhere in nature. "Spirits make the grass and plants to grow," said a very old Plains Indian. "Spirits cause the winds to blow and the clouds to float across the sky. Every animal and bird has a spirit."

To obtain some of this mystery power from nature, which was thought to be much stronger than human power, and to secure the lifelong protection of an individual spirit, every boy (and every girl in some tribes) spent a night or a few days and nights, alone, in a solitary place believed to be especially strong in supernatural power. Usually the longest vigil was four nights in the Plains tribes, five in the Plateau, for these were mystic numbers. Fasting and thirsting, the child waited for a voice to speak to him. If unsuccessful, he went again and again between the ages of six or seven and fifteen.

The most important event in a boy's life was securing the aid of a powerful spirit.

When a spirit spoke to him and appeared in his dream, it was usually the spirit of an animal in human form. It taught him his individual sacred song, instructed him about his special duties, and bestowed upon him some special gift, such as the ability to become a great hunter or great leader or to heal the sick. It also gave him some object—perhaps a feather, if the spirit was that of a bird—to be his talisman. A Blackfoot boy was shown certain objects which the spirit said he should make and care for in a particular way.

Buffalo, beaver, eagle, and bear, among the Plains tribes, bestowed especially strong power. The spirits of inanimate objects also gave power; for example, Pierre Pichette's Indian name, meaning "Hollow in the Sky," became his after he had received spirit power from "somewhere in the sky, somewhere in the clouds." Sun and thunder were the most powerful sky spirits.

The Indian terms for both a person's spirit power and his talisman have long been translated as "medicine." His talisman the boy placed in a skin bag, which was usually fringed and ornamented; he added other sacred objects to it, perhaps received in later dream-visions, as symbols of his power. The whole was called a "medicine bundle" or "sacred bundle." Its owner kept it close to him throughout life; when he prayed to his guardian spirit for guidance or strength, he held the medicine bundle in his hand or laid it on the ground before him. Among the Nez Percés and Kutenais, it was buried with its owner. Among the Plains Indians, it was sold when the owner became old (at a high price if he had been very successful), or it was bequeathed to a younger man, along with its songs and stories, its rituals and taboos, and its power. The transfer was made with ceremony and reverence.

Tribes and clans and societies also owned medicine bundles, differing from an individual's bundle only in their greater power, usually their greater size, and the greater veneration attached to them. Each group had its special songs, a story, and often a ritual. A "medicine man," or shaman, and a "medicine woman" had exceptional mystery power, received perhaps from thunder or the dwarfs, perhaps from several lesser spirits in different visions. (See the Kalispel story, "Spirit Power from the Little People," and the Crow story about "Long Hair, the Great Medicine Man.")

Adults as well as youths had dreams and visions, as will be seen in several stories. The medicine men had them oftener than other people and were therefore able to heal the sick, to give advice to a war party, to call the herds of buffalo to their people, to bring rain by prayer in times of drought, even to foresee the future. All dreams were to be heeded by everyone, for they were messages from the spirits. Thus dreams were an important part of Indian religion.

Dreams and visions, spirit helpers and supernatural experiences, sacred bundles and religious ceremonies, events in history—these and other aspects of the lives of the Plateau Indians and of the Plains Indians are revealed in the stories they once told around their home fires on winter evenings.

II. A Sahaptian Tribe: The Nez Percés

❧✖❧

W HEN SEVEN MEN, scouting ahead for the Lewis and Clark Expedition and weak from hunger and hardships, crossed the Bitterroot Range into what is now northern Idaho, they found about thirty double lodges of Nez Percés on the plateau above the Clearwater River. The time was September, 1805, and the women were digging their winter supply of camas roots. Three small boys, the first to see the bearded strangers, ran in fright and hid themselves in the tall grass. In a short time, men and women gathered round "with much apparent signs of fear." But they gave buffalo meat and dried berries to the famished scouts and sent food to the main party of explorers.

These were the first white men the Nez Percés had ever seen; their traditions of the event are related at the end of this section. The explorers fashioned dug-out canoes along the river, left their horses with Chief Twisted Hair, and made the rest of the journey to the Pacific by water. A Nez Percé guide took them down the Clearwater and then down the Snake River, with its many rapids, to its junction with the Columbia. Two old chiefs accompanied them as far as the Cascades of the great river, to pilot them around the rapids and to explain their peaceful intentions to the Indians along the shores.

On the return of the expedition in the spring of 1806, they were met with eagerness and the giving of gifts, including four "elegant" horses to the captains. They stayed with the Nez Percés during most of May and June, waiting for the snow to melt in the mountains. Three young men of the tribe guided them over the most difficult part of the journey eastward. In their journals, Lewis and Clark praised the Nez Percés for their hospitality and generosity, their honesty, intelligence, cleanliness, and high moral standards. Seventy-five years later, when Kate McBeth was a missionary among them, she found many evidences of their affection for their first white visitors.

Lewis and Clark estimated the entire Nez Percé population at about six thousand. The tribe lived in different bands and villages, each band having several chiefs, one of whom was considered the leader. More than forty subdivisions (or bands) are listed by John R. Swanton as having had their permanent villages along the Clearwater, the Grande Ronde, the lower Salmon and the lower Snake rivers, and along Wallowa Lake and its tributaries. The Nez Percés' roaming territory extended from the Bitterroot Range of the Rockies westward to the Blue Mountains of eastern Washington and Oregon.

The tribe was the largest and most powerful of the Indians speaking the Sahaptian language. Among the other members of the Sahaptian linguistic family are the Yakimas, the Walla Wallas, the Klickitats, the Umatillas, and the Cayuses, of central Washington and adjacent Oregon.

The Nez Percés' name for themselves is *Nimipu* (pronounced "Ni'mee-poo" by Otis Halfmoon). The word means "the people." "In the old language that died with the old Indians of my childhood," added Halfmoon, "our name was *Choo-pin-it-pa-loo,* meaning 'people of the mountains.'" Lewis and Clark wrote, "They call themselves *Cho pun nish* or Pierced Noses" (September 20, 1805); "the ornament of the nose is a single shell of the wampum" (May 13, 1806). David Thompson, exploring and trading in the region in 1810, seemingly was the first to record the name *Nez Percé,* which he learned from French-speaking trappers.

But Kate McBeth, who was a missionary among them for many years, wrote: "The Nez Percés deny that they ever did, as a tribe, pierce their noses. Occasionally one did." Today, members of the tribe informed about their culture think the name was given them because some French-Canadian interpreter misunderstood the designation in the sign language, or perhaps because some early white man saw among them a few members of some tribe that did pierce the nose.

In 1836 the Reverend Henry Spalding and his wife came to the Clearwater valley to begin a Protestant mission among the Nez Percés. There they established the first school and the first church in Idaho, taught the Indians the elements of agriculture and of homemaking, set up the first printing press in the Northwest, and on it printed a primer and the Gospel of Matthew in the Nez Percé language. In 1869 the Jesuits started a mission in the area. By the time of the gold rush into northern Idaho in the 1860's, the Nez Percés had such skill in agriculture that they supplied miners with eggs, corn, and beef.

The peaceful relations established by the Lewis and Clark Expedition continued for more than seventy years. In 1847, when Cayuse Indians killed Marcus Whitman, his wife, and twelve others at the Protestant mission about one hundred miles west of the Spalding mission, the Nez Percés guarded the Spaldings, and as soon as traveling was safe, they escorted their missionaries to Fort Walla Walla. (One of those protectors was the great-uncle of Otis Halfmoon.)

In spite of repeated uprisings by several neighboring tribes in the 1850's and 1860's, in spite of miners' encroachments upon Nez Percé lands during the gold rush, in spite of outrageous and unpunished acts of the whites against the Nez Percés and their possessions, peace-loving and prudent chiefs were able to restrain their embittered and angry men from fighting.

But hostilities broke out in 1877, after whites demanded the fertile Wallowa valley of northeastern Oregon and after the government, reversing a Presidential order of 1873, commanded young Chief Joseph and his band to give up their ancestral land there and move to the Lapwai Reservation in northern Idaho. They were ordered to move in May, when their horses and cattle, and even their people, were widely scattered, and when the Snake River, which they had to cross, was at its springtime high. "Let us wait till fall," asked Joseph. But General Howard refused permission.

In spite of Joseph's determination to avoid bloodshed, three young hotbloods from a Salmon River band (not from Chief Joseph's band) slipped away on an errand of revenge. The result was war. The Nez Percés fought bravely, but their warriors were outnumbered by each of four armies. After the surrender of Chief Joseph, whose character, skillful maneuvering, and masterly retreat almost to the Canadian border won the admiration of the commanding officers pursuing him, he and his followers were taken to Indian Territory (now part of Oklahoma).

In 1885 those who had survived the hardships and malaria were brought back to the Northwest. Joseph and 150 of his people were placed on the Colville Reservation in northeastern Washington, with tribes that spoke different dialects of another language; 181 were taken to the Lapwai Reservation. Today a few Nez Percés live on the Umatilla Reservation in Oregon. Others still live near Nespelem on the Colville Reservation (where Chief Joseph was buried). But most of them live near the Clearwater River, in or near their ancient villages of Lapwai, Kamiah, and Kooskia.

When Lewis and Clark came to the region, they were impressed by the large herds of excellent horses. Sometime in the eighteenth century the Nez Percés had obtained the first horses from the Shoshonis of southern Idaho. Soon after 1690, the Shoshonis had obtained horses from the Pueblo Indians of New Mexico, who had obtained theirs from Spanish settlers.

The Nez Percés soon became expert riders and then famous breeders of superior horses. They had been fascinated by a white mare in their first herd and were very fond of the horses with spots on their white rumps. The men rode the spotted horses in parades and in war and soon learned that they were valuable for trading. By selective breeding, the Nez Percés greatly increased the number of their spotted horses (now called Appaloosas, because of the nearby Palouse River), known for their gentleness, hardiness, and speed.

In their native religion the Nez Percés showed great reverence for the sun and the earth. "All the products of the earth are the children of the sun, born of the earth," they told Kate McBeth. Before eating, they expressed gratitude silently by turning a vessel of food around as the sun turns. When the first salmon came up the streams in the spring, the head chief called the people together for worship. Holding a fish up to the sun, he turned it in the direction the sun travels around the earth, while all the people chanted, "O Father Sun, bless the fish. O Father Sun, bless us." Then they dug a hole and the chief placed the salmon in it, while the people chanted, "O Mother Earth, bless the fish. O Mother Earth, bless us." Feasting and religious dancing followed.

Similar ceremonies were observed when the first roots were ready for digging in spring, when the first berries were ripe, and when deer were plentiful. Before going out to hunt their horses and before going out to hunt game in the mountains, they always acknowledged the sun as their great leader.

The most sacred ceremony of the Nez Percés was the Guardian Spirit Dance, carefully prepared for in autumn and held for several weeks in winter in the long-houses of several villages. Both men and women participated, singing the songs given them during the guardian spirit quest or inherited songs. Each person began his song and dance alone; then others took up the words and joined in the singing and dancing. Costumes, actions, painting of the body, even yelps and cries, often suggested the sacred animal that had given a person his spirit or power song. Edward Curtis' account of the Nez Percés includes several of these "medicine songs"—songs to the sun, the morning star, the eagle, the elk, etc.—with the Nez Percé words and both literal and free translations. Curtis considered songs "the essentials of religion" among the Plateau Indians and others.

At the Guardian Spirit Dance, a young man, after consultation with his father or uncle and with a medicine man of his band, might make known the guardian spirit that had appeared to him in his boyhood vision; he would then sing, for the first time in public, the song the spirit had taught him. Thereafter he was usually called by the name of his protector. The chief purposes of the Guardian Spirit Dance were to bring the people into close, friendly relations with the animals, birds, and other natural objects, and thus to increase each person's supernatural power.

Only a vague and changing boundary line in Indian thought separated man from his relatives among the animals and birds—his "little brothers." "When the world was young"—so old Indians often began their tales—human beings and animals and birds all spoke the same language. Indians believed that even after animals and birds lost their power of speech, they could understand what human beings said to each other and to them. An Indian understood the signs of birds and wild animals so well, said Otis Halfmoon, that through them he could foretell weather changes, the coming of strangers, and deaths.

"The birds that sped through the air were the messengers between man and the invisible power that animated all things," wrote Alice Fletcher, a government agent who lived among the Nez Percés in 1889. "The wind was the breath of the universe . . . , the living force within, the breath of life."

Because of this close relationship between the Indian and nature, it is not surprising that most of his tales were about animals and birds. Rather, they are about the "animal people" or "animal persons," as English-speaking Indians refer to them today. These mythological beings lived on the earth when it was young, "when people had not come out yet." They had many of the characteristics of their smaller descendants in today's world. Yet they could reason and talk, and they lived as the people telling the tales lived. In any story, a mythological character may change his appearance and his personality, so that at any point he seems human and at another point an animal.

In Nez Percé mythology, as in that of other Plateau tribes, Coyote is the principal character, and many of the tales about him are similar to some told by the Columbia River and other Western tribes.[1] As a culture-hero in Nez Percé tales, Coyote killed monsters that were troubling his people, and he broke the beaver's dam across the lower Columbia so that the salmon could come up the river and its tributaries. But in one Nez Percé fire myth, it was Beaver that secured

---

[1] Many of these appear in *Indian Legends of the Pacific Northwest*. Because of the wealth of material for this volume, I have avoided giving in detail variants of stories published in the Washington-Oregon volume. They can be located in the Source Notes.

the fire and shared it with certain kinds of trees along the Grande Ronde River. As a trickster, Coyote changed the appearance of several animals and birds while they were sleeping, and then with his close companion Fox sat down to laugh about the changes in coloring and features.

In a myth strikingly like the Greek myth of Orpheus and Eurydice, Coyote, mourning for his wife, went to the land of the dead. The death spirit finally allowed him to take his wife home but forbade him to touch her until after they had crossed the fifth mountain. At their camp on the fourth mountain, Coyote embraced her and she disappeared forever. So people do not return from the dead. This version Archie Phinney recorded from his mother. In another Nez Percé version, Coyote went to bring back his daughter and her husband, who had been burned to death by the five Salmon brothers. The theme of a journey to the land of the dead is found in the mythology of other Northwest tribes and of many peoples throughout the world.

There used to be a good many myths and legends about landscape features in the Nez Percé area, an Indian living near Lapwai told me, but most of them are now forgotten. Most of the Nez Percé traditions that follow I recorded from Otis Halfmoon and from Lucy Armstrong Isaac. Then an old man on the Umatilla Reservation, Mr. Halfmoon had spent the winters of his childhood in a village at the confluence of the Salmon and the Snake rivers. He had long wanted to write a book about his people and had actually written a few pages. Mrs. Isaac had learned the traditions from her father, Ralph Armstrong. Orphaned by the Nez Percé War of 1877, he was often called "my boy" by Chief Joseph. In 1898, Armstrong was graduated with highest honors from the Carlisle Indian School. For a few beliefs and customs recorded by him, see "Armstrong" in the bibliography.

Coyote and the Monster of the Clearwater

THIS VERSION of the most popular Nez Percé tale was related in 1955 by Otis Halfmoon. The final details were added by Oliver Frank while he was pointing out the topographical features mentioned in the story. An older Nez Percé, Ralph Armstrong, wrote that the monster's head lay where the village of Spalding is now located, its tail reached beyond Kooskia (several miles up the Clearwater River), its "eyes and ears were on the very spot where the Lewis and Clark party camped in 1805, on their way to the Waters of the Setting Sun." When the monster had swallowed so many of the ancient "animal persons" that more were inside its stomach than outside, wrote Armstrong, the council sent Silver Salmon down the Clearwater, Snake, and Columbia rivers to ask Coyote for help. With variations, this tale was told by Montana Indians also: among the Flatheads, the location was the Mission Valley; among the Crows, the valley of the Big Horn River. Neighbors of the Nez Percés used to relate a similar tale about a beaver monster that once lived near the junction of the Palouse and Snake rivers. Several Columbia River tribes had a similar tradition about the struggles of Coyote with a giant beaver that once lived in Lake Cle Elum, high in the northern Cascade Mountains.

COYOTE CAME UP THE COLUMBIA into the Snake River and up the Snake to the Clearwater. In the Clearwater valley he saw the monster he had been told about, and soon he decided what he would do: he would trick the monster into swallowing him.

So he made a strong rope and climbed to the highest peak in the Wallowa Mountains. With his rope he tied himself up there, and then he howled a challenge to the monster. Coyote was so far away that he looked like a blade of grass on the mountain top. The monster saw him, desired him, and drew a deep breath. But the thing he wanted did not move.

Then Coyote, carrying his rope, crossed the Snake River to the Seven Devils Mountains. There he tied himself again, and again he howled a challenge to the monster. The monster tried to suck him in, as he had sucked in the other animal people, but Coyote did not move. He was tied fast to the peak.

Then he moved into the Salmon River mountains, nearer the

monster. Above Whitebird he made a ridge that looked like a saddle. After he had tied himself to a mountain, he put some bushes over his head and peeped over the ridge.

He called down to the monster, "You can't swallow me."

The monster looked up at the place the voice came from, but he could see nothing except some bushes on top of the ridge. Coyote stood up and called again, "You can't swallow me."

The monster took a deep breath and tried to swallow him, tried to suck him in. But Coyote did not move. Then the monster knew who was challenging him. "You are Coyote," he said. "I have been waiting for you for years. I will swallow you."

That was what Coyote wanted to hear. So he cut the rope and let the monster's breath pull him down the mountain. On the plateau near Grangeville, he took some white paint out of his bag, pulled up a rosebush, and poured the white paint in the hole where its roots had been.

"A human race is coming," said Coyote. "They will need white paint for buffalo hides and many other things."

The monster took another deep breath, and Coyote was pulled on toward the Clearwater valley. He took some kouse roots from his bag and scattered them. He scattered many of them on the north side of Tolo Lake, between Grangeville and Cottonwood. "The human race will dig kouse roots for food," said Coyote.

The monster kept on sucking in his breath and Coyote kept on moving toward him. On the high cliff overlooking Camas Prairie, he took the camas roots out of his bag and threw them into the valley below him—many roots or bulbs. "The human race, the new people who are to come, will dig roots here for their food," he said.

That is why Camas Prairie used to be blue with camas every spring.

Closer and closer, Coyote was drawn to the monster, just as he wished to be. At last he was near its mouth. The huge jaws opened wide, and down Coyote went, swallowed just like a worm. Inside, he met Rattlesnake. Rattlesnake became angry and tried to bite him. But Coyote trampled on him and flattened his head. Grizzly Bear attacked him, but Coyote flattened his head. He scolded Rattlesnake and Grizzly Bear for not killing the monster. Coyote saw Black Bear also, but Black Bear was kind to him. He saw many other creatures down inside the monster's stomach. Those who had been there a long time were nothing but bones with skins wrapped around them. Those who had been there a short time looked as if they were gradually having life sucked out of them.

Coyote pulled chunks of fat from around the monster's heart and fed the people who could eat. Then he talked to them. He showed them all the openings in the monster's body—the ears, the nostrils, the mouth, the eyes.

"This thing is going to die," he told the people. "As soon as it dies, rush for the opening nearest you. Each of you take with you some of the bones of the dead people."

Then Coyote took from his bag five knives and began to cut the cords that fastened the monster's heart to its body. The monster tried to persuade him not to kill, but Coyote hacked away. He broke four knives. "Be ready to leave," he said to the people as he picked up the fifth knife. With the fifth knife he cut the last cord and the heart fell down. The monster was dead.

All the people left the monster's stomach. Coyote went out also. Muskrat got caught by his tail in some opening, but Coyote pulled him out. He jerked him so fast that he scraped some of the hair from Muskrat's tail. That's why part of Muskrat's tail has no hair today.

Outside the monster, Coyote rubbed himself and wiped the sweat from his face. All the people he had freed admired him. All their friends who had not been swallowed by the monster thanked him and admired him.

"I am not through yet," Coyote told them. "Bring the bones that you took from the monster's stomach."

The bones were placed on the ground, Coyote stepped over them five times, and they all came to life. Then Coyote cut the monster into pieces and threw the pieces in all directions, as far as he could throw them.

His friend Kots-kots the Fox stood watching him.

"From these pieces," said Coyote to Fox, "I will make a human race to live on the earth."

The legs, which he had thrown over the Rocky Mountains, he turned into the Blackfeet. "You shall be the Blackfeet. You shall be tall, long-legged people."

Of the scalp Coyote made the Crow Indians. "You shall be the Crow Indians. You will be proud of your long hair."

Of other parts of the monster's flesh and bones he made the Flatheads and the Bannocks and the Sioux Indians—all the tribes.

When he thought Coyote had finished, Fox asked, "Who is going to live in this country, the best country of all?"

"Why didn't you ask me sooner?" replied Coyote. "I would have saved some flesh for people here. But bring me some water from the river, and I will finish my work. This will be my greatest creation."

So he took blood from the monster's heart, mixed it with water, and sprinkled it up and down the valley.

"You will be the Nimeepoo," he said. "You will not be a large tribe, but you will be powerful in fighting and in everything else. People made from the blood of the heart will be brave and strong."

Then Coyote said to Fox, "Let us leave the heart and the liver here in the valley. They will be history for the new human race."

Coyote turned the heart and the liver into rocks. You can see them today, in the Clearwater valley between Kamiah and Kooskia. On the north side of the valley, on the brow of a hill, are Coyote's fingerprints. He left them there when he wiped his hands after creating the human race. They, too, are history.

Today the Nimeepoo are called the Nez Percé Indians.

❋

The Beginning of Summer and Winter

THIS MYTH, RECORDED IN 1896, is similar to one told by the Yakima Indians, who were related to the Nez Percés by language. The Yakima myth tells about the struggle between the five Walla Walla brothers, who brought the cold east wind, and the five Chinook brothers, who brought the warm west wind.

Other Columbia River tribes related parallel myths. Five is the usual number in them.

L ong ago, when the world was young and people had not come out yet, there lived in the warm southland a family of five brothers and their sister. They were surrounded by sunshine and flowers and the music of birds. The brothers, who were hunters, were always successful. They never went hunting without bringing back some meat.

Their sister stayed at home, mending their clothes and preparing their meals. She was always nicely dressed in buckskin that she had ornamented with elks' teeth and had painted with yellow powder.

In the northland there lived a family of five brothers and their sister. They lived in the midst of ice and snow. These brothers also were hunters, but they had so little success that they were often hungry. One time when their food supply was almost gone, the brothers said to their sister, "You will have to go to the five brothers in the southland. When you reach them, you will say, 'We are all very hungry. My brothers have sent me to ask for food from you.'"

At first the girl refused to go, but her brothers insisted. After many persuasive words from them, she started south, carrying in her hands some large icicles. Her brothers used icicles as spears. As she approached the southland, traveling in the form of a large black cloud, the five southern brothers saw her. The oldest said to their sister, "Paint yourself gorgeously with yellow powder, and sprinkle over your dress the perfumes of flowers. When the girl from the north comes close, go out and meet her. When you get to her, shake yourself."

"Yes, my brother," she replied.

When she was ready, the girl of the south walked out to meet the girl from the north. The black cloud made the air chilly and uncomfortable. The girl of the south smiled gently and shook her dress. From it flew fine dry powder and the sweet fragrance of summer flowers. Instantly the icicles which the northern girl planned to use as weapons fell to the ground. The black cloud scattered. Soon the particles of what remained were lost to sight.

How the girl returned home is not known, but when she told her brothers what had happened, they were angry. "Let us challenge the southern brothers to wrestle with us," they said to each other.

They sent their challenge, and the five southern brothers accepted it. When it was almost autumn, the two families met half way between their homes. The sister in each group took with her five buckets. In the buckets of the southern girl was hot water; in the buckets of the northern girl were ice and cold water. Each planned to throw the contents of her buckets at the feet of the wrestlers.

When everything was ready, the oldest northern brother wrestled with the oldest southern brother. They were so evenly matched that for a long time neither was able to throw the other. Suddenly both heard the sound of rushing water. The northern girl emptied one of her buckets, and the cold water made the northern man fight harder. Then the girl from the south threw hot water at the feet of the wrestlers. The ice melted, and immediately the southern man overcame his rival. The oldest brother from the north lay on the ground dead.

At once the next oldest from the northern family ran up to the victor and began to wrestle with him. In a short but fierce struggle he overcame the southern brother. The oldest brother from the southland also lay on the ground dead. One by one the brothers from each tribe wrestled with a brother from the the other tribe. After a while, only the youngest in each family was left alive.

For five days these two wrestled, neither of them able to overcome the other. On the sixth day the southern boy got tired and almost fell, but in some unknown way he regained his feet. Then they decided to stop for a while. The southern boy went to his home and stayed there for five moons.

At the end of that time he traveled north and met the northern brother at the place where they had fought before. This time the southern boy easily defeated the northern boy and drove him far back into the cold land. For about six moons the southern brother had possession of the lands of the northern family. At the end of six moons the northern boy returned, and the two wrestled for one whole moon. This time the southern boy was defeated and driven home.

Even today the two continue to wrestle for mastery of the land. When the southern wrestler defeats the northern one, we have summer. When the northern wrestler defeats the southern one, we have winter. Two battles are waged every year. Just before spring, the southern boy conquers the northern boy; in the autumn, the northern boy conquers the southern boy. Each rules the land for a few months.

✳

Coyote Arranges the Seasons

THIS TALE WAS RECORDED from Sam Slickpoo in 1954. A variant of it concerns the moon instead of the sun. In the Nez Percé language, as in the languages of the Interior Salish, the same words are used for the sun and the moon, except for modifiers to indicate the "day sun" and the "night sun."

IN THE EARLY TIMES, Sun was too hot. Often it scorched the earth, and the people were uncomfortable.

"I could be a better Sun," Coyote thought to himself. "I will take its place."

So he tried to catch Sun. He traveled west to seize it, but when he got there, it dropped out of sight. He traveled east to meet it, but when he got there, Sun was high over his head. He made a boat and traveled east by water, but when he got there Sun was in the middle of the sky.

At last he went to Frog with his problem.

"Help me get hold of Sun," Coyote said to Frog. "Can't you go up to the sky and bring Sun down?"

"I think we can if we work together," answered Frog. "You throw me against Sun. I will grab it with my four hands and bring it down to earth."

So Coyote took hold of Frog and threw him with all his might at the Sun. Frog seized Sun and pulled it down to earth. While Frog was on his journey to the sky, Coyote had planned what he would say. He used his special powers and made some places to show Sun. When Frog came back, Coyote welcomed Sun warmly.

"I am very glad to see you and to talk with you," he said to Sun. "Your father and my father once camped near here. Would you like to see the place where they camped?"

Coyote led Sun to a good camping place, scraped off the earth, and showed him the ashes of an old campfire. He pointed to five old tipi poles. "Our fathers lived in this tipi," said Coyote.

Then he led Sun to the remains of the sweat lodge on the river bank. The framework of willows was still there, and also the rocks which had been heated for the sweat baths.

Sun was convinced that their fathers had been friends, and so he was willing to be a friend of Coyote and to camp with him. When night came, they lay down to rest. Coyote had planned to kill Sun as soon as he was asleep, and so every once in a while he would look over at his companion, expecting to find him sleeping. But Sun was always awake, always had his eyes wide open, just as in the daytime.

Coyote kept on with his plan to kill Sun. He made a big knife and hid it under himself. He knew it was not good enough, and so he waited for a few more nights. He slipped away from Sun during the day and made another knife. This one was made of flint. Again the two lay down to sleep, and again Coyote kept watching for his chance. Again Sun lay with his eyes open. But one time when Sun was looking in another direction, Coyote took his flint knife and cut off Sun's head.

Then Coyote went up to the sky and became the sun. But he soon found that he did not like to spend all of his days traveling across the sky.

"I'll have to bring Sun back to life," he said to himself. "I'll put his head beside his body. Then I'll straddle him three times and so bring him back to life."

That's what he did. He stepped three times across the body and the head, they grew back together, and Sun came back to life. Sun yawned and stretched.

"Oh, I have enjoyed my rest," Sun said. "I'm not going to work so hard again."

"That's right," replied Coyote. "I'm not going to let you. You will never again be as hot as you used to be. You will be warm in summer but not scorching hot.

"I am going to divide the year into four seasons. Summer will be the warm season, when you will shine all day for long days. Autumn will be a medium season. Winter will be your time to rest. Spring will be another middle season, when you will be getting yourself ready for Summer again."

But Winter was not satisfied. He thought he should control a longer part of the year than Summer controlled. So he and his four brothers challenged Summer and his four brothers to a wrestling match. Winter won, and all the Summer brothers were killed. The earth was very cold for a long time.

But one of the Summer brothers left a baby son. His mother and grandmother took the child south to live. When the baby grew to boyhood, he often asked about his father. But his mother would not answer him. "Where is my father?" he would ask. But his mother would not reply.

She encouraged him to become strong. Every day he took a sweat bath in the sweat lodge, so that he would obtain the power of Heat. From the sweat bath he plunged into the river, so that he would obtain the power of Cold. When he became a young man, he was very strong and had as his special helpers the powers of Heat and of Cold. One day he said to his mother, "I think I am prepared to meet anyone and anything."

His mother was glad. "Now I will tell you about your father," she said. And she told him also about the wrestling match between the five Winter brothers and the five Summer brothers.

Her story made the young man eager for revenge, and he challenged the five Winter brothers to a wrestling match. One at a time he fought them. He overcame the oldest brother and cut off his head. He overcame the second brother and cut off his head. The third and the fourth Winter brothers also he killed. But he let the youngest one remain alive.

"Because you are so young," the young man said, "I will let you live. We will share the year between us. You will be in power half of the time, and I will be in power half of the time."

And that is the way it has been ever since.

✖

Origin of the Sweat House

THE SWEAT HOUSE or sweat lodge, known to probably all the tribes north of Mexico, was very important in the ceremonial life of the Plateau and the Plains Indians. Among many tribes, nothing of significance was undertaken by an individual or by a group without the sweat bath and its accompanying rites, which included prayers and songs.

Even the construction of the simple lodge, in the old days, was done according to ritual. Anyone who built it irreverently or abused it in any way would have ill luck. It was a low, dome-shaped structure, with a framework of arched willow saplings. If it was for permanent use, this framework was covered with several layers of bark, earth, and grass. If for temporary use—near a summer camp, for example—it was covered with skins or blankets. The entrance usually faced a stream or lake. Stones were heated red-hot near the entrance and then were pushed into a pit dug inside the lodge. The bather or bathers crawled in, closed the entrance, poured water on the hot rocks, and bathed in the steam. They sweated from ten to thirty minutes (customs varied somewhat), all the time chanting songs and prayers to the spirit of the sweat house. Then they ran out and plunged into the stream or lake or, in winter, rolled in the snow.

The sweat-bath had purposes besides physical cleanliness. It was to purify the body and propitiate the spirits before war or any other serious undertaking; to invigorate the body after a hunt; to cure illness by influencing the spirits of disease; and, in some tribes, to enjoy the company of other men appreciating the luxury of the steam bath. The Crow Indians usually thought of the sweat lodge as an offering to the Sun. By some of the Plateau tribes, the sweat house was personified, almost deified. This Nez Percé account of its origin was recorded in 1896.

Long ago, in the days of the animal people, Sweat House was a man. He foresaw the coming of human beings, the real inhabitants of the earth. So one day he called all the animal people together, to give each one a name and to tell him his duties.

In the council, Sweat House stood up and made this speech: "We have lived on this earth for a long while, but we shall not be in our present condition much longer. A different people are coming to live here. We must part from each other and go to different places. Each of you must decide whether you wish to belong to the animal beings that walk or that fly, that creep or that swim. You may now make your choice."

Then Sweat House turned to Elk. "You will first come this way, Elk. What do you wish to be?"

"I wish to be just what I am—an elk."

"Let us see you run or gallop," said Sweat House.

So Elk galloped off in a graceful manner, and then returned.

"You are all right," decided Sweat House. "You are an elk."

Elk galloped off, and the rest saw no more of him.

Sweat House called Eagle to him and asked, "What do you wish to be, Eagle?"

"I wish to be just what I am—an eagle."

"Let us see you fly," replied Sweat House.

Eagle flew, rising higher and higher, with hardly a ripple on his outstretched wings.

Sweat House called him back and said to him, "You are an eagle. You will be king over all the birds of the air. You will soar in the sky. You will live on the crags and peaks of the highest mountains. The human beings will admire you."

Happy with that decision, Eagle flew away. Everybody watched him until he disappeared in the sky.

"I wish to be like Eagle," Bluejay told Sweat House.

Wanting to give everyone a chance, Sweat House said again, "Let us see you fly."

Bluejay flew into the air, trying to imitate the easy, graceful flight of Eagle. But he failed to keep himself balanced and was soon flapping his wings.

Noticing his awkwardness, Sweat House called Bluejay back to him and said, "A jay is a jay. You will have to be contented as you are."

When Bear came forward, Sweat House said to him, "You will be known among human beings as a very fierce animal. You will kill and eat people, and they will fear you."

Bear then went off into the woods and has since been known as a fierce animal.

Then to all the walking creatures, except Coyote, and all the flying creatures, to all the animals and birds, all the snakes and frogs and turtles and fish, Sweat House gave names, and the creatures scattered.

After they had gone, Sweat House called Coyote to him and said, "You have been wise and cunning. A man to be feared you have been. This earth shall become like the air, empty and void, yet your name shall last forever. The new human beings who are to come will hear your name and will say, 'Yes, Coyote was great in his time.' Now what do you wish to be?"

"I have lived long enough as Coyote," he replied. "I want to be noble like Eagle or Elk or Cougar."

Sweat House let him show what he could do. First Coyote tried his best to fly like Eagle, but he could only jump around, this way and that way. He could not fly, the poor fellow. Then he tried to imitate the Elk in his graceful gallop. For a short distance he succeeded, but soon he returned to his own gait. He ran a little way, stopped short, and looked around.

"You look exactly like yourself, Coyote," laughed Sweat House. "You will be a coyote."

Poor Coyote ran off, howling, to some unknown place. Before he got out of sight, he stopped, turned his head, and stood—just like a coyote.

Sweat House, left alone, spoke to himself: "All now are gone, and the new people will be coming soon. When they arrive, they should find something that will give them strength and power.

"I will place myself on the ground, for the use of the human beings who are to come. Whoever will visit me now and then, to him I will give power. He will become great in war and great in peace. He will have success in fishing and in hunting. To all who come to me for protection I will give strength and power."

Sweat House spoke with earnestness. Then he lay down, on his hands and knees, and waited for the first people. He has lain that way ever since and has given power to all who have sought it from him.

✳

The Great Flood

THE CONCEPT OF A GREAT FLOOD that once covered the earth is found in almost every mythology in the world. When the first missionaries came to the Northwest, they found that many tribes had traditions about the Deluge. Some of their flood stories, recorded in detail, tell of people being punished for evil-doing and of a few being saved on one of the giant peaks of the Cascade Range. The first of the following fragments was recalled by Otis Halfmoon, the fourth by Lucy Armstrong Isaac. No detailed flood story from the Nez Percés has been published, and none is known today.

THE GREAT FLOOD, some people say, took place long before the human race was created, back in the days of the animal people. It rained for a long, long time. The valleys were filled with water, and the animals lived on the tops of the hills. Some of the animals were saved, but the big animals perished. That is why people have found the bones of big animals along the Salmon River and big hip bones near Lewiston. Watermarks and driftwood carried by the flood have been found on Steptoe Butte in southeastern Washington.

OTHERS SAY that the great flood came in the early days of the first Indians. Some of the people along the Clearwater River were saved because they climbed a high mountain east of them. But many were drowned, those who could not or did not reach the top. The crest of that mountain is hollow, like a bowl. The water came nearly to the rim of this bowl but stopped there. All who reached the bowl were saved. Stone mortars, pestles, and other grinding implements have been found there, as well as horn spoons and other things.

YA-MAS-TAS, a mountain near Moscow, Idaho, is where the Nez Percés took refuge at the time of the great flood. All the other places but that one were under water. You can see up on that mountain still the stone in which they pounded their kouse roots. People say it looks just like one of their old mortars.

STEPTOE BUTTE STOOD above the waters at the time of the great flood, and many Indians were there saved from drowning. Below the top, there used to be a water line, the mark of where the water had once been.

The Nez Percés call the butte *Yamustus,* which means "Holy Mountain." About 1910, I went by train to the Spokane Fair. As we approached Steptoe, the old people crowded to one side so that they could see Yamustus.

The Origin of Fire

MOST NORTH AMERICAN INDIAN TRIBES, like other peoples throughout the world, had one or more myths about the origin of fire. Probably the simplest of the Nez Percé fire myths is this one related by Lucy Armstrong Isaac: Coyote's son used to kick a stump in such a way that fire would start and would jump out. At last the son said, "I'll fix it so that each person can make his own fire. He can rub two sticks together." And then he showed the first people how to do it.

A very different kind of story about the origin of fire is this one handed down in the Reuben family of Nez Percés.

Long ago the Nimipu had no fire. They could see fire in the sky sometimes, but it belonged to the Great Power. He kept it in great black bags in the sky. When the bags bumped into each other, there was a crashing, tearing sound, and through the hole that was made fire sparkled.

People longed to get it. They ate fish and meat raw as the animals do. They ate roots and berries raw as the bears do. The women grieved when they saw their little ones shivering and blue with cold. The medicine men beat on their drums in their efforts to bring fire down from the sky, but no fire came.

At last a boy just beyond the age for the sacred vigil said that he would get the fire. People laughed at him. The medicine men angrily complained, "Do you think that you can do what we are not able to do?"

But the boy went on and made his plans. The first time that he saw the black fire bags drifting in the sky, he got ready. First he bathed, brushing himself with fir branches until he was entirely clean and was fragrant with the smell of fir. He looked very handsome.

With the inside bark of cedar he wrapped an arrowhead and placed it beside his best and largest bow. On the ground he placed a beautiful white shell that he often wore around his neck. Then he asked his guardian spirit to help him reach the cloud with his arrow.

All the people stood watching. The medicine men said among themselves, "Let us have him killed, lest he make the Great Power angry."

But the people said, "Let him alone. Perhaps he can bring the fire down. If he does not, then we can kill him."

The boy waited until he saw that the largest fire bag was over his head, growling and rumbling. Then he raised his bow and shot the arrow straight upward. Suddenly, all the people heard a tremendous crash, and they saw a flash of fire in the sky. Then the burning arrow, like a falling star, came hurtling down among them. It struck the boy's white shell and there made a small flame.

Shouting with joy, the people rushed forward. They lighted sticks and dry bark and hurried to their tipis to start fires with them. Children and old people ran around, laughing and singing.

When the excitement had died down, people asked about the boy. But he was nowhere to be seen. On the ground lay his shell, burned so that it showed the fire colors. Near it lay the boy's bow. People tried to shoot with it, but not even the strongest man and the best with bow and arrow could bend it.

The boy was never seen again. But his abalone shell is still beautiful, still touched with the colors of flame. And the fire he brought from the black bag is still in the center of each tipi, the blessing of every home.

❈

Preparing for the New People

THE FOLLOWING STORY was related by Lucy Armstrong Isaac.

COYOTE WAS ALWAYS SAYING, "A new race of people are coming." Sometimes the animal people would ask, "What will become of us then? Where will we go?"

When Coyote felt sure that the new people were coming soon, he called a gathering of the animal people.

"We will pick out names for us," said Coyote, who was the first chief. "And we will decide how we will make our living, what we will do, and where we will live when the new people come."

Coyote himself wished to be Buffalo.

"Who will be a buffalo?" asked Fox, who was second chief.

"I will," answered Coyote. He tried to act like a buffalo but could not.

"You're not good enough to be a buffalo," Fox told him. "You will have to be Coyote."

Buffalo went out and acted like a buffalo, so he was named Buffalo.

"Who will be Beaver?" asked Fox.

"I want to be Beaver," answered Frog.

"Then swim across this stream and chew the trees down," said Coyote.

Frog could swim, but he could not chew the trees. He just stood and looked at a cottonwood tree. Then Beaver swam across and chewed down a tree.

"Yes, you will be Beaver," said Coyote and Fox.

Then Frog wanted to be Rabbit. "I can jump like a rabbit," he said. But he could not jump far enough.

"You're just a frog," he was told.

Cricket wanted to be a buffalo bull but he could not act like one. So he was Cricket. Some other creature became Buffalo Bull.

One of the little birds wanted to be Eagle but could not fly high enough. Meadow Lark wanted to be all kinds of birds.

"I can't give you that power," said Coyote. "But you will be able to speak all kinds of languages."

So he gave Meadow Lark an arrow necklace, all yellow and black, to wear round his neck, and made him able to speak any language he wanted to.

"Now we will decide where we will live and where we will go for the winter," said Coyote. "Human beings will soon be here. I will go where there is a good place for a den."

"I will find a hole in the mountains where I can hide in the winter," said Bear.

"I will build my nest high in a tree," said Eagle. "There I will be safe from human beings."

"We will build our nests in the trees, too," said the little birds. "People can not get us there."

"I will live close to some stream," said Beaver. "I can hide part of the time in the water. I will build for high water and for low water. I can always keep building."

Next day the new people came out of the ground—not just our people, but all people. And they spread over the earth.

When the human beings came, all the animals became silent. No longer did they have the power of speech.

Origin of the Lolo Trail

THE LOLO TRAIL is known in Northwest history as the old Indian trail which the Lewis and Clark Expedition followed when crossing the Bitterroot Range from the headwaters of the Missouri to the headwaters of the Columbia River. Also, Chief Joseph and his followers made their masterly retreat over the Lolo Trail in the Nez Percé War of 1877.

LONG AGO, a Nez Percé boy was lost in the mountains, where his people had gone on a hunting trip. Winter came on and he had no place to go. The animals saw him, and knowing that he would die if they did not help him, they called a council to decide what should be done.

"I will keep him," said Grizzly Bear. "I have no children of my own."

So she took the little boy to her home in the rocks. They slept there all winter, in her dry den which was well bedded with shredded cedar bark and soft decayed wood. In the spring Grizzly Bear said, "Now we will travel."

She took the boy eastward over the mountains—the Bitterroot Mountains, they are called now. Before winter came again, they returned over the mountains to the dry den in the rocks. Two snows they lived there together. Then Grizzly Bear was killed. But the boy stayed in the mountains, wintering in the bear's old home. After a time—no one knows how long—he was found by his people and taken back to his own country. He was able to show his people Grizzly Bear's trail over the mountains. They followed that trail when they went over to the buffalo country, and it has been known by the Indians ever since.

Some say that the boy returned to the grizzly bear people and never again was seen by his own people. On a hunting trip he had pointed across the canyon and said to his companions, "See that mist over there? That is where the grizzlies live."

The following summer he disappeared. His family thought that the Grizzlies killed him because he had betrayed them to the hunters.

✖

The Guardian of Lolo Hot Springs

THESE MAY HAVE BEEN the hot springs that Captain Clark observed in September, 1805, a few days before he reached the Nez Percés. He put his finger into the water and at first could not bear the heat.

NEAR THE HOT SPRINGS which are along the Lolo Trail, a hunter named Thunder Eyes killed a deer. As he was skinning it, he heard a loud whistling, like the whistle of the squirrel that lives on the ground. Thunder Eyes said to himself, "Eh! that is a loud whistle! There must be a big ground squirrel near by."

He kept on skinning the deer. Soon he heard the loud whistle again—and again—and again. "I will have to see what it is, this thing that makes such a loud whistle," thought Thunder Eyes.

He followed the sound through the morning sunshine, as he walked softly. When he reached a spot from which he could see the hot springs, he was startled by the sight of a great snake standing in the water. Its head and neck were the size of a man's thigh, and it was striped with yellow, blue, red, green, white, black—every color. It was a fine-looking snake, and it was whistling. When it caught sight of Thunder Eyes, it slowly sank below the surface of the water.

Thunder Eyes went to the spring and put his finger into it. The water was too hot for him; he wondered how the snake could live in it.

"Now I know that this spring is good water," he said. "My grandfather used to say, 'Where is found a good spring of lasting water, there will be found also the rattlesnake. He makes the water good.'

"No rattler is ever found in a spring of bad water or at a place where the spring has gone dry. I am glad I came to see what made the loud whistling." ✖

The Water Mysteries in Waha Lake

THESE TRADITIONS about Waha Lake, a little lake in the mountains above Lewiston, Idaho, were recalled by Lucy Armstrong Isaac in 1954. *Waha* means "beautiful." From as far away as Lapwai, Nez Percé boys were sent to Waha Lake for their solitary guardian spirit quest.

WHEN APPROACHING WAHA LAKE, you used to see a woman sitting beside the water. She was dressed in buckskin. As you came nearer, she would walk into the water and disappear. Foam would come up and there would be a little whirlpool.

One time when a man was out hunting, he shot a buck but did not kill it. The wounded deer ran toward Waha Lake and then out into the middle of it. After taking off his moccasins and his trousers, the man waded out a little way. Soon he felt something pull him into the water. Looking down, he saw a big red crawfish, then many big red crawfish. So he waded back to shore, picked up his moccasins and trousers, and hurried away. He was scared.

When he thought he was a safe distance from the lake, he looked back. The buck had disappeared. Where it had gone down, water with fur on it began to circle around. The last time the man looked back, the whole lake was covered with fur, and the fur was being blown by the wind.

The man never went to Waha Lake again. He told the rest of the people about his experience, and they never went there either. They were afraid of it.

Near Waha Lake is a little lake surrounded by willows and bushes and bulrushes. One time a woman was digging kouse near there. She had her baby with her. In the middle of the day, when she stopped to eat, she decided to bathe in the lake and to bathe her baby also. Both of them disappeared. Next day, when she did not come home, people went to the lake to look for her. They found her clothes and the baby's cradle board, but they never found the bodies. Some creature in the lake had seized them. So the Indians did not go there again.

�֍

Legend of Joseph Mountain

THE WALLOWA COUNTRY, the mountains and valleys loved by Chief

Joseph, is in northeastern Oregon. Old Joseph, father of the more famous chief, is buried at the foot of Wallowa Lake. This legend of the origin of the lake and of the largest mountain beside it was related by Otis Halfmoon.

MANY YEARS AGO, before the white man came here to live, an old chief of the Nez Percés went toward the sunrise to visit another tribe. When he returned to his home in the Wallowa country, he gathered his people together.

"The palefaces will come out here, to our hunting and fishing grounds," he told them. "They will want those shining rocks in our mountains."

"Let us kill them," counseled the young men.

"We can not do that," replied the chief. "They are too many. They would come in great bands and kill us all."

The wise men and the young men held many councils. At last it was decided that the shining rocks should be gathered in one pile and buried. For many moons the people worked. At last all the shining rocks were piled in a great pile beside the Wallowa River.

"But how can we bury them?" the young men asked. "How can we dig enough dirt to cover such a big pile? We must leave no signs of our digging."

Another council was held. A new plan was made. Again people worked for many moons. The snow came, and the snow melted. At last the work was done.

The people had carried great rocks and boulders, from all around, and had mingled them with the small shining rocks. A big mountain stood where the pile of shining nuggets had been.

At the foot of the mountain lay a deep lake, formed by the broadening of the river. Silver Lake, the Nez Percé people called it, as an ever constant reminder of the treasure which they had buried among the boulders.

Years later, after Joseph became chief of the Nez Percés, the mountain which his people had made was called Joseph Mountain.

The Strange Creatures in Wallowa Lake

PEOPLE USED TO SEE strange sights in Wallowa Lake early in the morning. If a person was very quiet, he might see a great herd of strange animals grazing on the shore of the lake. Some of the animals were buffaloes; some were blue and white elk; others were deer without horns. Some of them were so strange that people did not know their names. Great numbers of these animals lived in the lake.

If the person watching them made the slightest noise, the animals stampeded for the water. Bellowing, whinnying, barking, snorting, they plunged into the lake and churned the water into foam. But soon all would be peaceful once more, and the animals would not be seen again for a long time.

CATTLE USED TO BE SEEN coming up out of Wallowa Lake, also black bears. Crabs or lobsters of great size and of dangerous strength lived in the water and often came out on the shore. Sometimes they carried calves down into the lake. These crabs or lobsters were dangerous to people also.

When a white man settled in the Wallowa country, he lost some of his calves. He thought that a Nez Percé had taken them, and so he watched his stock at night. Early one morning he saw a heifer fighting one of these lobsters, and he shot it. Then he knew that Indians had not stolen his calves.

These frightful beings lived in the deepest part of the lake. One time a man saw one of them. He said that it was floating on the water above a deep and dark hole, and that it had great flippers with which it could dig and scoop out dirt and rocks like a steam shovel. The deep place where the man saw it is near the center of the lake and is very dangerous for canoes. The Indians knew where it was and thought they knew when the lobsters might pull them down. So they avoided passing over the place.

These dangerous beings finally disappeared. Whether they were killed or traveled to the ocean, no one knows.

LONG AGO, a young Nez Percé, hunting far up in the Wallowa

48

Mountains, surprised a huge horned monster. The monster fled, and the hunter followed it. On and on they ran, until they reached Wallowa Lake. The monster plunged in, and its pursuer followed.

Both swam rapidly and soon reached the middle of the lake. There the monster paused. Just as the hunter reached out to fight with it, the monster sank below the surface of the water. It was never seen again. The man swam about for a few minutes, and then he too sank and never rose again.

His children and their children, for many generations, believed that sudden death would come to anyone who dared go near the middle of the lake.

∾ Long ago, a young chief of an enemy tribe loved a Nez Percé maiden, the daughter of a chief. She loved him, but her father would not consent to their marriage. He would permit her to marry no one but a young man in their own tribe.

But the lovers continued to see each other secretly. One summer evening, when the shadows were deep, the young chief came down the mountain to the east shore of the lake. There he took his canoe from its hiding place and paddled across to the spot where the girl had promised to meet him. She joined him, and again the canoe moved softly out into the lake.

Suddenly they heard a shout from the beach. A Nez Percé guard had seen them. Almost at once, many canoes shot out in pursuit of the lovers. Just as the boats reached the middle of the lake, the waters heaved and a monster serpent leaped into the air. It swallowed the pursuing canoes, one after another, and then sank below the surface as suddenly as it had come.

But the lovers escaped. They reached the young chief's lodge in the land of the rising sun beyond the Shining Mountains.

Ever since then, the Nez Percés have stayed away from Wallowa Lake. Even today, the old men of the tribe will not fish in its waters. They go to the streams that flow into and out from the little lake, but they do not go upon the lake itself.

The Stick Indians

THE NEZ PERCÉS, like other tribes in the Northwest, have traditions about a race of dwarfs. Many Indians today refer to them as "the Stick Indians" (because they lived in the woods, it is thought); others call them "the Little People." The following details about them were recalled in 1954 by Lucy Armstrong Isaac, who had learned some of them from her father and others from a very old neighbor.

THE STICK INDIANS were just like human beings except that they were small. They wore deer skins wrapped around them, and they made strange sounds out in the woods. They lived in the deep woods, but they went anywhere and everywhere. Some day when the lumbermen cut down the trees in the deep forest, they will probably find where the Stick Indians live. The Nez Percé name for them is *Its'te-ya-ha*.

Sometimes the Stick Indians would rub themselves with a certain kind of grass and make themselves invisible. But sometimes they were visible. One time my grandmother's father found one of them, a tiny boy, dead on a flat rock. Once when my father was a boy, he was camping with his uncle and aunt. They were out hunting. One evening there was a storm, with thunder and lightning. Uncle Titus said to my father, "Cover yourself up. A strange visitor is coming."

My father and his aunt pulled their blankets over their faces, but my father found a hole in his blanket and peeped through it.

"Don't look!" warned his uncle.

But when the strange visitor came, my father looked. He saw a little man with very small eyes and a wrinkled face. He had long hair, uncombed, and he wore nothing but a deer skin wrapped around his waist and hanging down over his knees.

"Give me something to eat," the little man said to my father's uncle.

So Uncle Titus gave him some deer meat and some salmon. The little man took them and went away. Next day my father's face was swollen, as punishment for having peeked at the little man.

Sometimes the Stick Indians would whistle around the house. People would put out bits of salmon, and next morning the salmon would be gone. The little people had picked it up. Sometimes they would hoot so much like owls or howl so much like coyotes you would think they *were* owls or coyotes. Sometimes they would kidnap Indians; people who disappeared were thought to have been kidnapped by the Stick Indians.

These little people were very strong. An old white man told my father-in-law about an experience he had with one of them. The white man's sheep and calves were disappearing at night. He could find no tracks of them, although he looked every morning. So he stayed up one night, watching. Very early in the morning, just as it was beginning to get light, the white man saw a little man standing on the limb of a tree. He was holding two calves under each arm.

"There was nothing I could do with him," the white man said. "He was too strong for me."

One time when some people were huckleberrying near Mount Adams, they locked their baby in their car, for safety. No one else was in the car. While they were picking berries, they heard the baby cry. They went to the car and found that the baby was gone. Then they heard it cry from another direction. They went over there, and there they found it. The Little People had taken the baby out of a locked car.

This did happen.

✾

The Help of the Spirits

OCCASIONALLY, as the following story reveals, a person was given spirit power without an all-night vigil in a solitary place. This narrative, once told as a true story, was related by Otis Halfmoon.

"Snake Indians" is the common English name for the Northern Shoshonis. They called the Nez Percés "kouse-eaters"; the root of the kouse was a favorite vegetable of the Nez Percés and of their neighbors.

YEARS AGO, at the time of the spring salmon run, a Nez Percé family was camping at the mouth of a creek that flows into the Wallowa River, in what is now northeastern Oregon. All were busy

—the men catching the salmon, the women cleaning and drying it for the winter food supply.

One morning, just at dawn, they were surrounded and attacked by a party of Snake Indians. Almost helpless against the larger number, the Nez Percé men were killed and scalped, and one girl was taken captive. The Snakes carried her away with them, traveling over the mountains and down the canyons until they reached the Snake River country across from where Weiser is now. The journey took them several days.

"We have a girl from the kouse-eaters," said the warriors to the people of their village.

When night came, the Snakes were afraid the girl might escape. So they had her lie down between two women in the big tipi, and then they tied the girl's legs and arms to the legs and arms of the women beside her. Soon all the people in the big tipi were asleep— all except the Nez Percé girl. She lay tense and full of fear.

Suddenly she heard a voice. "You aren't going to die, little girl. Those strings aren't strong to me. I could chew them, and I give you the power to chew them."

A long time the girl lay wondering about the voice and the message. Then she heard the voice again.

"Little girl, I gave you the power to get away. You can hide."

Again the girl lay wondering about the voice and the message. When she heard it a third time, she knew that a spirit was speaking to her.

"There is nothing to fear little girl. This is the plains country, the country of thunder and lightning. And I give you the power to control thunder."

So the girl started chewing the rawhide thongs that bound her to the sleeping women. She chewed off the string from one arm, from the other arm, from one foot, from the other foot. She was free!

She heard the voice again, with a last message. "Thunder is my outlet here."

The girl lay quietly for a few moments. Soon she heard a roll of thunder. Then another and another, closer and closer. Lightning flashed. The wind blew. People who had been sleeping in the open rushed inside the big tipi. The smaller tipis were blown down. There was much excitement in the camp, but the women who had been tied to the girl still lay sleeping. The spirit that had spoken to her had made them sleep.

In the midst of the excitement the Nez Percé girl got up and slipped out of the tipi. Thunder still rolled, lightning flashed, and now rain was falling. Except for the flashes of lightning, the night was so dark she could see nothing, but she walked quite a distance in the darkness. When morning came, the clouds opened up.

"I am free," she said to herself. "If the powers don't disappoint me, I can find my way home."

She started north, into the sagebrush country. Soon she heard a noise behind her and, looking back, she saw a cloud of dust.

"The Snakes on horseback!" she thought. "What shall I do?"

"Hide!" she heard a voice say. "I give you power to hide."

Then she knew that her guardian spirit was leading her, and she hid in the sagebrush. The horses came closer and closer, their hoofs pounding and stirring up a great cloud of dust. But no one saw her, and the horses jumped over her. After a while the men returned, walking their horses this time, and grumbling and mumbling that they would find her in camp, after all. Even after they had passed by her, the girl remained hidden among the sagebrush. She heard the men shouting and yelling as they looked for her in the camp and then searched through the valley and the flats around the village.

All day she lay there, becoming stiff and hungry and very thirsty. At twilight two wolves came to her, and one of them said kindly, "Come on, little girl. We will take you home. One of us will stay in front of you, the other behind. We will protect you. But first you must eat something."

So she ate some of the food the wolves had brought her and then walked along between them. She felt well protected as they journeyed along the trail. After a while she saw the Wallowa Mountains, blue in the distance. "Soon I will be home," she said, but it was really several days before she reached home.

When they came to the place where she had been captured, she saw an old man lying near where their campfire had been. She recognized him as her father and tried to cover up his body. Near the place where her mother had been pounding kouse, she found some roots in a hole in the rocks. Taking some of them, she soaked them in water and ate them. She and the wolves rested there quite a while. Then they went on toward the Cold Spring country, over the mountains and down into the brushwood country.

Nez Percé scouts, always on guard now and always watching, saw something far away on a ridge.

"It looks like a fly moving," one scout said to the other. "But it comes along and then seems to fall down."

"I see two animals with it," said another scout, "one in the lead and one behind. They look like wolves."

The guards sent a scout out to get a nearer view, and he sent a message back: "The one in the middle is a human being. Looks like a woman walking. She's about all in."

Soon he sent another message to the village: "The girl that was captured last year is coming home."

Then the wolves slipped away into the bushes. They had brought the girl safely home. The people of the village, going out to meet her, found that she was just skin and bones. They carried her to her mother's tipi, and there she almost faded away.

"*Wat-ku-ese,*" her mother called her. "She has escaped and returned home."

She had been gone from the spring salmon time of one year until the spring salmon time of the next year.

❦

Prophecy of the Coming of the White Men

"Throughout the northern region west of the Rocky Mountains one hears in almost every tribe a tradition that before the appearance of the first white man, a dreamer, or in some instances (and nearer the truth) a wandering Indian of another tribe prophesied the coming of a new race with wonderful implements."[1]

This Nez Percé prophecy was related by Lucy Armstrong Isaac.

A N OLD MAN in Lapwai—I forget his name—used to see the future in his dreams. He would see white-faced animals a little bigger than deer coming over the hill. They would come down Thunder Hill, between Lapwai and the Clearwater River. Behind the white-faced deer was a white-faced man.

"Another kind of human being is going to be here soon," the old man would tell his people.

Other men laughed at him.

"We are going to have some writing given us," he told them. "We must have our ears open so that we can understand it. A white-faced man will explain it. We will have seven sleeps, and the seventh day will be a holy day.

"The earth will be plowed up. There will be many ways of going fast to other places. People will go fast on the land and fast in the air, like big birds."

People laughed at the old man's dreams, laughed at what he said would happen. But everything he prophesied came true.

This is a true story, not a myth or legend.

❄

The Wandering Nez Percé

HAR-HARTSE-TOOTSI HIMSELF told Otis Halfmoon's father this story of his wanderings. Both were from the Salmon River country. The old man made his journey before the coming of Lewis and Clark, probably some time in the late eighteenth century.

H AR-HARTSE-TOOTSI SAID he had often wondered where the sun comes from, so he decided to find out. Taking horses, moccasins, and enough food to last for a long time, he started east. For ten snows he traveled toward the rising sun, traveling across plains

[1] Edward S. Curtis, *The North American Indian*, VIII, 76.

and over mountains. Always he saw the sun farther on. He came to a big river, went down it to another big river and on down the second river. He still had his horses.

Along the way he met many Indians. Some of them wanted to kill him, but for some reason they decided to leave him alone. At last he decided to give up trying to find where the sun came from.

Along the way he saw white people, also. They had hair on their faces, and they seemed to be eating fire. He thought they were some kind of grasshopper, because they were always chewing and spitting something brown.

One winter he stayed where some people were kind to him. He thought the place was called Cincinnati. Some people there were good; others were bad and wanted to kill him. Where did all these strange people come from, he wondered.

Then he went down another river, clear to the mouth of it. There he saw a different kind of people. They wore big hats and little blankets. He stayed there for a winter. When he looked across the river, he saw the sun rising, still a long distance away. So he started west.

He saw much sand and cactus bigger than pine trees. He came again to the people with the big hats and the little blankets and stayed with them for five winters. He married there among the Indians and had several children.

Then he started north and in time reached The Dalles on the big river, the Columbia. From there he came up the rivers and back to his own country, the Salmon River country.

"How many years were you gone?" my father asked.

"About twenty," replied Har-Hartse-tootsi.

That winter the people had the winter dance, as usual, in the long lodge. It was big enough for seven fires. All were dressed in their regalia, the singers in the middle, the people dancing round the fires. The man who had taken the long journey taught them two dances which he said he had learned from the Spanish people. He told many stories of the things he had seen.

Until he died, a very old man, he told people stories about the many strange things and strange people he had seen on his journey toward the rising sun.

⌘

Lewis and Clark among the Nez Percés

When Kate McBeth came to the Protestant mission among the Nez Percés of Idaho in 1879, the story of the coming of the Lewis and Clark Expedition in September, 1805, was such a favorite around the home fires and the camp fires that even her school children knew it. Mrs. Lizzie Lowery, interpreted by Oliver Frank, related the first of the following traditions in the summer of 1952. She was then about ninety-five years old.

Lewis and Clark discovered our country. The people of my village ran away when they first saw the white men. They were afraid of their beards, for they had never seen people with hair on their faces. And they had never seen mules before. They thought the mules were some kind of overgrown rabbits.

Watkuese saved the Lewis and Clark men from being killed. *Watkuese* means "escaped and returned to her own country." The girl had been captured and taken away to some place in the east—somewhere on an island. Her baby was born there, a little boy. When he was six or seven months old, able to sit up and crawl around, she decided to come home to her people. She only knew that she should follow the sun. She tied her baby on her back and crossed the water on a drifting log. Then she walked toward the setting sun. For a long, long time she walked. She used elderberries for food. Old Grizzly Bear went with her and protected her part of the way, and Chipmunk protected her part of the way. When danger came near, Chipmunk made a fog so that nothing could see her. Some white people helped her, too.

Somewhere along the way, her baby died and she buried him. She kept on following the sun, and so she came back home to her people. That is why she is called Watkuese.

She was in one of our villages when Lewis and Clark came from across the Rising Sun Mountains. She heard the men talking about killing the white men, and she begged them not to because white men had helped her. So our people made friends with Lewis and Clark and gave them food. They started trading what they had. They helped the white men across the river and escorted them part of the way.

THIS SECOND TRADITION was related by Otis Halfmoon, the third one by Elizabeth Wilson, of Kamiah, Idaho. The black man mentioned in these accounts was Captain Clark's Negro servant, York. Some who saw him, Sam Tilden recalled, thought he had been smoked.

ONE TIME, when a band of Nez Percés from where Lewiston is now were over in the Flathead country, several of them had the same dream. Their dream caused them to make this prophecy: "Some day strange people will come over the mountains from the rising sun. They will wear something on their heads with feathers on it. They will eat dogs. They will eat horses. They will mark out lands. They will plant things. They will come to the Clearwater River. Some day they will cause us lots of trouble."

Most of the people did not believe the dreams. They had heard about a long trip one of their old men had taken to distant places, where he had seen strange people, and they thought that the dreams were influenced by this story.

Then they heard that strange men really were coming down the river from Kamiah. Billy Williams saw them first. They had hair on their faces, and they wore hats with red feathers. The reality was just like the dream.

Some of the Nez Percés wanted to kill the strange-looking men, but they were afraid of the black man who was with them. He had shining eyes that rolled around in his head. "If we kill these others," they said, "the black man will surely kill us." So they let the strangers come on. They reached the place where Lewiston is now and stayed there for a few days. Some Indians helped them; others wanted to get rid of them.

The Nez Percés farther up the Clearwater River also had been frightened. Some wondered whether the strangers were human beings at all, and they wondered what had burned up the black man. Especially frightened were the Indians near Kamiah, who first saw the strangers when the black man was paddling a canoe. One woman was so panic-stricken that she ran away and left her baby fastened on his cradle board, leaning against a tree. She had put him there while she was working. After a while her husband slipped back from the woods and got the baby. Chief Lawyer always laughed when he told his part of the story; he had been that child on the cradle board.

❧ EARLIER, up the Weippe River above the Clearwater River, some people had wanted to kill the strangers right away. They were scared of the white men, and they were scared of the black man. "What had burned him up?" they wondered. But they would have killed all the strangers if it had not been for Watkuese.

When she was a girl, she had been taken captive during a fighting. The Nez Percés were beaten. She was taken east and there was sold to some white people. Perhaps they were Canadian-French.[1] They had fair faces, blond hair, and light-colored eyes, blue or green. She had hiked all the way home. On the way her little boy died of starvation.

When the strangers came to Weippe Prairie, she was there, sick in bed. She heard the commotion and asked, "What's the matter?"

"Some strange people have come. They have pale faces and eyes like the eyes of a cooked fish. One of the men is black and looks like an evil spirit. Everybody is plumb scared. The chiefs and all the other men are having a council. They have passed the pipe around. They plan to kill all these white men."

"Bring the head chief to me," said Watkuese. "I must talk to him right away."

[1] The Nez Percé word for *French* was pronounced *Ah-Lime'ah* by Mrs. Wilson.

When he was brought to her tipi, Watkuese told him, "These are some of the people who were good to me. When I was captured, I was taken many sleeps away. Indians sold me to white people. They were good to me. They helped me start home.

"When I was coming all that long journey, when I was hungry, white people fed me. When I was sick, white people took care of me. They will be kind to you, too. Don't be afraid of them, and don't harm them. They did no harm to me. Go up close to them and make friends with them."

The chief went back to the council and told the men what Watkuese had said. They held their meeting for a long time. Finally they agreed, "We will save them."

Watkuese died very soon afterward—that very night, I think. If it had not been for her, all the Lewis and Clark men would have been killed.[2]

[2] After reading Bernard De Voto's abbreviated edition of the *Journals of Lewis and Clark* the following winter, Mrs. Wilson wrote to me: "What I told you is a true Indian story about Lewis and Clark's outfit. But none of it is mentioned in the book. I gather that it was never explained to them how close they were to being killed and that this one woman saved their lives. I suppose they had no way of knowing what was going on. They mention that they were kindly treated, but it might have been otherwise."

III. Salishan Tribes: The Flatheads, the Kalispels, and the Coeur D'Alênes

❦

SHORTLY BEFORE the members of the Lewis and Clark Expedition reached the Nez Percés, they had spent three days with a band of Flathead Indians in the Bitterroot Valley of what is now western Montana. These people also had received them in a friendly manner and had shared their only food at the time—berries—with the first white men they had ever seen. The Flatheads' oral history of the coming of the explorers will be found near the end of this section.

A few years later, David Thompson, of the Hudson's Bay Company, thought the Flatheads colorful in their fringed buckskin garments decorated with beads and porcupine quills. He described the people as "meticulously clean, amiable, truthful, upright." Another Hudson's Bay man, Ross Cox, coming upon a small village of Flatheads in 1812, was "charmed by their frank and hospitable reception." After a winter with them, he recorded that they were "honest, brave, quiet and amenable to their chiefs, cleanly . . . [and] decided enemies to falsehood of every description." Ferris of the American Fur Company (1830–35) was lavish in his praise of the Flatheads, enumerating nine "manly virtues that have no parallel in the Rocky Mountains."

The Flatheads, the Kalispels, and Coeur d'Alênes belong to the large Salishan linguistic family of the Northwest. In language and culture they are closely related to the other Salishan tribes of the Plateau (the Spokane, the Sanpoil, the Okanogan, and others), less closely to the numerous Coast Salish tribes, who live west of the Cascade Range.

The term "Flatheads" is misleading, for these people never had the practice of changing the shape of their babies' heads, as did some tribes west of them. At least three explanations of the name have been given, each of which seems plausible. The Flatheads' name for themselves is Salish; its meaning is forgotten, although the last syllable seems to mean "people."

The Kalispels, meaning "camas people," were given the name Pend d'Oreilles ("Earring people") because, when first seen by French-Canadian traders and trappers, most of them wore large shell earrings. Never numerous, the Kalispels lived in present-day northern Idaho, on Lake Pend Oreille, Priest Lake, and nearby rivers. David Thompson, who built a trading post among them in 1809, wrote that they prided themselves "on their industry, and their skill in doing anything, and are as neat in their persons as circumstances will allow, but without Soap there is no effectual cleanliness." He praised them also for their morality and their chastity.

The Kalispels and the Flatheads have lived together peacefully for centuries, and today on the Flathead Reservation of western Montana, where most of them live, they think of themselves as one people. Their oral literature and other aspects of their culture are nearly identical; even differences in their dialects have almost disappeared. A few Kalispels still live in northern Idaho and adjacent Washington.

The Coeur d'Alênes lived south of the Kalispels, in present-day Idaho, chiefly along Lake Coeur d'Alene and the streams that flow into it and out of it. They once extended into Washington, almost to the waterfalls in the present city of Spokane. Their name for themselves is *Skitswish,* the meaning of which is unknown. The name *Coeur d'Alene*—that is, "Awl heart" or "Stingy hearted"—developed from trade with French-Canadians. Some say that it was a Skitswish chief's description of a trader's heart; others, that it was the *voyageurs'* description of these Indians, whom they found shrewd in trading. Most of the tribe now live on their reservation south of the city of Coeur d'Alene.

All three of these tribes were converted to Christianity by Jesuit missionaries. After three delegations of Flatheads had journeyed to St. Louis in the 1830's to ask for religious teachers whom wandering Iroquois Indians had told them about, a young Belgian priest, Pierre

Jean De Smet, volunteered. In the spring of 1840, the Jesuits sent him to the Indians of the northern Rockies. In a few years he and other Jesuits had established missions and schools among the Flatheads in the Bitterroot Valley (at Stevensville), among the Coeur d'Alênes, and among the Kalispels, first along the Pend Oreille River and then in Mission Valley. Both the last one—St. Ignatius Mission, serving the Kalispels and the Flatheads—and the Coeur d'Alêne mission are still active. In his long and informative letters to his superiors, Father De Smet had only words of praise for these people, who always greeted him with warmth and joy.

These Salishan tribes observed several native religious ceremonies even after missionaries came among them. In the spring when the first bitterroot and camas bulbs were dug, but before any of them were eaten, the Coeur d'Alênes gathered together, and the chief of a camp prayed a long prayer of gratitude to Amotken, the Creator, who lived on the highest mountain; the chief also offered Amotken some of the roots on a tray or in a basket. A similar ceremony was held when the first important berry crop was ripe. The chief prayed first to the sun and then to the earth. After the prayer, the people often danced for a while and then ate of the first fruits. The Flatheads also thanked Amotken in "first fruits" ceremonies.

A Thanksgiving ceremony, years ago, was performed by the Coeur d'Alênes at the end of the harvest, when all the roots, berries, and salmon were preserved and stored for the winter. They thanked Amotken for the plentiful harvest and asked him for another the next year. Then they prayed to the sun for success on the buffalo hunt, which was about to begin. Among the Flatheads and Kalispels, after the collective buffalo hunts began, the "first bison" ceremony was important; on the winter expedition, the flesh of the first buffalo was ceremonially roasted, and prayers were offered by the head chief.

The Midwinter Festival, the most important religious ceremony of the Flatheads and Kalispels in pre-Christian days, consisted of the Camas Dance and the Bluejay Dance. The Camas Dance was a merry occasion of feasting, dancing, and prayer for a plentiful supply of roots in the spring. People were often married at this time. The festival lasted for four days. After four days of rest, the serious Blue-jay Dance began, in which prayers were offered to all the guardian spirits. The ceremony is described among the stories in this section.

Very few of the traditional tales of the Flatheads, Kalispels, and Coeur d'Alênes have been published. A brief account of Flathead mythology was written by Father Gregory Mengarini, who in 1841 assisted Father De Smet in establishing a mission in the Bitterroot Valley. A part of this account, never published until 1955, is the first story in this section. Another part, about giants, is as follows:

➤ SINCHLEP, the prairie wolf [Coyote], was regarded as the most powerful and favorable to mankind [of all the animal "geniuses"]. To show the power and favor of Sinchlep, their ancestors reported that there was a time when a large portion of the earth was inhabited by a set of giants, terrible men, who killed everyone they met with, for which they were called *Natliskeliguten,* which in the ancient language means killers of men; that Sinchlep in pity for the smaller people, went through all the earth, killed every giant, and converted them all into large stones; and even of late, when the Flatheads in crossing the mountains saw a basaltic rock standing upright on the top, they said to one another, "Keep aside, there is *Natliskeliguten,* killed by Sinchlep," and every large piece of Silex they saw around was for them a fragment of an arrow of the killers of men. . . .

"Fully half of the Flathead stories," wrote H. H. Turney-High nearly a century after Mengarini, "deal with these giants, and easily two-thirds mention them." They had amazing strength. Once when a small hunting party came upon a giant asleep in the forest, they tied him with ropes of buffalo hair, sat upon his chest, and beat him until he wakened. Then he laughed thunderously, burst the ropes, and sent the men flying through the air as he rose to his feet. Seizing one of them by the ankle, he tossed the man across the Missoula River.

Giants were visible to the human eyes, but they usually avoided being seen. They gradually decreased in number because, some say, there was not enough food for such huge creatures.

Coyote is the principal character in each of the eleven Flathead tales published by Louisa McDermott in 1901, the only collection from that tribe in print before this one. He was said to be a great chief and was usually dressed in "nice clothes, all beaded and trimmed in shells." Often he was assisted by his friend Fox. Coyote killed the giant who was causing the animal persons to starve to death. He killed another giant on a butte near Stevensville. He made the falls in the Spokane River to keep the salmon from coming to the Pend d'Oreille people, whose chief had refused to allow him to marry any girl in his tribe.

The Coeur d'Alênes used to relate a creation myth similar to the final episode in the Nez Percé "Coyote and the Monster of the Clearwater River." This monster was near the mouth of the Palouse River, a tributary of the Snake. (The Palouse Indians told variants of the story.) After a long fight with the monster, Coyote killed it, cut up the body, and from each part made a different tribe—from the scalp, the Crow Indians with their long hair; from the legs, the tall Blackfeet, and so on. In a fragment recalled by Julia Nicodemus in 1954, a giant walking along the coast saw the body of a big monster. The giant cut it into little pieces and threw them as far as he could. Each piece turned into an Indian village, complete with smoke from the lodge fires. The ribs became the Nez Percés; the heart, the Coeur d'Alênes. The Spokane Indians and the Coeur d'Alênes, said an elderly member of both tribes, used to relate almost identical fireside stories.

A large proportion of the Flathead-Kalispel tales in this volume are from two sources: Pierre Pichette and Bon Whealdon. Pichette, a Flathead full blood, cut off from normal activities by blindness, was persuaded about 1905 by a white judge to become an authority on the traditions and customs of his people. From his elders came the stories he related in the summer of 1953, the year before his death. He had long hoped to write a book about his people. Bon Whealdon, who had a strain of Delaware blood in him, first came to the Flathead Reservation in 1907. A few years later, he began collecting the traditions of his Salish neighbors, conversing with the old Indians in the Chinook jargon, which he had learned in childhood, but depending chiefly upon an educated half-blood as his interpreter. It was his custom to record a story from a group of elderly people, encouraging them to correct each other, meanwhile carefully listing the names of all participants. If he recorded a story from just one person, he checked his notes with other full bloods.

Surprising in his collection is a group of myths in which the culture-hero is Bluejay, an important character in the mythology of several tribes along the coast of Oregon and Washington. Now we can only wonder whether these myths were connected with the Bluejay Ceremonial Dance. We can only wonder whether there is any connection between the Bluejay myths and the Flathead tradition that their ancestors migrated from the banks of a river that flows into the Pacific Ocean. In oral records, where is the dividing line between history and myth or legend?

❊

In the Beginning

"OF THE CREATION OF mankind there are probably as many stories as there are tribes," wrote George Gibbs in 1865, in the first extensive study of Northwest Indian mythology. The following creation myth of the Salish or Flathead Indians was sent to Gibbs by Father Gregory Mengarini. The Salish believed, wrote Mengarini, that the "earth is flat and surrounded by water, like an island; the sky is a huge hollow mountain, covering the earth like the covering of a kettle. . . . When the Salish Indians saw the whites the first time, they thought them the sons of Amotken and hence immortal, until one of them was killed by Blackfeet."

BEFORE THE WORLD was created, a son was born to a very powerful woman, Skomeltem. The son's name is Amotken, which means "he who sits on top of the mountain," for his home is on the summit of the covering of the earth. Amotken created heaven and earth and mankind. He created other worlds also, worlds under and above and around us. His mother lives alone on one of those worlds beyond the waters.

The first human beings that Amotken created became very wicked and turned a deaf ear to his teachings and his warnings. Angry with them, he drowned all of them in a great flood. Then he created a second tribe, twice as tall as the first. But they became even more wicked than the first people, and so Amotken destroyed them by fire from heaven. He created a third tribe; when they became as wicked as the first, he destroyed them by a pestilence. The fourth tribe would have been destroyed also had not Amotken's mother begged him to let them live. She so softened the anger of Amotken that he promised never to destroy his creations again.

Until the time of the fourth tribe, the world was in darkness, for there was no sun. Believing that the sole cause of their wickedness was the darkness, the people held a council to discuss the matter. These were the animal people—animals that could reason and talk. All of them refused to be the sun except Sinchlep, or Coyote. He was the smartest and most powerful of the animal people. But when Coyote was the sun and passed over the land, he saw what everyone was doing. And he called out, so that all might hear, even the secret doings of people. The evildoers angrily took Coyote by the tail, which at that time was very long, and brought him back to the ground. They told him that he could no longer be the sun.

Crow then offered to be the sun. But as he was really black all over, he gave very little light. People laughed at him. Unable to endure their ridicule, Crow gave up the task in shame.

Amotken, though invisible, had several sons, one of whom was Spokani. Seeing the people's need for light, he sent Spokani down to be the sun. Spokani, wishing to marry a woman from the earth, landed in a camp of Flatheads. People thought him very handsome but so different from themselves that they refused to admit him to their lodges.

Disappointed, Spokani left the place. Nearby, he saw a family of frogs to whom he complained about the treatment their neighbors had given him. One of the frogs, very large and fat, said that she was willing to marry him; she would be happy to become the wife of Amotken's son. With a jump she attached herself to one cheek of Spokani.

The neighboring people, seeing the disfigured cheek, were so angry that they tried to kill the frog with sticks, but they could not. She remained on Spokani's cheek. She begged him to leave the earth and become the sun at once.

And so Spokani became the sun. To revenge himself for the contempt of the people, he does not allow them to see him closely during the day but covers himself with a shining robe. As night approaches, he removes his robe, crosses the waters under the earth, and then only shows himself as he is. Then he is the moon. The spots on the moon are the frog on his cheek.

⚜

Amotken and Coyote

FROM INTERVIEWS with Lassaw Redhorn, Quequesah, and Domicie Michell, Bon Whealdon obtained the following information about pre-Christian beliefs of the Flathead and Kalispel Indians.

THE SUPREME ONE in our older beliefs was given several names: *Amotken,* Big Spirit Above, Sky Chief, Power of the Upper World, and Highest Mystery. "Amotken" and "Highest Mystery" were the names generally used in praying to the Supreme One and in praising Him. Amotken was the Creator of the sun, the earth, and all living things. The sun was the symbol of Amotken. The Salish were never worshippers of the sun, as were some other tribes.

When asked if the sun was Amotken, an old Indian replied, "No, no, the sun is Amotken's child who helped us. We look at the sun and thank Amotken for it. The sun is our very good friend."

Amotken created Coyote to be his special helper, and assigned to him the welfare of all Indians. Coyote was to overcome the evil work of Amteep, the wicked chief of the lower world. Once Amteep tried to bring famine upon the earth by blighting the berries, fruits, and vegetables. So Coyote persuaded the salmon and the trout to seek places of spawning in the fresh-water streams, and he taught the Indians how to catch and prepare fish for food.

When Amteep emptied his parfleche, his rawhide bag containing diseases and illnesses, Coyote brought healing herbs from the upper world and planted them upon the earth. When the plants were ready for use, he taught the medicine men how to prepare them and how to use them in healing.

When Amotken saw that the people needed more food, he told Coyote to bring buffalo to the plains, and to teach the Indians how to make bows and arrows and how to kill the great animals. Then Coyote showed them how to use the meat and the tallow. When Amteep blew his icy breath over the land to freeze the people, Coyote taught them to make clothing, bedding, and tipis from the warm robes of the buffalo.

During the early days, before Coyote was created, Amotken often appeared in person upon the earth, in order to teach the people to live better. Then he took the form of an elderly man, a white man. While Amotken was on the earth, there were no deaths, no suffering, no misfortunes of any kind. Winter did not come. Roots and fruits and berries were plentiful. Amteep and his evil helpers were unable to come up into the earth world.

"All people should live in peace," Amotken told the medicine men. "All men are brothers."

IN A LESS religious version of these traditions, Pierre Pichette told of a power contest between Coyote and a Stranger whom he met in a pleasant meadow. The Stranger proved to be the Creator. The story ends as follows:

＞ THE CREATOR TOLD Coyote to prove his power by lifting a rock that lay near them, a rock about the size of a person's head. Coyote jumped at it, thinking that he could lift it easily.

He tried and tried, but he could not lift it. He tried to roll it, but he could not move the rock at all.

The Creator stood looking at him and then spoke: "You have found out for yourself that you can do nothing with that little rock. You can't move it. All you have told me is false. When I said to you, 'Lift that rock,' you tried to lift the whole world. You have failed. I am the one who is taking care of the world. Everything is under my care.

"Now listen carefully. Hereafter you will be called the Sachem of beasts and of everything. And you will have power, granted through me, to do many things. Hereafter you will travel through the country. On your way you will meet evil beasts and scorpions that have great powers. I am granting you power so that you will be able to destroy these monsters. I am sending you into this country for the purpose of destroying them.

"In generations to come, the human race will live in this country, free from the monsters, and happy. They will increase in numbers, and you will help them. You will teach them what I tell you to teach them.

"You will be killed by the monsters many times, but I give you a companion to help you—your cousin Fox. Fox will be able to bring you back to life by jumping over you. And you can protect yourself by taking other forms—the form of a human being or an animal or this and that. When you need to change into another form, just call upon your powers to change you.

"Now you know why you could not lift that rock. Now you know that I have more power than you have."

That is how Coyote became a great sachem. The Creator made him one.

⌘

Origin of the Moon and the Sun

TALES OF HOW the sun and the moon were obtained and placed in the sky are numerous in the mythologies of the North American Indians. Parallels with at least different parts of this Kalispel myth were once related by several Interior Salish tribes. On the Coeur d'Alêne Reservation, Julia Nicodemus told me a variant of the first half; Stanislaus Aripa, a variant of the second half.

L ONG AGO, when the world was very young, the moon was the play-
thing of a certain tribe of animal people. One day Coyote said
to Antelope, "Let our sons go out and learn how to steal the moon."

He and Antelope lived together, and each of them had four sons.
Following their fathers' instructions, the eight young men went up
into the mountains, each in a place by himself, to fast and to obtain
the help of his spirit. Again and again they were sent out. At last
Coyote said, "Our boys should be wise enough now to steal the moon."

When the eight young men reached the open space where the
animal people were rolling the great round shining ball, they hid
themselves at one end of the play field. Now the owners of the moon
knew that the boys were coming to steal it. They rolled it toward
the boys, sure that it was too heavy for anyone to take away. But the
Coyote brothers, one at a time, rolled it toward their home. The
owners of the moon caught up with the Coyote brothers and killed
them, one at a time. The Antelope brothers took the moon from the
youngest Coyote, and they ran so swiftly that no one could catch them.

When they reached home and told Coyote that his four sons had
been killed, Coyote began to cry loudly. "Put out the fire and give
me that moon," he said to the Antelope brothers. They obeyed him,
he took the moon back to its owners, and they gave him his sons,
restored to life.

One day Sapsucker said to his grandmother, "Let me go and steal
the moon." So he set out. When the moon people saw him coming,
they knew his purpose and began to laugh.

"Roll the moon toward little Sapsucker," said one of them. "Let's
see what he can do with such a big thing."

When it reached him, he lifted it with difficulty and staggered off
with it. Again the people laughed. "Let him go as far as that ridge.
But if he passes over it, we will kill him."

They did not know that Sapsucker was very clever. When they
reached the top of the ridge, they saw him and the moon at the top
of the next hill. He had rolled the moon down the first slope, and

its momentum had carried it almost to the top of the second slope. Sapsucker flew over the valley and pushed the ball the rest of the way. The people ran after him until they were tired out, and Sapsucker rolled the moon to his home.

Sadly the people started home without the moon. "Let us make a new moon," they said. "And let us place it in the sky."

"Who will be the new moon?" someone asked.

The people discussed and discussed the matter. Finally they decided that Yellow Fox should be the new moon, and Yellow Fox agreed. They put him in the sky, where he was to shine by day as well as by night. But he made the days so hot that they took him down.

Then they asked Coyote, "Do you think that you would be a good moon?"

"Yes, of course," he replied. "I would like to be the moon, for then I can see everything."

So they placed Coyote in the sky. He did not make the days too hot, but he did see everything. And whenever he saw anything wrong being done, he called out loudly the name of the person and the wrong thing he was doing. The people who wished to do things in secret demanded that Coyote be taken from the sky.

Two young men in the tribe—nicely dressed young men—were desired by four Frogs. The Frogs wanted the two young fellows as their husbands but did not know how to get them. One Frog made a plan. She made everything in the forest wet, so that the young men could find only one dry place in which to sit. That was inside the cedar-bark lodge of Frogs. Instantly one Frog jumped on the face of one of the men and stuck there so fast that he could not remove her. The other Frogs blinded the other young man in one eye.

When the people tried to help the two men, they could do nothing. The blinded one said, "I think I should be the sun. I am ashamed to go about as a man with only one eye."

"I will be the moon," the other man said. "I do not want to go among people with this Frog on my face."

So the people placed the two up in the sky, to be the sun and the moon. The spots we see on the moon are the Frog still sticking to the young man's face. The sun, as we all know, has only one eye.

❆

Creation of the Red and the White Races

THIS CREATION MYTH can not be a very old tribal tradition, for the Flatheads who saw the Lewis and Clark party in 1805 were puzzled by the strange appearance of the men. These Indians did say, however, that they could go in six days to where white traders came and that they had seen bearded men who came from a river a six days' march north of them. Stories about the creation of the races, sometimes including the black race, are found among tribes as far apart as the Assiniboines of Alberta and the Chickasaws of our southeastern states.

According to Salish myths, Old Man Coyote was the figure of good, and Mountain Sheep was the symbol of evil.

LONG, LONG AGO when the world was young, Old Man in the Sky drained off the earth which he had made. When he had it crowded down into the big salt holes, the land became dry. About the same time, Old Man Coyote became lonely and so went up into the Sky Land to talk to Old Man. Old Man questioned him.

"Why are you unhappy and crying? Have I not made much land for you to run about on? Are not Beaver, Otter, Bear, and Buffalo on the land to keep you company? Why do you not like Mountain Sheep? Did I not place him up in the hills, so that you need not fight? Why do you come up here so often, just to talk?"

Old Coyote sat down and cried many more tears. Old Man became very cross and began to scold. "Foolish old Coyote, you must not drop so much water upon the land. Have I not worked many days to dry it? Soon you will have it all covered with water again. What is the trouble with you? What more do you want to make you happy?"

"I am very lonely because I have no one to talk to," Coyote answered. "Beaver, Otter, Bear, and Buffalo are busy with their families. They do not have time to visit with me. I want a people of my own, so that I may watch over them."

Old Man replied: "If you will stop this shedding of water, and stop annoying me with your visits, I will make you a people. Take this rawhide bag, this parfleche, and carry it to the mountain where there is red earth. Fill it full and bring it back to me. Hurry!"

Old Coyote took the bag and traveled many days and nights. Finally he came to a mountain where there was much red soil. Though weary after his long journey, he managed to fill the parfleche. Then he was sleepy.

"I will lie down to sleep for a while. When I awaken I will run swiftly back to Old Man in the Sky."

Coyote slept so soundly that he did not hear Mountain Sheep come along and look at the red soil in the bag.

"Foolish Coyote has come a long distance to get such a load of red soil," Mountain Sheep said to himself. "I wonder what he wants it for. I will have fun with him."

He dumped the red soil out upon the mountain. Then he filled the lower half of the bag with white earth and put some red soil on the upper half. Laughing to himself, Mountain Sheep ran away to his hiding place.

When Old Coyote awakened, he tied the top of the parfleche and hurried with it to Old Man in the Sky. The sun was going to sleep when he arrived. It was so dark that they could scarcely see the soil in the bag. Old Man in the Sky took the dirt and said, "I will make the soil into the forms of two men and two women."

He did not see that half the soil was red and half white.

"Take them to the dry land below," he said to Coyote when he had finished shaping them. "They are your people, and you can talk with them. So do not come up here to trouble me."

Old Coyote put the new people in the parfleche and carried them to dry land. In the morning when he took them out to put breath into them, he was suprrised to find one pair red and the other pair white. Instantly he knew the trick that had been played upon him.

"I see that Mountain Sheep came while I slept," Coyote said. "What shall I do now? I know that I can not keep these two colors together."

So he carried the white ones to the land by the big salt hole. The red ones he kept in his own land, so that he could visit with them.

That is how Indians and white men came upon the earth. And that is why Coyote was a friend of the Indians.

✼

The Origin of Death

NEARLY ALL North American Indian tribes whose folk tales have been published have some explanation of the origin of death. Coyote is the central character in such myths among the Plateau tribes and some others. This is a Kalispel myth.

COYOTE'S DAUGHTER became ill and died. Grieving and wandering around, Coyote came to a little hill. From the top of it he could see a stream below him and signs that someone lived there. Going down, he saw two long lodges on the other side of the stream and heard the sounds of a gambling game being played inside.

"Take me across the river!" he called out.

But no one answered. Coyote lay down on the bank and yawned sleepily. Someone heard him yawn, but still no one offered to get him. When he yawned a second time, the people looked out of the lodges and said, "Someone is calling. Go across and bring him over."

As Coyote watched the canoe coming across the stream toward him, he saw that the person paddling it was his daughter, the one who had died recently.

"Why are you here?" she asked. "I think you should not have come. But get into the boat. Close your eyes first."

Coyote had noticed that the canoe was only a framework of bark, but he closed his eyes and got in. Half way over he thought, "I should like to know how things are going."

When he opened one eye, the canoe began to sink.

"Shut your eye quickly!" said his daughter. "If you don't, we will sink."

Coyote obeyed. As soon as they landed on the other side, they went into one of the lodges. It was empty, for the gamblers were in the other lodge.

"You must not look at the game," Coyote's daughter warned him.

"I won't," Coyote promised. "I won't leave you, for I have been lonely for you ever since you died."

Yet all the time he was thinking in his heart that he would slip in and watch the game.

Both Coyote and his daughter lay down and went to sleep. Sometime later Coyote awoke, heard the sound of gambling, and noticed that daylight had come. Seeing that his daughter was still sleeping, he tiptoed into the other lodge. There he saw two groups of people playing the stick game. All had their hair tied up on their heads, with some sort of weed caught in the knots.

Observing that one side had no good players, he sat down among them. At first no one paid any attention to him. So he made himself look like them by tying a weed in his own hair. When his side was almost beaten, he entered the game. Each time he guessed the correct hand. Then he sang his power song, juggled the bones, and gathered in all the counters but one.

Just then his daughter woke up, heard her father's voice, and entered the lodge. As she came in, the other gamblers guessed, they lost their last stick, and all fell back dead.

"Why did you not obey me?" asked his daughter. "I told you not to come in here. You have killed my children and your grandchildren. If they had won, you and your side would have died, and they and I would have escaped from this place of the dead.

"You come with me now, into my lodge."

On the floor of her lodge lay a bag filled with something. She did not tell him what it contained.

"You must go home now," his daughter told him. "Take this bag with you. Do not open it before you get to the top of the hill on the other side of the stream."

Coyote promised, put the bag on his back, and started to the boat. On the other side of the river, he again placed the heavy bag on his back and started climbing. But something in it hurt his shoulder. Hot and tired when half way up the hill, he stopped to rest.

"I wonder what is in that bag," he thought to himself. "I'll untie it, peep in, and then tie it up again."

But the moment there was a small opening, a child leaped out and ran off. Coyote followed as fast as he could run, but he could not catch the child. As Coyote was returning to the bag, he saw another child jump out. This one also he could not catch. Then a third child jumped out of the bag, and a fourth. Coyote did not follow them, thinking that he should tie up the bag before others leaped from it. But he found the bag empty. It had contained only the four children.

"I will have to go back to my daughter and tell her what has happened," Coyote said to himself.

When he reached the river, he could see no one and could hear no sound. He shouted loudly but received no answer. A second time he shouted. His daughter came out from her lodge and called across to him. "I told you not to look inside that bag. If you had waited until you reached home, you would have found your grandchildren in it. But now you have lost them forever. And I am lost too!"

Sorrowfully Coyote turned away.

When the daughter had died, the spirits had carried her to the land of the dead. There she had become the mother of their children. The gambling game in the lodge was to decide the question of life and death. If the children had won, life would have conquered and there would now be no death.

✖

Medicine Tree Hill

"THERE WAS one large pine tree on top of the hill just west of Mc-Carty's bridge in Hell Gate cañon," wrote a frontiersman, "on which the Indians hung small articles of bead work, bear claws, strips of red cloth, queer-shaped stones, bunches of white sage, pieces of buffalo scalp, small pieces of bone, etc. There was another such tree in the Bitterroot valley 50 miles above Stevensville. The objects were hung on these trees as the Indians passed on their way to the hunting grounds and were placed there to invoke the aid of the Great Spirit to make game plentiful and to make them successful in their enterprises."

The following legend, recorded by a pioneer, is about the first of these two "medicine trees." It was near Missoula.

MANY YEARS AGO a young Indian, while slowly climbing a hill, learned that he was being pursued by enemies. Needing rest, he found a sheltered spot, hung his medicine bundle on the limb of a pine tree, lay down in its shade, and fell asleep. He was awakened by the yells of his enemies. They had discovered him and had instantly begun to shoot their arrows at him. He saw that he was surrounded by warriors.

To their surprise and to the surprise of the young Indian, not an arrow touched him. All veered off and flew in another direction before they reached his body. Knowing that he was being protected by the talisman in his medicine bundle, he shot his own arrows from his bow. Every arrow found its mark. Many of his enemies fell dead. When his quiver was emptied, more arrows came into it. The young man continued shooting and killed a large number of warriors.

One of his enemies noticed the medicine bundle hanging on the tree. Seeing the slaughter around him, he knew that the young man's power was coming from that bag. So he made a dash for the tree, seized the medicine bundle, and threw it away. The very next arrow shot from an enemy caused the young man to fall to the earth, dead.

Since that battle, Indians never passed the tree without hanging upon its branches some token of awe and reverence.

Even today, as well as in the frontier days of Granville Stuart, the spot is called Medicine Tree Hill.

The Ram's Horn Tree

THE SECOND of these "medicine trees," the one in the Bitterroot Valley, was known as the Ram's Horn Tree. Probably the fur trader Alexander Ross, who saw it in 1823, was the first white man to describe it: "Out of one of the pines . . . about five feet from the ground, is growing up with the tree a ram's head, with the horns still attached to it; almost the whole of one of the horns, and more than half the head, is buried in the tree; but most of the other horn, and part of the head, protrudes out at least a foot. . . . All Indians reverence the celebrated tree, which they say . . . conferred on them the power of mastering and killing all animals; hundreds, therefore, in passing this way sacrifice something as a tribute to the ram's head."

Sometime in the 1890's, said a pioneer of the region, a white man cut off the horn. The bark has grown over the spot, but a scientific test has indicated that the horn is still embedded in the tree. Here is Pierre Pichette's version of a myth explaining the origin of the shrine. The Nez Percés also told the story, and they left gifts at the medicine tree on their way to the buffalo country.

ONE DAY COYOTE, after a long journey, was traveling up the Bitterroot Valley. Hungry and tired from his long trip, he paid little attention to where he was going. As he came near a big yellow pine tree, he heard a small voice cry out in pain, "Oh, you have broken my leg! It hurts terribly. When you stepped on me, I was about to tell you something important. Now I won't."

Fluttering around Coyote's feet was Meadow Lark. One leg was broken, and she was groaning in pain. Coyote felt sorry for her. Sitting down beside her, he said in a kind voice, "Stop crying. I will mend your leg so that it will be as good as ever."

He broke off some willow twigs and bound them on the bird's leg, wrapped the twigs with fine bark, and then rubbed the leg. With his powers, Coyote made the leg as good and strong as ever.

"Now that you are on your feet again," he said to Meadow Lark, "won't you tell me your secret?"

"Yes, I will. And I thank you for healing my leg.

"This is what I planned to tell you. Not far from here lives a large mountain sheep, very powerful and very quick. He has fought everyone who has passed this way. You must not go farther, for the ram will hurt you if you do."

Coyote thought about Meadow Lark's warning for a while, but at last he decided to continue his journey. "I had better prepare myself to fight with the ram," he said within his heart. So he sang his power song and through his powers he got a magic flint knife.

"Now that sheep can not harm me," he said, as he started on, carrying his flint knife.

Almost at once he heard a great roaring sound. Looking up, he saw on a cliff above him a huge ram, pawing and snorting. Coyote decided to take his stand beside a big yellow pine. The ram surprised him by reaching the tree at the same time.

Coyote began to get a little worried. "What are you going to do to me?" he asked.

"I'm going to fight you. That's what I am going to do."

"Why?"

"Just because it is your turn," roared the ram. "I have fought everybody who has tried to come through this mountain pass. Now you are here, and it is your turn."

Coyote collected his wits and spoke calmly. "You must be very powerful. How do you fight? What are your weapons?"

"I *am* very powerful," answered the ram. "And I fight with my horns. With my sharp horns."

"Prove your power," said Coyote. "Prove your power first by striking this tree. Then you may do with me as you wish."

The mountain sheep was very proud of his strength and was very glad of this chance to show it. He stepped back a few feet, snorted a challenge to himself, and then charged at the tree at full speed. He struck it a few feet from the ground, struck it with such force that one of his horns passed entirely through the trunk.

While the ram was struggling to free himself, Coyote rushed forward, took out his knife, and cut off the head. The body fell to the ground. Then with just a touch of his flint knife, Coyote cut the head from the horns that were sticking through the tree. He picked up the head and hurled it across the valley against a high cliff. The blood of the ram splashed on the rock, and at once the face of a human being appeared on the cliff, looking toward the yellow pine tree.

Then Coyote made a prophecy: "This face on the cliff will be seen by generations to come. It will be a reminder of what has happened here. Many generations of people will pass this tree with the ram's horn in it, and it will become a wishing tree. If they will offer beads and feathers and moccasins, or this and that, and if they will make a wish with their offering, that wish will come true. They may wish for good luck or for food or for health—for anything they want—and it will be granted to them.

"If anyone makes a wish for ill luck, just to show off, that wish also will be granted, even if he asks for death."

And it came to pass even as Coyote prophesied. For many generations people passing through the Bitterroot Valley saw the face on the cliff and left their offerings with the tree. When I was a boy, the Indians gathered each summer at the Medicine Tree for ceremonial dances. They hung offerings on the tree and through it prayed to the Great Power for special benefits and blessings.

Years ago, a lumberjack tried to get the ram's horn out of the tree, but he could not. He did break off the point of the horn that had stuck out several inches beyond the bark.[1]

�֍

How Missoula Got Its Name

INDIAN STORYTELLERS used to speak of "tying up a myth" at night, like a canoe, and of tying one myth to another. The following story is made up of two Coyote episodes tied together. They were told, years ago, by Duncan MacDonald, son of Angus MacDonald of the Hudson's Bay Company. His story of the Jocko Valley is condensed in the first two paragraphs because some details in it are similar to the Nez Percé "Coyote and the Monster of the Clearwater"; other details omitted are similar to part of "The Ram's Horn Tree." Locally, the part of the Clark Fork of the Columbia that flows through the city of Missoula is called the Missoula River. The water of the Little

---

[1] In Sophie Moiese's recollections, interpreted by Louis Pierre in 1955, Coyote's struggle with a mountain sheep was the brief, concluding episode in a long story about Coyote's killing monsters in the Jocko and Bitterroot valleys. She ended her tale with this personal note: "When I was a child, the skull and face were still there. When I was a young girl, people told me to put some of my hair inside the sheep's horn, so that I would live a long time. That's why I am nearly ninety years old."

Jocko also eventually reaches the Columbia. In a variant of this tale, Coyote planted two tamarack trees which still grow near Arlee and are the only ones in the immediate area.

W AY DOWN ON THE COLUMBIA, a landslide formed a great dam across the river, a dam so high that salmon could no longer come up to the headwaters in the mountains. The salmon were sorry, and the people in the land of the Salish were sorry. When Coyote heard of their hunger and their distress, he went down the Columbia to the dam and struck it a mighty blow. The water was freed, and so were the salmon. They came up the Columbia and up its many tributary streams, as they had done before the dam was made. Coyote walked along the banks of the rivers, all the way to the Jocko, to see that the water was clear in every stream.

Near the mouth of the Jocko, Meadow Lark warned Coyote of a powerful monster, a huge rattlesnake monster that swallowed everyone who came its way. Its jaws were the bluffs between Dixon and Ravalli, its tail was the canyon which reaches to De Smet, and its stomach was the Jocko valley. Meadow Lark told Coyote how to guard himself against the strength of the monster, how to destroy it, and how to let the people out of its stomach.

All of the animal people escaped, but some were changed by the struggle. Until that time, all of them—Ant and Deer, Gnat and Buffalo, Trout and Elk—were the same size. Those who escaped through the snake-monster's mouth, which it opened wide in its agony, or through its eyes, or through its ears got out easily. Not crowded and pressed, Buffalo, Moose, and Elk are still large.

Deer, Goat, and Beaver were squeezed a little, and so are not as large as they used to be. But they were not pressed out of their original shape. The animals that escaped through the tail, the narrow gorge, however, were in great numbers and so were crowded and pressed. That is why Trout and Fly, Gnat and Wood Tick are very small. Ant was the last to get out; when she was half way out, the monster's body collapsed and she was caught in the middle. That is why Ant has a small waist, even today.

When Meadow Lark saw the animals coming, she sang her song of happiness, the song which we now hear as the sun rises. But she still limps when she walks because Coyote stepped on her leg and broke it.

In the Jocko Valley you can still see the heart of the monster—a low, round butte east of Arlee. It was shaped like a heart until Coyote stabbed it when he was inside the monster. West of Ravalli are high bluffs where Meadow Lark had her nest. On these rocks, you can see the form of a man with a dog beside him, figures which have been there ever since Coyote killed the rattlesnake monster. On the cliff on the other side of the river are the same figures. Both are monuments to the monster and his dog. The monster's dog was Grizzly Bear.

After he had killed the monster in the Jocko Valley, Coyote had to go through the dense forest which then stood between where Arlee and Evaro are now. On the way he saw his cousin Fox.

"Stay on the trail," Fox warned him. "No matter what you see or hear, stay on the trail."

Coyote promised and went on through the woods and up the hill. Soon he heard the sound of voices singing, but he stayed on the trail. The farther he went, the more pleasant the singing sounded. But still he remembered Fox's warning and his promise. When he came out of the forest, he learned the source of the music. In a mountain meadow, bright in the sunshine and colorful with flowers, he saw a group of girls singing and dancing.

Coyote thought he had never heard music so beautiful or dancing and girls more pleasing to look upon. He started toward them. The girls invited him to join them, and soon he was in their circle, each hand clasping the hand of a pretty girl. As they danced, their circle moved closer to the stream that flowed through the meadow. When they reached its bank, the girls swung their hands and dropped Coyote into the water. They danced on and left him there, drowning.

Fox, doubting Coyote's ability to heed his warning, had followed close behind him. When he found Coyote's body in the stream, he first thought that he would let his cousin stay dead. But almost at once he felt sorry, pulled Coyote out of the water, stepped over him, and restored him to life.

"Why don't you get even with those girls?" Fox asked him.

"How?"

"Only through fire," replied Fox. "Join the dance again and set fire to the grass."

Coyote followed Fox's suggestion, the grass flared up, and the beautiful dancing girls were burned to ashes.

Almost at once Coyote was sorry for what he had done.

"Oh, I wish I had not killed them!" he moaned. "What can I do?"

But he did not have the power to restore them to life. All he could think to do was to gather up their ashes and scatter them on the water. Up to that time the stream had been quiet and placid. But the moment the ashes touched the water, it sparkled in the sunshine. Whenever ashes drifted to the bank, trees sprang up—aspen trees, with leaves that dance in the sunshine.

And so the stream became known as *Il-mis-eul-etsch-em,* which means "the Land of Shining Waters." That is how Missoula got its name. You can still see the meadow near Evaro, the sparkling waters, and the dancing leaves of the quaking aspen trees.

☙ "Coyote was a great friend of the Indians," added the narrator. "He taught them all they know about woodcraft, provided them with string for their bows so that they might shoot strongly, gave them flint for their arrow points so that their shots might kill. He stocked the streams with fish and saved the animals of the forest, so that the Indians might have game to hunt."

✳

Why There Are No Salmon in Lolo Creek

THE FLATHEADS' NAME for the Clearwater River of northern Idaho was *Epsumclee,* meaning "Salmon River." Their name for Lolo Creek, a tributary of the Bitterroot River in western Montana, was *Tumsumclee,* meaning "No Salmon River." Pierre Pichette related this version of an old Flathead myth about the area. Along Lolo

Creek, the Lewis and Clark Expedition camped in September, 1805, and again in June, 1806. They called it Travelers Rest Creek. Lewis mentioned in his journal that there were no salmon in it.

COYOTE WENT THROUGH the Jocko Valley, up the Bitterroot River beyond where Missoula is now. When he got up in the Bitterroot Mountains, about where Lolo Creek is, he stayed quite a while resting.

One day after close study about his travels, he said to himself, "Well, now here's something to think about. I came up all those rivers on the setting sun side of the mountains, and the salmon followed me. They followed me because of my special power. But there are no salmon in this creek and there are none in the Bitterroot River. I wonder what I can do to get salmon in these streams on the rising sun side of the mountains."

Coyote lay there and thought and thought.

"Over the ridge is the Epsumclee, where there are plenty of salmon. I can get a fish from that river, bring it over the ridge, and put it here. Then there will be food for the people in this part of the country."

So one day Coyote went over the range and down to Epsumclee. There he caught a big salmon. "Here's what I'll take back," he said. "If I can get it up there alive, there will be salmon in the Bitterroot Valley forever."

While he was resting and thinking, Coyote heard a voice speaking to him: "Yes, you can do that. But if you fail, nothing can be done. You will have to work hard and do as I tell you. Cover the salmon with fresh, green grass. Carry it over the range. And be sure not to stop until you get to the other side of the range. Remember—don't stop!"

Coyote saw no one, but he heard a voice. "I can easily do that," he said to the voice.

"Don't forget. Don't stop at all," repeated the voice.

Coyote started on his return journey. He went and went and went. He became tired, and his pack got heavier and heavier. He became very tired, and also thirsty. At last, when he looked up to where he was going, he saw the top of the mountain not far ahead.

"I'm just about on top," he thought. "I guess it won't hurt if I stop and rest awhile."

So he sat down, took the pack off his back gently, and put it down on the ground carefully. Somehow the salmon got out of his pack. Coyote grabbed it, but it was so slippery it slid out of his hands. It dropped on the ground and slid away from his reach.

Where the salmon touched the ground, a spring at once gushed forth. Soon it formed a stream of swiftly flowing water. Coyote tried to catch the salmon, but the stream carried it down the west side of the range, back into the Epsumclee.

When Coyote got back up to the top of the range, he said, "Hereafter this stream will be called Tumsumclee because there are no salmon here. The people who live near it will have to go over the range to get their salmon. They will make a trail over the mountains and travel over it to catch salmon in the Epsumclee."

Coyote felt very unhappy because he had failed to put salmon in Tumsumclee. "If I had been able to do it," he said to himself, "the salmon would have been a benefit to the people who are to come. I wonder what I can do?"

Suddenly while he was sitting there, an idea came to his mind. "Here's what I can do. From this spot right here, a spring will bubble out. It will be a warm spring. In generations to come the spring will be for the benefit of the people. If people who are sick or diseased will wash in the spring, they will be cured. In that way I will do good for the people here."

And so warm springs gushed forth. Today they are called Lolo Hot Springs and are a few miles north of Lolo Pass. Tumsumclee is now called Lolo Creek. The Lolo Trail was made by the Flathead Indians going over the Bitterroot Mountains to get salmon from the streams west of the range.

❋

Coyote's Prophecy Concerning Yellowstone Park

PIERRE PICHETTE's long account of the jealous struggle between Coyote and Grizzly Bear has been condensed in the following tale. Elderly

Flatheads told Pichette that their ancestors went to the area of Yellowstone Park to get obsidian for arrowheads. That the last part of this tale is of comparatively recent origin is evident from the mention of the horse and probably also from the reference to the geysers. In 1833, Ferris visited the geysers, accompanied by two Pend d'Oreilles (Kalispels).

"The Indians who were with me [he wrote] were quite appalled and could not by any means be induced to approach them. They seemed astonished at my presumption in advancing to the large one, and when I safely returned congratulated me upon my 'narrow escape.' They believed them to be supernatural and supposed them to be the production of the Evil Spirit. One of them remarked that hell, of which he had heard from the whites, must be in that vicinity."

WHEN Coyote left Medicine Springs above the Medicine Tree in the Bitterroot Valley, he had a long way to go. For a long time he traveled, until he became so tired and hungry and thin he decided to take a rest. Lying in the shade of some trees, he heard a voice. Drowsily he listened to someone shouting in the distance. He sat up when he heard the voice shouting his own name.

"Coyote! Coyote! Coyote!"

The voice came from the sky. Looking up, Coyote saw Golden Eagle going east.

"I'm on my way, Coyote, to a place where the people are gathered. It's far away—several ridges east of here. It's too far for you. You just lie where you are. Here I go."

Golden Eagle flew on and was soon out of sight.

"I wonder why no one told me about that meeting," thought Coyote to himself.

He yawned and stretched his arms. "Grizzly Bear!" he said aloud. "I wonder if Grizzly Bear called the meeting. I will see if he is chief of the camp. He is always trying to get ahead of me."

He stood up, stretched his legs, and began to walk slowly. Then he walked a little faster and soon found himself able to run at full speed. In one day he passed over eight ridges. Unnoticed, he reached the gathering of the tribes in a valley of what is now Yellowstone Park. Eagle had already arrived and had told the people that Coyote was far away and would not attend the meeting.

Coyote entered a little tipi that stood apart from the rest of the camp. There sat an old woman.

"Oh, my little grandchild," she said to Coyote, "so you have arrived. Probably you are tired. Sit down here and have a good rest."

After he had rested a while, he said to the old woman, "Grandmother, I am hungry. I want you to go to the head chief and ask him to give you some of his best food. Tell him I sent you."

"Oh, no, I can't do that, my little grandchild. The head chief is Grizzly Bear. He's quick-tempered and cruel. I'm afraid of him."

"You must go, grandmother."

Finally she went to Grizzly Bear's tipi and was given some dried meat. But it was not his best food and so Coyote threw it on the ground.

"I don't want that," said Coyote. "Go back and tell him I want some of his *best* food."

A second time the grandmother went, and a second time Coyote threw the dried meat on the ground. The third time the grandmother went, Grizzly Bear asked, "Who is your grandchild?"

"Coyote," she replied.

Grizzly Bear became frightened and gave her some of his best food. Coyote ate it.

After he had rested a while longer, he said to the old woman, "Go to the chief and tell him I am borrowing his little drum, his hand drum."

Grizzly Bear sent one. Coyote beat on it a few times and then threw it down. "Tell him I want his *best* drum."

The next drum the chief sent pleased Coyote. "Yes, this is the best one," he said when he beat it.

Then he started his power song. Beating the drum and singing his song, he walked around the camp. The tipis were placed in a circle. The second time he walked slowly, and asked his powers to send him rain. As soon as the rain came, he asked his powers to send cold.

Then he ordered the chief to walk around the camp, and he ordered the dogs to bite him. Before Grizzly Bear got all the way round the camp, he was bleeding and so worn out that he lay down and died.

Next day the sub-chiefs invited all the important people to come to the chief's tipi to choose a leader for the whole tribe. They were really glad to get rid of Grizzly Bear, for he had been cruel. Most of the people wanted Coyote; he had showed them what powers he had. But Coyote would not accept.

"I have not finished the work I was sent to do," he explained. "I can not be chief at present. I have to go back to the people in the west. But I will select a chief for you. I select Golden Eagle. He will be a good leader, kind-hearted and helpful. You will get along well with him, always.

"Tomorrow I must start back west. Before I leave, I will have something to tell all of you. Come back here tomorrow morning."

Next day, Coyote prepared himself for his journey westward over the mountains. The people were sorry to lose him, but they were happy about having Golden Eagle as the new chief. A man in the tribe offered Coyote a gray horse.

"Here's a horse to take you where you are going, Coyote."

"Thank you. I accept the horse gladly. Now I am ready to leave, and here is what I have to say:

"In generations to come, this place around here will be a treasure of the people. They will be proud of it and of all the curious things in it—flint rocks, hot springs, and cold springs. People will be proud of this spot. Springs will bubble out, and steam will shoot out. Hot springs and cold springs will be side by side. Hot water will fly into the air, in this place and that place. No one knows how long this will continue. And voices will be heard here, in different languages, in the generations to come."

After prophesying these things, Coyote got on his gray horse and struck out for the west. When he came to the valley now called the Jocko, he noticed the branch he was using as a whip. At Dixon he threw it down and from it grew a plum tree.

"In the generations to come," prophesied Coyote, "there will be plum trees growing right here."

And there are. That is why the Indians called Jocko River the Creek of the Wild Plum Trees.

⌘

The Great Flood in the Flathead Country

THE GREAT WATER first came to the valley where Flathead Lake has remained until this day. The flood grew bigger and bigger, spreading over all the lower lands. Most of the people were drowned in the valleys, but others fled to the highest mountain. As they climbed, the water followed them. At last all the land was covered except for the solitary peak where a few Indians had gone for refuge.

Then the chief said, "I will try to stop the water. I will ask my guardian spirit to help me."

He shot an arrow toward the ground at the edge of the water, but the arrow floated away and the flood was not stopped. He sent a second arrow. It also floated away and the waters continued to creep upward. He sent a third arrow. It stayed in the ground at the very edge of the waves. The water reached the third feather on the shaft of the arrow but went no farther.

Gradually the water went down, the tops of the mountains appeared, then the hills, then the valleys. The flood water that remained formed Flathead Lake.

And so a few people were saved. Their wise men prophesied that through them the tribe would grow again, but that after several generations they would all perish from the earth.

⌘

Sheep Face Mountain

McDONALD PEAK in the Mission Range of the Montana Rockies was called by the Indians "Sheep Face Mountain." On its brow is a formation of granite that bears a striking resemblance to the head and face of a huge sheep, quietly lying down but keeping watchful eyes on the mountains near him. Bon Whealdon recorded from four Kalispel-Flatheads this myth explaining the formation.

WHEN THE WORLD WAS YOUNG, old Mountain Sheep was brutal toward all the tribes of animals, birds, and fishes. Before long, they hated him very much.

Whenever he saw the birds flying down to drink or to bathe at the edge of the stream, he rushed up to frighten them away. If he saw fish on their way up the creeks, he turned the water into new channels, so that the fish died in the shallow pools along the old creek bed. Often he loosened stones in the trails so that deer, elk, and goats, walking that way, slipped and fell to death at the foot of the cliff.

Most of all he hated the young of every tribe. When he found bear cubs playing on some mountain ledge, he watched until the mother bear left them for a few minutes. Then he would rush in and butt them over the ledge, into the canyon below. Often he trampled under his sharp horns a family of young skunks. By striking trees with his head, he was able to jostle eggs and young birds from their nests, so that they were killed on the rocks below.

The Indians, also, he treated with brutality. If he saw hunters down at the bottom of a canyon, or climbing a mountainside, he would start an avalanche of boulders tumbling from the peaks to bury them. When he found a patch of ripe huckleberries that might be visited by berrypickers, he would run among the bushes and brush them with his head, until he had shaken off the ripest berries.

Among all the animals, birds, fishes, and Indians, he had not one friend. Only two did he fear—Chief Old Man Coyote, who was wise and good, and Chief Eagle of the Mountains, whose beak and claws were sharp and tearing. Mountain Sheep always tried to avoid Coyote and Eagle. At last all the animal, bird, and fish tribes became so desperate that they gathered for a council at Post Creek.

"One thing we must do," they said. "We must kill Mountain Sheep before he destroys all our people. But we are not wise enough to make plans to destroy him. Will our two great friends, who are wise and good and powerful, lead us? Will they tell us what to do?"

Chief Eagle of the Mountains had flown down for the council, and Chief Old Man Coyote also was present. They knew that the people's plea was for them. Old Man Coyote spoke: "Chief Eagle and I have talked. We know what must be done, and we know how to do it. We must restrain this enemy of all living things, but we do not have the power to destroy him. He was with us when life came to us all. Chief Eagle, whose sight is clear, and I have chosen the place where he shall be forced down—still alive but powerless to hurt people.

"Mountain Sheep now takes his sleep in the sunshine, on the rocks west of the ice field on the highest peak. East Wind will come quickly and make the ice and snow stiff there. The men of the valley, the birds, and the animals must go swiftly to the mountain where the Sheep lies. Each one will carry as large a rock as he can. They will place the rocks on the back and on the hind quarters of the Sheep, but the head shall be left uncovered. So when the people see the head, they will say, 'This is our enemy.' We shall weight him to the earth with the weight of all our rocks, so that he can no longer move about to destroy us."

Quickly all the tribes did as Coyote and Eagle had planned. Then all were happy, and said to each other, "This thing that is evil is now kept down by our good rocks that we carried and placed upon it. Mountain Sheep can never harm us again."

❈

The Mystery People of Flathead Lake

Bon Whealdon recorded this tradition through an interpreter from four elderly Kalispel-Flatheads in 1923. When Joseph MacDonald told him the same tradition, he called Whealdon's attention to two distinct types in stature, head formation and features among the old Salish on the reservation. *Su-appi* is the Salish term for white man. Their name for Flathead Lake is *Sit-kait-koo*.

You are our friend and are not here to laugh at our tales. Soon we shall all go to the Spirit Land. Our sons do not care for the old ways and the old stories of the Indians. We tell what our grandfathers' grandfathers passed down about the strange people of long, long ago. Put our words into the *Su-appi* language, so that our sons'

sons may know them. When they come to us in Spirit Land, they will say, "The old men spoke true words."

Then we and the Mystery People will reply, "Yes, the words came from whole tongues, not from forked tongues."

Where did the Salish first come from? We know only the story our old men told our men down from the beginning: the first Salish were driven down from the country of big ice mountains, where there were strange animals. Fierce people who were not Salish drove them south. So in our stories our people have said, "The river of life, for us, heads in the north."

After many generations, the Salish held the grounds from way west, eastward, and past the red-paint caves near Helena. Then our warriors were so many that the three enemy tribes of the Dakotas dared not fight us. The west tribes by the Great Salt Water Mystery were our friends. With them we traded.

After a long, long time, men in strong canoes came up the rivers from the great river which flows into the Great Salt Mystery. The men were not *Su-appi* and not true Indians. They brought with them their women, who were Coast Indians, and their children. The women's heads and the children's heads had been pressed flat with boards when they were babies.

There were not many of these people, and they troubled no tribes. They lived on fish, small game, berries, and roots. They made their homes on the islands in the lake, and they did not hunt far from water. Our people liked them. Sometimes they would paddle west and be gone a long time, all the summer moons. When they returned, they brought with them much dried red salmon, which they traded to our fathers for buffalo pemmican, bitterroot, carrots, and camas.

They were skilled in curing sick people and knew how to make good medicines from roots, seeds, and leaves of plants. They showed our old men how to make good healing salve by mixing deer tallow and balsam pitch, boiling it over low fire and then putting it into hide bags until used. This salve cured cuts and deep wounds quickly.

They taught our old people, whose eyes were weak and sore from much tipi fire smoke, to wash their eyes with clean water and then to put in them a little clean bear oil. They made tea from the bark of the chittim tree and drank it when they wanted to clean out their insides. They told our people not to throw filth near the water they drank and to keep their bodies clean.

At that time our people got their fire-starters in two ways: by rubbing two sticks together and by taking embers from trees hit by lightning. Both were slow, slow ways. The Mystery People taught all the river tribes the right rocks to strike together in order to throw sparks into dry leaves, pitch wood, and moss for quick fires. They told our women to dry or bake or roast fish and meat. Raw and frozen fish, they said, cause sickness.

Where did the Mystery People come from? And what became of them?

We know only what their old men told our old men. "Our fathers," said the Mystery People, "came from a land beyond the Great Salt Mystery. The winds blew on the sails of their big salt canoe, and carried them far. They were lost. In many sleeps they came to the mouth of the great river and toward land. Another storm broke their big canoe. The Indians along the shore treated them kindly.

"Soon a bad sickness came to all the Indians along the rivers. Many, many people went to the Spirit Land. Our fathers told the Indians not to use sweat baths for this sickness, and not to plunge into cold water, or they would all die. They stopped their sweat baths, and many got well. All the Indians were happy to have our first men as friends and gave them wives, canoes, paddles, bows, arrows, and spears. Afterwards, our fathers thought that perhaps they might find people of their own kind inland, so they went eastward up the rivers and on to Flathead Lake."

That is all we know about the Mystery People. They were smaller than the Salish and the Nez Percés and the Coast Indians. Their features were finer, but their color was the color of Indians. They were kind people, good to women and children, and they liked to laugh and to play. They knew many things which they taught our people.

Long ago all this happened, long before the *Su-appi* came. The first Mystery Men died. Their sons' sons and daughters married Salish people. In time, no Mystery People were left on Flathead Lake.

When the first *Su-appi* came, they saw with the Salish a few old Mystery Men with flat heads. So they called us Flatheads. They thought all Salish had flat heads, but that is not true.[1]

Burning Star Jumps into the Lake

THE TWO INDIANS who related this story to Bon Whealdon in 1924 thought that Burning Star was a meteor that had plunged into Flathead Lake long ago.

THE WORLD WAS VERY YOUNG when this story took place. It was before our grandfathers' grandfathers' days, but there were people who saw these things. They saw the burning star race through the air and jump into the lake now called Flathead Lake.

One darkness, when the people were in their tipis, they heard a star shrieking in terrible pain. Going outside to see why it was making such crying, they saw that it was burning up. The light of the flames brightened all the sky and the land as if it were day instead of night.

The people saw Star running swiftly down to the lake and jump

[1] A skeleton and artifacts found with it in a grave near Forest Grove, Montana, in 1934, seem to have a relationship with this story. They are now at Montana State University. The bones "indicate a racial type shorter than the modern tribes, but much more muscular and powerful." Three tubular beads of sheet copper "of great antiquity," unlike any copper in the area, a dentalium necklace, an ear ornament, a small obsidian point—these artifacts caused Turney-High to conclude that "it can probably be said that western Montana was at one time inhabited or visited by people with physical and cultural affinities with the older people of the coast."

From details given him by elderly informants, Turney-High thought this a possible migration legend: One of two bands fishing in a river near the coast, seemingly just below the southern border of Oregon, traveled eastward for days until they reached the banks of a river, apparently the Owyhee. They followed this stream to the Snake River, which his informants positively identified. They followed it to the mouth of the Clearwater (site of Lewiston, Idaho), went up the Clearwater to its source streams, crossed over the Bitterroot Mountains by way of Lolo Pass, and reached a country already occupied by a band of Kalispels. The Kalispels received them peacefully, moved north, and left the Bitterroot Valley to the newcomers. In fact, it was "the traditional home in the minds of many Flatheads." Gradually, over the centuries, the two groups became one.

into the deep water near Wild Horse Island. Immediately a thick cloud rose from the water and hung over the lake.

Our people were very much frightened and would not go near the shore. "The Water Mystery," they said, "has reached out with its strong power, has pulled the Star from Skyland, and has taken it into the lake. If we go near it, it will pull us in also."

But the Mystery People of the Lake, the Canoe People, said, "No, it is not the Water Mystery which pulled Star, for water mysteries have no influence over sky and land mysteries. Foolish Salish, do you not know this? We, too, saw Star burning in the sky, and we heard its cry of pain as it jumped into the lake to put out its flames. Not being made of fear, we paddled our canoes close. The water was warm, and many, many cooked fish floated on the waves."

Tribes that lived many sleeps away also saw Burning Star and its light. Only the Mystery People of the Lake were not afraid. So our fathers sometimes called them "the Fool People." Perhaps they meant "the fool-hardy people."

These are true words.

⌘

The Bluejay Ceremonial Dance

"THE DANCE OF THE BLUEJAY is probably the principal expression of the hopes and woes of the Montana Salish," stated the anthropologist Turney-High in 1933 in his description of this annual ceremonial dance. "When the time for the ceremonial has arrived, all members of the tribe who have some ailment to be cured, some ambition to be fulfilled, as well as those who are merely interested, assemble in the *sumesh* lodge." Led by the shamans—the "medicine men"—the dancing begins. It "consists of regular hops in the same rhythm as the music." The music is vocal, accompanied by rattles made by stringing deer hoofs on thongs.

The traditional rites were discontinued in 1938 because of the passing away of most of the elderly full bloods and the lack of interest of the next generation. The Salishan tribes on the Colville Reservation in northeast Washington also held the Bluejay Dance annually until some time in the 1930's. After the following account of the ceremonial dance are four myths that seem to explain why the Blue-jay was thought to give strong *sumesh,* or spirit power.

W HEN WE WERE young men, the Bluejay, or *Kwas-Kwee,* rite was held each December or January, when spirit power is strongest. It was always observed in a large medicine tipi or log cabin away from the presence of curious white men, small children, and Indians who were evil in their living and unclean of habit and person; for Bluejay would not show its power if undesirable people were present.

Before the ceremony began, those who were to participate went through a process of purification. This cleansing was done for a three-day period before the actual meeting. It consisted of numerous sweat baths, fasting, chanting of spirit songs, and prayers to the heavenly beings interested in man's welfare.

For some reason long forgotten, the sitters, while in session, must not have any objects of metal on their bodies or in their clothing. So they had to wear buckskin clothes or drape robes and blankets about them.

In the old Salish language we would chant for a long time:

Come, power bird. We are prepared.
Show yourself. Prove your power.

Then Bluejay would some into the center of the tipi and do many things for us. He would cure disease, tell us where to hunt and trap, and warn us about our enemies.

The last night—the third one—Bluejay would give different powers to different people. Some men would have dream-visions. Some men would be able to walk, with bare feet, on burning coals without blistering or burning the skin. Some would be able to hold flaming embers without blistering or burning the skin. Some would be able to go a long way in snow and freezing weather, without being cold or becoming sick.

Yes, we know the old ways of Bluejay and our people. We speak not with forked tongues. It was good.

Bluejay Brings the Chinook Wind

THE CHINOOK WIND is a warm wind of the Northwest. In January or February or March, it may melt overnight the ice-locked rivers and strip the lower lands and slopes of their snow. The name was first given to a warm wind that blew from over the village of Chinook Indians to the trading post of the Hudson's Bay Company at the mouth of the Columbia.

WHEN THE WORLD was very young, Amotken, the Creative High Mystery, gave a little part of the Salish country to Thunderbird. This was the North Crow Creek Canyon of the Mission Range. Thunderbird was happy to have an area of her own and to know that her long-time enemy, Coyote, could not enter it. There had been much jealousy between the two. Now she was free to lay her eggs and to hatch her young without being troubled. There in North Crow Creek Canyon she gave birth to her three daughters: Bluejay, Crow, and Magpie.

Thunderbird was kind to people when they came from the valley of the Bitterroot to hunt, to fish, and to gather huckleberries in her canyon. If a storm was coming through the East Pass, she would warn the people to leave. Her deep thunder noises were her warning to them.

All went well for a long time. Then a careless hunter failed to put out his campfire, and a great fire spread through Thunderbird's canyon. The forest on the canyon floor was destroyed; the flowers and the berries were burned; the deer, elk, and birds left the canyon. Worst of all, the creek became smaller and smaller, and then dried up.

Thunderbird was much annoyed by the destruction of her canyon country. Angrily she beat her huge wings against her breast and thundered out punishment against the people of the valley.

To the cold Northeast Wind she said, "Stand in the pass. Blow hard. Blow your chill breath down my canyon and out on the valley. Drive away the people who have destroyed my country."

So at each darkness, Northeast Wind came and blew his cold breath into the valley. Soon the grasses and the plants died, and ice came upon the big lake in the Salish country, the one now called Flathead Lake. Shivering with the cold, the people went into the Bitterroot country. Animals and birds took refuge there also, as did Bluejay, Crow, and Magpie, the daughters of Thunderbird. Nothing with life remained in the valley.

After many snows had passed, Thunderbird's anger softened. Then she became lonely, and she longed to see her daughters, the Indians, the animals, and the little birds. Again she spoke to Northeast Wind. "Cease blowing your icy breath, and go. Too long you have punished the valley. If you will go, perhaps my daughters, at least, will come to see me."

Almost at once a great stillness came over the land. A scout felt the silence and reported to the Salish chief living at the place where the warm waters flow.

"The icy wind blows no longer in the valley," the scout told his chief. "And Thunderbird in the canyon is making a noise like sobbing."

Then the head chief said to his people, "When the land becomes warm again, we shall go back to our old homes in the valley. Will Coyote tell us how we can please Thunderbird so that she will hasten the warming of our country?"

But Coyote, not liking Thunderbird, replied, "Let the big bird with the big noise sit forever in the region she has made desolate. I shall not help."

Then Bluejay, who loved the Salish people, offered her help. "Coyote is old and lazy," she said. "He thinks of nothing but of filling his stomach with salmon. So he has become a deceitful boaster like my sisters, Crow and Magpie. I myself will help the Salish and make glad the heart of my mother, Thunderbird."

So at the right time, Bluejay flew west to ask Chinook Wind to warm the valley and help her friends. Chinook Wind's heart was warm and kind.

"Gay and good little bird," he said to Bluejay, "I will hasten to the relief of your friends if you will show me the way."

So Bluejay flew before the Chinook Wind until they came to the valley below the Mission Range. There Chinook Wind blew his warm, moist breath a long, long time across the land. The ice melted, grass and flowers grew, trees came to the Mission Range, deer and elk returned to the canyon.

Thunderbird was happy. "How can I repay you, little daughter?" she asked.

Bluejay answered, "Keep your temper down, my mother, so that the innocent will not suffer with the careless ones."

❆

Bluejay and the First Skin Tipi

LONG, LONG AGO, before the Salish and the Kutenais had tipis, guns, ponies, and white man's tools, they lived in a miserable manner. Their homes were in caves and in holes covered with bark and soil. There they suffered much from rain and from melting snow dripping into their shelters. Their brush wickiups also gave little protection from storms.

One year they suffered from hunger, too. They found few fish in their own streams, few salmon in the streams west of the Bitterroot Mountains. Berries were scarce; roots and bulbs were not as plentiful as usual. In the buffalo country, enemy tribes kept our people and their friends from going on the yearly buffalo hunt.

The Salish people—that is, the Flatheads and the Kalispels—had to depend upon killing many deer and elk for their winter supply of meat, tallow, and hides. They would have to go to the Swan Valley country for the game, and they would have to carry it back across the Mission Range before the mountain trails and passes were filled with snow.

Six of the best hunters were chosen to kill the game. All the other able-bodied men, women, and youths carried to the home valley, on their pack-boards, the meat, tallow, and hides, of the deer and the elk, and also the pelts of the bear, otter, and beaver. The pelts would be used for robes. Many pack-trips were made, back and forth, across the mountains. The season grew late. A snowstorm might come any day.

At last the leader of the hunters said to the leader of the packers,

"I think we have plenty of supplies now. This can be your last trip home. My men and I will stay a few days longer to get more hides and robes. Then we, too, will return home."

In two days the hunters had as much as they could carry out. But just as they were ready to leave, a blinding snowstorm came, very suddenly, driven by a cold northeast wind. Travel was impossible, and so the hunters took shelter in a thicket of small spruce trees. It was now bitterly cold, and the men knew they were in danger of freezing to death.

Hugging the ground beneath the spruce trees, they lamented, over and over, "Now we die. Now we die."

Suddenly they heard the voice of Bluejay, friend of the Salish people. "Quickly, quickly tell the men not to sleep," Bluejay said to the head man. "Tell them to stamp their feet on the ground, to swing their arms and beat their hands together."

The men followed her directions and became warm again.

"Now I shall tell you how to make a shelter against cold winds and storms," said Bluejay. "You must work swiftly, for night will come soon.

"Four of you will place hides together so that they overlap along their edges. Take some pointed bones and punch holes through the overlapping parts. Make some thongs from other hides, and lace them through the holes. Draw the thongs tight and knot them. You have many skins; so make a large piece from several laced together.

"While four men are working with the hides, the other two will find a strong spruce tree about the height of two men and will break off the lower branches."

Both groups of men quickly did as they were directed. Then Bluejay spoke again: "Now take the big piece of hide you have laced together and put it around the tree. The strong upper branches will spread the hide out and keep it from blowing together. Leave an opening at the top about two feet wide. At the bottom, put heavy rocks along the edges of the hides, to hold the skins in place.

"On the side sheltered from the storm you will need only a few rocks. There, cut an entrance hole in the hide and lace a flap cover."

Again the men followed the directions of their friend Bluejay, and soon they had a skin tipi standing among the spruce trees.

Bluejay spoke again: "Now take into your shelter many dry twigs, your skin bag of water, your food, your parfleches, and the rest of your robes. Go in quickly. Use your flints to make a low fire of twigs. The smoke will follow up the tree trunk and go out the hole at the top. You will have fire, food, water, and warm robes. The storm and the cold can not reach you inside the tipi.

"I will go to the valley to tell your people that you are safe. After four days you will come out to them. Then you will tell your people how to make a shelter like this one. Instead of using a living tree, tell them to cut poles, cross them, and tie them at the top. Show them how to stretch hides round the frame work of poles. It is a good shelter."

That is how the Salish people learned to make the skin tipi a long, long time ago.

✖

How Bluejay Saved the Buffalo Hunters

WHEN ENDING a factual account, said Bon Whealdon, old Indians always added, "It is good" or "These are true words." The following story, he thought, was based upon an actual incident of the early nineteenth century. "Bright Sky Bird," the father of Bluejay, was a mythological spirit bird from Sky Land; he had a sunny and kind disposition. The buffalo-berry shrub is a member of the oleaster family.

ONE AUTUMN our fathers made their preparations to join their relatives living in the Bitterroot Valley for the annual trip to the Judith Basin country to hunt buffalo. Our fathers had made peace with the Crows, Shoshonis, and Cheyennes, and from them had obtained our first guns and horses. At the time of this story, the Blackfeet tribes did not have guns or ponies. Being envious, they often tried to get these things by raiding our camps. As usual, the hunters left the elderly folks and the young children in a guarded place in the valley of the Big Bitterroot River.

How Bluejay Saved the Buffalo Hunters

As the men prepared for the buffalo hunt, Bluejay, friend of all the Salish, was very happy. She would go with her people, to share in their joys and sorrows. Also, by the time they would reach the buffalo country, the early frost would have touched the buffalo-berries and they would be sweet to the taste. Bluejay would feast on them.

She called to her half-sisters, Crow and Magpie: "Come. Let us go with our hunters."

But Crow and Magpie, being fat and lazy, refused, saying, "It is our duty to stay with the old people and the children."

Bluejay scolded them. "You are no good. Both of you are mean and boastful. You, Crow, are staying here just to steal food from the camp. And you, Magpie, plan to feed on some helpless, sick deer. Your father was the gloomy, black Dark-of-the-Moon Bird. I am glad that mine was the Bright Sky Bird."

So Crow and Magpie stayed with the old people. Bluejay went with the hunters. Traveling swiftly on their ponies, the hunting party came, in a few days, to the place of the mussel shell. Water and fuel were there for a good camp, and the sweet grass of the valley was good for their horses. Early every morning the men went out to the plains to shoot buffalo. The women were busy skinning, boning, and cutting the meat up for drying and smoking.

Bluejay spent her time eating buffalo-berries and telling the smaller birds about her happy home in the Flathead country, the *Sin-yel-min*. Evenings, she was happy in camp, chattering and teasing. She loved to sit in a cottonwood tree and scold the dogs until she had them barking. Then she would whinny like a colt to make the ponies answer. Amused by her happy, lively ways, the people would give her bits of buffalo suet to eat.

One day Bluejay strayed north to the camps of the Blackfeet and Blood people. Seeing the women at work, she drew near to watch them make buffalo pemmican. The men were out scouting, she learned, and the women were doing much excited talking. Listening from the tree tops, Bluejay heard them mention her people, the Salish. She learned that the Blackfeet and Blood warriors were planning to attack the Salish, to kill and scalp them, and to steal their guns, horses, and buffalo meat. The attack was set for the following morning, while it was yet dark.

Bluejay knew that she must warn her people quickly. Although they had guns, their warriors were few and the enemy's warriors were numerous. She must find a way to warn her friends.

Bluejay flew into camp just as the men, weary from their long and hard day on the hunt, were eating. How could she tell them of the danger? She did not know. So she went to her old friend Owl, who was sitting in a nearby tree. Quickly she told him her problem.

Owl knew the answer. "Your people are my good friends also. Let us warn their medicine man when he is sleeping. I will cause a vision-sleep to come to him early tonight. Then you whisper in his right ear and tell him what the evil ones are planning to do. Your own spirit power will make you able to speak so that the medicine man will understand."

Owl and Bluejay carried out their plans early in the evening. The medicine man woke quickly and told his people what Bluejay had whispered to him. Believing him and Owl and Bluejay, the chief at once made new plans.

"The enemy are too numerous for us to fight in the dark," he said. "Take down the tipis and load them quickly. Put the buffalo meat and the equipment on the pack ponies, and get ready to leave camp. We shall ride to the camp of our friends the Nez Percés while we have time."

Hurriedly the people followed the chief's directions, and when the Blackfeet warriors approached, they found the Salish camping place deserted. In the camp of the Nez Percés, our people found protection. Because of Bluejay and her friendship, the buffalo hunters were saved. It is good.

❋

The Great Canoe in the Sky

ALONG, LONG TIME AGO, when the world was very young, there were only a few stars in the sky. Now they are countless. Some of them are campfires which Amotken, the Creator, lighted for the spirits of Indians. Others are transformed animals or people from the earth world.

One group of five stars are five Salish Indians who once lived along the west shore of Flathead Lake. They were good friends and always did their work together. Together they hunted and fished and fought their enemies.

One summer they decided that their five canoes, old and rotten, were unsafe. "Let us build one big canoe," said the oldest of the friends. "Let us build one big enough for all five of us."

So they began to build a large canoe. As soon as it was ready for the water, they would paddle it across the lake to a shallow bay. "There are many fish in that bay," they said to each other.

While the men worked and talked about their plans, Bluejay watched and listened. Usually Bluejay chattered and did not listen, but now sorrow placed a heavy weight upon her tongue. These men were her friends. Bluejay knew that a terrible storm was on its way to the lake, and that it would arrive soon after the men had finished their canoe. If they should go out as they planned, they would surely drown.

Not knowing what to do, Bluejay flew to the big rocks where Old Man Coyote was standing. She told Old Man Coyote the cause of her sadness.

"What can be done?" she asked. "What can you do to save our five friends?"

"I have little power over the water," Old Man Coyote answered, "but I can prevent their drowning. The day for their departure for the Sky World has come. I will place them in the Sky World as stars together. They shall all be at work up there, five friends in their canoe."

So he lifted the canoe and the five men into the sky. When darkness comes, we can see them there, still working together as they did in life.

✳

The Origin of the Indian Drum

SUN LOOKED UPON his children and saw that they were quiet people. "I have given them many things," he said, "but their hearts always seem to be heavy."

He sent for Coyote and asked him, "Why are my people so quiet and their hearts so sad? I have given them many gifts—food and clothes and shelter; yet they are silent."

Coyote replied, "Your words are true, Father Sun. They have been given many things, but their hearts you forgot to make light. They hear the strong voice of the Thunderbird, the water talking to the falls, the yellow birds singing from the purple thistles. They hear the wolves on the ridges, the north wind whistling on their tipi poles, the buffaloes pounding the earth when they run. They have all these sounds in their hearts, but they can not tell them out and so lighten their hearts."

"What shall I do to make them express themselves?" Sun asked. "Will you go, Coyote, and call out the sounds from their hearts? I want my people to be happy as are my other children, the birds and the animals."

Coyote went back to earth again. Soon he met Beaver on the trail, and they talked about the people's sadness.

Beaver told Coyote his thoughts: "We will go to the tipi of the young hunter and steal from it all his elk hides and buffalo robes. He will want more, but it is the wrong season for him to go buffalo hunting. So he will go elk hunting. Then we will work our plan. It is a very good plan, brother Coyote."

The young hunter was angry when he found that all his hides and robes had been stolen. He asked Bluejay, "Who stole my hides while I was away?"

Bluejay replied, "Two old wise men carried them away. Why don't you get a wife to live in your tipi? If she is lazy, she will sleep on the robes while you are gone. Then the old men can not take them away."

The young hunter and his people went to the mountains to hunt more elk, and he killed a bull elk. When he carried it to his camp, a flame jumped out from the fire and burned off the hair. The young hunter was so disgusted that he threw the green hide over a pine stump. In the morning he went again to the mountain, where he stayed many days. When he came back to camp, the people said, "We have been waiting for you a very long time. Now we must go to our homes in the valley."

They started down the mountainside while the young hunter slowly gathered his things together. When he went to get his elk hide, he found that the sun had dried it fast over the hollow stump. He pulled at the hide, but it did not come away from the stump. He pulled again, but fell back upon a stone. Very angry at the hide, he picked up a club and struck it. It gave out a great noise like the voice of the Thunderbird. When he beat it fast many times, he heard many buffalo feet pounding on the prairie.

His people down the mountain heard the Thunderbird and the buffalo feet. They came running back to the young man, crying out, "We heard the voice of Thunderbird and the sound of many buffalo running on the plains. Why does this come from your camp? Have you made such strong power that you can call buffalo to the mountains? Where are the bird and the buffalo? We do not see them."

The young hunter told them, "The voices are hidden in the stump hollow, under the dried hide. When I beat upon it, their voices answer me. See and listen!"

Then the hearts of the people were light. As they made the voices under the hide speak for them, they danced round the stump. They found that the quiet voices in their hearts and the ones from the fire stump were the same. Then songs came out of their mouths, and Sun knew that his children were as happy as the birds and the animals.

✳

The Origin of Bitterroot

BITTERROOT WAS ONE of the staple vegetable foods of the Flatheads and neighboring tribes. It bears one rose-colored blossom, which opens only in the sunshine. Ordinarily it flowers in May, at which time the root is gathered and dried. The bitterroot is now the state flower of Montana. Its name has been given to a river, a valley, and a mountain range in the region where it is found in abundance.

IT WAS A TIME of famine in the land that is now known as the Bitterroot Valley. An old woman, the wife of a medicine man, was
grieved because her children were hungry. Without meat or fish, they
were slowly starving to death. They had been eating shoots from sunflower plants, but the only ones left were old and woody.

"My sons have no food," mourned the old mother. "Soon all of them
will die. I will go to a place where I can weep alone and sing the
song of death."

So she went to the stream now called the Little Bitterroot and sat
down beside it. There she bowed low until her face touched the
ground and her gray hair spread out upon the earth. Bitter tears fell
as she sang the song of death.

The Sun, coming up over the mountains overlooking the valley,
heard the death song. He saw the grieving woman and called to her
guardian spirit. "Your child sorrows for her starving people," the
Sun Father said to the spirit. "You must go to her. Comfort her with
food and with beauty out of dead things."

The guardian spirit took the form of a red bird and flew down to
the weeping woman. Softly he spoke to her.

"The tears of your sorrow have gone into the soil, and there the
roots of a new plant are being formed. The plant will have leaves
close to the ground. Its blossom will first have the rose of my wing
feathers and then the white of your hair.

"Your people will dig the root of the plant and will eat it. They
will find it bitter from your sorrow, but it will be good food for them.
They will see the flowers and will say, 'Here is the silver of our
mother's hair upon the ground and the rose from the wings of the
spirit bird. Our mother's tears of bitterness have given us food.' "

❈

Star Myths of the Coeur d'Alênes

MOST STARS WERE ONCE the people of the mythological age. When
the world changed, they were transformed into stars. The
Pleiades, for example, which the Coeur d'Alênes called by a name
meaning "Cluster," were once a group of people.

At one side of Cluster is a small star and behind it is a large red star. The small star was Coyote's favorite child; the larger one was Badger. Badger stole Coyote's child. Coyote pursued them, but just when he had almost reached them, they were transformed into stars.

A group of stars forming a circle, with one star at the side, were once a group of women cooking camas in a pit in the ground. The roots were nearly cooked, and the women were sitting around it, ready to take out the roots. Skunk went toward them with the purpose of spoiling the cooking, but as the women were surrounding the pit he could not get near. So he sat down at a little distance to wait for an opportunity. In this position all were transformed into stars.

Another group of stars is "the canoe." Five men were making a canoe. One man was working at each side of the canoe, one at each end, one between an end man and a side man. In this position the men were transformed into stars.

Another group was once a lake with a bird on it. Some hunters shot a goose, and as it died, it spread its wings over the water. All were transformed, including the goose with its wings outspread.

The Great Bear, or the Big Dipper, was once three brothers and their brother-in-law, who was a grizzly bear. The youngest brother liked the brother-in-law, but the older two did not. One day when they were out hunting, they told their youngest brother that they would kill the bear. The youngest brother determined to warn the brother-in-law, who had already gone hunting, but the other two followed close behind him.

Just as they were about to shoot at the grizzly bear, the youngest brother called out, "Brother-in-law, they are going to kill you!"

At that moment, they were transformed into four stars, which form the corners of the Big Dipper. Some people say that the four stars in the square are the bear and the stars forming the handle of the dipper are the three brothers.

※

Water Mysteries in the Coeur d'Alène Country

THE COEUR D'ALÊNE INDIANS, like other Interior Salishan tribes, had many traditions about "water mysteries" and "land mysteries." They were usually located in lakes, waterfalls, mountain tops, and sometimes in trees. At some of the passes in the mountains, near a land mystery, each traveler put down a stone; if he did not, he would have ill luck. Water mysteries were in the form of a huge fish or a huge mammal, or were creatures half mammal and half fish, or half fish and half human. Offerings were made to these mysterious powers, to appease them or to obtain their assistance. Most of the details in the following traditions the author recorded from Julia Nicodemus and Stanislaus Aripa, of the Coeur d'Alêne Reservation.

IN LAKE COEUR D'ALENE—In Lake Coeur d'Alene, near where Conklin Park is now, people used to hear strange noises. Beside a large stone in the deep water there, they used to see a mermaid. She had long hair, the body of a fish, and hands like the hands of a human being. Many people saw her there, between the stone and the shore.

Near Harrison was a bush where people would hang furs or other valuables. I think it was a small willow tree. People coming down the river would hang gifts there so that the water mystery would not make the lake windy. After a while, many things were hanging in the willow tree.

At the mouth of the Coeur d'Alene River, there used to be a water mystery with the form of a buffalo. One time when a man was paddling along the lake shore in the dark, his canoe suddenly stood still. Though he paddled as hard as he could, the canoe did not move. He looked around him, in the water and on the shore. He could see nothing, and so he paddled again. Still the canoe did not move.

The man felt along the bow of the boat and found that a horn was holding it on each side. Then he knew that the Water Buffalo had caught him. He put some beads on the horns and begged it to let him go. The buffalo settled back in the water, the canoe was freed, and the man paddled away.

Ever after, people left beads and other gifts on the bushes near that place and prayed to the water mystery not to harm them and not to make the lake windy.

One time Father Joset was in a boat with a group of men who, as usual, left gifts there near the mouth of the river.

"Put your beads away," said Father Joset. "That is just a superstition."

Water mysteries lived in other parts of Lake Coeur d'Alene. There, also, Indians left offerings and prayed for good weather on the lake and good luck in fishing.

❧ IN THE ST. JOE RIVER—One time, long ago, some women and girls were gathering serviceberries along the St. Joe River, in the mountains north of Lake Coeur d'Alene. Among them were four sisters, who, one hot day, decided to swim in the river. While swimming, one of them saw in the deep water what she thought was a large fish.

"Let's see who can reach it first," she said.

When the sisters reached the spot where the fish was, it went down. Immediately all the girls sank and were seen no more.

The women who were watching said to each other, "That was not a fish. That was the tongue of a water mystery."

Shortly afterward, some people were up on a mountain near the place where the sisters were drowned. On the shores of a little lake up there, they found the hair of the sisters. They reported the find to the girls' parents, and they went up there and took the hair away.

Then the people knew that a water passage connected the St. Joe River with the lake near the top of the mountain and that it was used by a water mystery.

❧ IN HAYDEN LAKE—Some years ago, when my father was young, a band of Coeur d'Alênes lived on the shores of Hayden Lake. They were happy there for a long time. But later, fish and wild game became scarce, berries and camas roots froze. The people were miserable, for there was little to eat.

A medicine man of the band advised them to leave the region, but they refused to go. As the years passed, fish and birds and deer became even scarcer. But the Indians would not leave the shores of the little lake. One moonlight night the chief of the band decided to try once more to get some fish for his people. He went out in his canoe, while his people watched from the shore. They saw him stand up in his boat and shout, "I have caught a fish!"

As they watched, the boat, moving slowly, began to go around in circles. Then it gained in speed. It went faster and still faster, making a whirlpool of water around it. Suddenly it leaped into the air and then plunged into the whirlpool it had made. Horrified, the people watched, helpless. They never saw their chief again.

"The Great Mystery Above is again telling us to leave," the medicine man said to the grief-stricken people.

This time they packed their tipis and all their possessions and left for a new home. They expected, year after year, to receive a message to return to their old home along the lake. But their medicine man never received such a message from the Great Mystery.

⌘

A Legend of Spirit Lake

PROBABLY, FATHER DE SMET was the first to record a tradition about Spirit Lake, one of the many picturesque lakes in northern Idaho: "The Indians regard *Kaniskee,* or Spirit Lake, with superstitious awe. They believe that the most lovely bride of every 'moon' is stolen by witches and borne to the sands near its shores."

Stories still told in the region are similar to the following, which was recorded in 1899. The Coeur d'Alênes used to relate a similar romantic tragedy about Hayden Lake: sweethearts from enemy tribes, in a canoe in the lake, were lost in a furious storm and the father of the girl was drowned when searching for her body. Ever after, the Indians avoided Hayden Lake.

TWO TRIBES were once camped on the opposite shores of Spirit Lake. For generations they had been enemies and had fought many fierce battles. Sometimes one tribe had been victorious, sometimes the other. Now there was a lull in the warfare. Each group was at peace.

One evening the son of the head chief, while canoeing on the lake, saw a beautiful girl from the enemy tribe, also canoeing on the lake.

This chance meeting was followed by planned, secret meetings, for the two had fallen in love. One moonlight night a fisherman from the young man's tribe saw the two canoes in the middle of the lake and investigated. So did a fisherman from the girl's tribe.

Both men were angered by the sight. Each reported to his chief and to his tribesmen, who also became angry. They wanted no marriage with their long-time enemy. Each tribe vowed to kill all of the other tribe, and fierce battles followed.

After a few days the young man's tribe was almost destroyed, and he was taken captive. What should be done with him? The chief and the elders held council and decided that he must be killed. He would be taken to the middle of the lake, heavy weights would be fastened to his neck, and his body would be lowered into the water. The girl protested, but to no avail. In the middle of the night, with torches and shouts and chants, the victors carried out their plan. Even the enemies of the young man said that he met his death bravely.

For several days the girl's tribe feasted and celebrated their victory. Then they crossed the lake, killed the remaining men in the enemy tribe, and captured the women and children. Again they feasted and celebrated their victories.

One night during the feasting, the girl slipped away from camp, rowed to the middle of the lake, and disappeared into the water. Next morning her friends found her canoe, her paddle, and her feathered headdress floating on the lake.

Now the Indians say that the lake is haunted. Once every year the spirit of the girl appears at night upon the water. She is dressed in white, and her long black hair hangs in folds about her body. She stands in a spirit canoe for a moment and then disappears.

Neither her people nor the people of the enemy tribe will fish in Spirit Lake or camp on its shores.

✄

Giants and Tree Men

GIANTS WERE FORMERLY COMMON in Coeur d'Alêne country. They had a very strong odor, like the odor of burning horn. Their faces were black—some say they were painted black—and the giants were taller than the highest tipis. When they saw a single tipi or lodge in a place, they would crawl up to it, rise, and look down the smoke hole. If several lodges were together, the giants were not so bold.

Most of them dressed in bearskins, but some wore other kinds of skins with the hair left on. They lived in caves in the rocks. They had a great liking for fish, and often stole fish out of people's traps. Otherwise, they did not bother people much. They are said to have stolen women occasionally in other tribes, but there is no tradition of their having stolen women in the Coeur d'Alêne country.

☙ OTHER SUPERNATURAL BEINGS that used to be seen in the Coeur d'Alêne and Spokane countries were called the Tree Men. They, too, had a strong odor. They dressed in buffalo skins and had the power to transform themselves into trees and bushes. Once, when a number of people were dancing in the Spokane country near a small lake close to present-day Cheney, they suddenly smelled a bad odor. One of them exclaimed, "That is the Tree Men!"

The people looked around and saw four men standing a little apart from one another and wearing around their shoulders buffalo skins, with the hair side out. As soon as they saw people looking at them, they disappeared. Four bushes stood where the four Tree Men had stood. Those four bushes could be seen until lately. Possibly the power of the people's glances killed them or prevented them from changing themselves back into men.

There are trees which have been in one spot a very long time. They really are Tree Men, although they seem merely trees to people looking at them. In other spots, trees and bushes change places or are sometimes absent and sometimes present. Often when these beings were seen and people approached them, they disappeared, and only trees or bushes could be found.

✖

The Little People

THE FIRST OF THE FOLLOWING traditions about dwarfs is from the Flathead Indians. The second group is from the Coeur d'Alênes, part of them recorded directly from Julia Nicodemus. Old Spokane Indians have the same traditions about dwarfs as the Coeur d'Alênes have. These Salishan traditions might be compared with the Nez Percé accounts of the Stick Indians and with Shoshoni and Arapaho accounts of the cannibalistic Little People.

THE FIRST INHABITANTS of the Flathead country were a race of dwarfs, who were about three feet tall. They looked much like Indians, except for their very dark skins and their small stature. Although originally their abilities were not supernatural, they were remarkable, for they possessed all the elements of civilization of Indians and of whites.

They owned herds of tiny horses, about three feet high and always a glistening black. The dwarfs did not ride these animals or burden them with packs. But when food ran short during the winters, the dwarfs killed them and ate them. When the dwarfs disappeared from ordinary life, their horses disappeared with them.

After the dwarfs were crowded into the highest mountains, some Flatheads think that they died out completely from life as people live it. They were said to sleep during the day in old craters in the mountains—or rather, they were thought to be actually dead during the daylight hours and to arise at night to dance and play.

After ages of this kind of rest, they acquired a great deal of spirit power. The Flatheads believed that anyone who obtained a dwarf as his guardian was unusually fortunate; consequently, old craters in the mountains were favorite places for the quest of the supernatural guardians.

The Flatheads always speak respectfully of these original inhabitants of their country.

≈ IN THE OLD DAYS, many dwarfs lived around Rosebud Lake. It used to be surrounded by dense forest with much underbrush. Trees and bushes were so thick that people could get through them only with difficulty. That's the kind of place the dwarfs liked.

In the evenings my family would sometimes hear sticks beating against the trunks of trees. My grandparents would say, "The dwarfs are hitting the trees." We children would be afraid.

Sometimes people saw the Little People. Some people said that they wore brown suits with pointed brown caps. Others said that they were red all over and were dressed in red. They went up and down trees very quickly, always head first. In the trees, they walked with their feet on the under side of the branches, their heads hung down, but their caps were still on their heads. They carried their babies upside down on board carriers.

Sometimes people would be awakened suddenly by the crying of dwarfs in the night. They were a nuisance then, for they would wail and wail.

People approached by the dwarfs lost their senses, and when they came out of their stupor they found themselves leaning against a tree, upside down. Sometimes they missed part of their clothing and, on looking around, saw it hanging high up in the trees. Sometimes the dwarfs took food away and hid it. Sometimes they took bags of camas and tied them to the ends of branches of trees. But they never kept anything they had taken, and they never hurt anyone. They just liked to play tricks.

Dwarfs of another kind were about the size of small boys. They lived in cliffs and in rocky places in the mountains. In the old days, they were very numerous in the Coeur d'Alêne and Nez Percé countries. They dressed in squirrel skins and used small bows and arrows. They often shouted when they saw people, and in this way often led hunters astray.

Spirit Power from the Little People

Few people among the Kalispel-Flatheads would reveal their experiences in getting their spirit power, lest it leave them or destroy them. But because of the friendship between H. H. Turney-High and Charlie Gabe, an old medicine man of the Kalispel tribe, Gabe told his experience to the anthropologist. Charlie Gabe died in the winter of 1936–37, at a very old age. In 1955 his power as a medicine man was still remembered on the Flathead Reservation. The Yakima Indians of central Washington also believed that strong spirit power might be obtained from the Little People who, long ago, made the pictures on the rocks near Naches Pass, in the Cascade Mountains, and kept them freshly painted.

WHEN CHARLIE WAS about fourteen years old, he and his mother, very poor, were living among the Flatheads. In early summer he fasted for days and then started to climb a mountain, in search of his power. He wanted to obtain unusual power, and so he determined to climb to the highest peak for his solitary vigil.

On the second day he was higher than most men go. There, certain signs made him feel that his efforts were to be rewarded. Near the summit of the mountain, where no lake could be—above the tree line and up the face of a big rock—he saw a little lake. Playing beside its banks were some white muskrats—another sign that some supernatural power was near.

When the boy reached the topmost peak, he fell exhausted and laid his head on a cottonwood log. Now the cottonwood tree is a valley tree, belonging on the banks of the Bitterroot River. The boy recalled the stories of the Great Flood and of the cottonwood log which it had left on the mountaintop. But the Flood had been long, long ago, and this log was freshly cut. So Charlie forced himself to his feet, for he knew that spirit power was close at hand.

At the summit he found a large hole. Looking over the edge of it, he saw the Little People preparing to dance. He went down into the crater and there—at first—no one paid any attention to him. But when all the preparations had been made, the chief of the Little People invited the boy to the festival. All night they danced. When morning came, the chief cried, *"Ce hoi!"* And everyone stopped. They rested throughout the day, seldom speaking, but using a language of their own when they did. Four nights they danced, and four days they rested.

Then the boy knew he had been on the mountain long enough. Before starting down, he seized one of the Little People and tried to take the dwarf home with him. But the Little Person escaped. A second time Charlie caught the Little Person and got him half way down the mountain before he ran away. The third time also he escaped. The fourth time the boy was successful. He carried the Little Person to his home in the valley and hid him in his lodge.

"With the fourth attempt," said the Little Person to the boy, "you captured me. Well, you must now keep me and feed me for four years. Then you must take me back to my people and free me. When that time comes, I will tell you something good."

And so it happened. The Little Person was kept hidden and was fed with the best food the boy could find. When the four years had passed, Charlie carried the dwarf up the mountain. This time the climb was much easier than it had been when the boy was alone. At the mountaintop Charlie placed the Little Person at the edge of the crater.

"I have been your guest for four years," said the dwarf. "From now on when you are in trouble or when you need anything, think hard about me. I will come to your aid. You need not suffer danger any more. Also, I will give you my power whenever you want to help someone else."

And so it was. Charlie became a great medicine man, revered by both the Kalispels and the Flatheads. Like the other medicine men of the region, he always refused payment for his services.

⌘

How My Grandmother Received Her Healing Power

PIERRE PICHETTE SAID that the following account of his grandmother's experience is "not a legend or a myth, but a true story." Both his mother and her mother were great medicine women. His mother's talisman was a bear's claw and a little of the fur. Before telling the story, Mr. Pichette gave a little information about the power quest, or guardian spirit quest, among his people. To get their powers, children were usually sent up on a red mountain, the highest mountain near Stevensville. Up there lies a poplar log left by the great flood of long, long ago. Though the tree lies uprooted, it has leaves every spring.

A child sent there in search of his special power was told to build a circular wall of rocks around himself and to lie down inside the circle. Some spirit would appear to him in the form of a human being or a bird or an animal and would give him an object of some kind. If the child should *take* the object, instead of being given it, the rock wall would disappear. The spirit would give him a special song, and would tell him what his spirit power would be and when he could reveal what his guardian spirit was. If he should reveal the secret before the specified time, he would suffer misfortune, possibly death. Usually, a child was carefully prepared for the guardian spirit quest, but occasionally the experience came without special preparation.

Mr. Pichette told the story as if his grandmother were speaking. Her name was Mary Sdipp-shin-mah, meaning "Fallen from the Sky."

W HEN I WAS A LITTLE GIRL, five or six years old, my mother said to me one day in huckleberry-picking time, "Tomorrow morning we will go up on the high mountain and pick huckleberries."

Next morning she got a horse and we rode double up the mountain. On the way, I told my mother that I saw a spot with many nice, big huckleberries. But she said, "No, we will go farther up the mountain."

Late in the afternoon we were on a high ridge. There we got off the horse and started picking huckleberries. After a while my mother said to me, "You stay here and pick. And you may eat as many berries as you wish. I am going farther up the mountain. I will not be gone long. Nothing will harm you."

I picked some berries, and then I sat down and ate them. The sun set, but Mother did not come back. I called and called for her. Then it got dark, and I was frightened. I cried and cried and cried. Then I walked farther up the ridge, crying and crying. After a little rest, I went a little farther. I slept for a while and then I climbed a little higher, still crying.

When the sun came up, I was very tired and sat down on a ridge, facing a gulch thick with forest. I thought I heard something down there, so I stopped crying and listened. I thought I heard the voice of a human being. I listened and listened. Then I saw something coming toward me, coming where the trees were not so thick.

A woman and two children were coming. I felt pretty good, now that I knew people were near me. The three turned into the brush, out of sight, but I could still hear them. The boy and girl were playing and having fun. Soon the three of them came right to me and the mother said, "Well, little girl, what are you doing here? You must be lost. We heard you crying, and so we came up here to give you help."

The mother was a middle-aged woman, well dressed in buckskin. Around her shoulders the buckskin was painted red, and she wore trinkets. The little boy and the little girl were pretty little fellows, clean and also well dressed in buckskin.

"Don't cry anymore, little girl," the mother said. "You come with us."

I jumped up and went with them. The children tried to get me to play with them, but I stayed near the mother.

She told them, "Leave your little sister alone. She is too tired to play."

When we got to the bottom of the gulch, where the bank was not steep, we stopped to get a drink. I stooped over and drank for a long time, for I was very thirsty. When I finished and sat up, I was alone again. The mother and the children were gone. I cried again until I heard the mother's voice say, "Don't cry, little girl. Come up here."

They were sitting on a bank, and I climbed up to them. Then the mother said, "Now we are going to take you back to your people. When you grow up, you will be a good medicine woman. I give you power over all kinds of sickness. I give you power to heal people. I give you special power to help women give birth to children. But you must never try to do more than I tell you to do. If you do, you will be responsible for suffering and even for death.

"That is all I can tell you now. I have given you your power. These two are your little brother and little sister. I am your mother."

I glanced away and when I looked back, the mother and children were gone. Instead, a grizzly bear sat there beside me, with two little cubs. The mother bear stood up and said, "Now we are ready to take you to your people. Get on my back."

I did. How fast we went, I couldn't say. After a while she stopped and said, "Your people are near here. Walk on a short distance, and you will see them."

And I did.

Now you know why I never accept payment for healing the sick or for helping women in childbirth. My power was not given me for reward of any kind. And I cannot tell anyone how I heal the sick.

✳

The Vision Before the Battle

To REPRESENT the warring aspect of Indian life, the following Flathead narrative has been selected, not only because of its interest as a story, but because it includes a dream—very important to Indians— and also because it was found among the memoranda of Angus MacDonald. MacDonald was Chief Trader of the Hudson's Bay Company in what is now eastern Washington, northern Idaho, and Montana, from 1834 to 1870. An old Flathead chief, wrote MacDonald, related this story to him one night beside a campfire in what is now Montana.

MANY YEARS AGO a small band of my people were camped on the plain of the Cold Spring, not far from Hell Gate. On that plain, generations and generations had held their races every year— foot races and then horse races after the Salish had horses.

From the summit of the mountains east of the plains, we could see far across the valleys of the Jocko, the Missoula, and the Bitterroot rivers. From those mountains the enemies of my people also could look down upon our land. For days they would sit there, watching, spying, hoping to see some unprotected Salish in the valleys below.

On the day my story begins, a day in early summer, the women and children of the little group were digging the bitterroot on the plain. A small group of men sat inside a large tipi, smoking and telling stories about their adventures on the hunt and in war. Another group lay on the grass outside the tipis, enjoying the blue sky, the forested mountain slopes, the snow glistening on the mountain tops. An atmosphere of peace filled the little camp.

Suddenly, one of the men lying on the grass saw what he thought were five buffalo bulls grazing on the slope of Hell's Gate Mountain. In a moment the camp was stirred to wild excitement. Every man, except the very old, mounted his fastest horse and started in pursuit of the buffalo.

But when they reached the spot where the buffalo bulls had been seen, they could find no trace of the animals. Instead, in the loose earth on the mountainside, they saw something alarming—the print of human feet. Quickly and anxiously the men turned their eyes to the camp below. There in the sunlight they saw the enemy at their deadly work of killing people.

Stung by grief and by anger at being tricked, the men whipped their horses and rushed down the mountain and over the plain. But before they could reach the camp, the enemy had finished the slaughter and were in flight. Every person the hunters had left in camp had been slain—old men, women, children.

One of the buffalo hunters was the father of three little girls. Because he had no son, all his love was centered on them. They and their mother he found lying in their blood, their little bags of bitterroot strewn around them. The father sank down to the earth beside them, overcome by grief and bitterness. On the mountain pass his enemies were already disappearing. Overhead the sun was shining brightly, as if nothing sorrowful had happened.

Fiercely the father spoke to the sun. "You saw this happen! Why did you give light to the murderers? Why did you let them slay my innocent ones? You dry the sands. You harden the stones. Help me to avenge my children."

Silently he rose, dug a shallow grave, placed his four loved ones in it, and covered them. Then he climbed the highest peak, the one that overlooks the valley of Missoula, the Camas Plains, and Flathead Lake. On the summit of that peak he walked and talked for days and nights. He talked to the forest below him, to the canyons which hold the winds, to the distant peaks that really seemed close to him, to the lake, and the sky and the moon.

Most of all he talked to Amotken, the power of the Upper World, the Cause of life and death. Again and again he prayed to Amotken for power to avenge the death of his loved ones. One morning, a strong wind swept from the mountains which stand toward the setting sun. Out from the heavy murmur following the wind came the voice of *Alla-la-lee-meah,* the old woman who controls the storms and hurricanes.

"You are here?" the voice asked the man.

"Yes, I am here," he answered sadly.

The voice spoke again. "Yes, you are here, and you are here in earnest. Heed my words. Go to the hot spring that boils from the earth on the other side of the Camas Plain. Wash your whole body in that spring for four days. Be clean as you have never before been clean. See that your nails and hair, your joints and the grooves of your flesh are thoroughly clean.

"On the morning of the fifth day, when the dawn beats up her first light, be on the top of the mountain that is east of the hot spring and nearest to it. That is the mountain of the Rattlesnake's house. There a friend will tell you more. If you wish to succeed, you must do everything that he tells you.

"But before he gives you instructions, his voice will reach you four times from the sky. He will offer you something. Refuse it. A second thing. Refuse it. A third thing. Do not refuse it. Now go. Remember what I have told you. I am Alla-la-lee-meah."

The man then descended the mountain, tied his bow and quiver upon his head, and swam the river that ran between the high mountain and the Camas Plain. At the hot spring he bathed himself as the voice had directed. Before dawn of the fifth day he stood, thoroughly clean, on the top of the mountain of the Rattlesnake's house. From there he saw day and night touch one another. The sky was spotless. The bird of the three songs and of the earliest day spoke to him.

Suddenly the man was forced to sit upon a rock, where he felt as if he were tied to it. He felt a pressure upon him, and he heard a solemn voice in the sky, far off, toward the dawn. The sun was still hidden from sight, but the snow on the mountaintops was reddened by its rays.

A fourth time the man heard the voice in the sky, and the cry seemed to touch him. Then he saw a shape like a man, walking on the mountain, a shape powerful and beautiful to look upon. His hair, dark as an Indian's, was twisted and hung down to his shoulders; its points were a brown-crimson, as if scorched in hot blood. The spirit's form was red and smooth, and his face glowed like a stream of Northern Lights. A wreath of flowers encircled his head, and a long red feather in it stood erect. The spirit stopped in front of the man.

"My son, you are here?" he asked.

"Yes, I am here," the man answered.

"You are saved from man," the spirit replied. "I meet your life."

Then he took the feather from his wreath and offered it to the man. Remembering the words of *Alla-la-lee-meah,* the man turned his head away and refused the feather. The spirit threw it on the mountain and it became a pointed reed, growing from the earth. Then the spirit offered the man the wreath on his head. But the man turned his head and refused the wreath also. So the spirit threw it upon the mountain, and it stood up, a tall, red willow.

Then he took from his mouth a thing like a burning yellow iron and hung it on the man's neck. Some long hairs, like the hairs from a man's head, were attached to it and hung from it.

The spirit spoke again. "These hairs are the lives of your enemies. I give them into your hands. Fear not, my son. I have pitied your grief, followed your steps, and observed your watchings. Your weeping will be stopped, and your sorrow will be avenged. I will go with you to battle. Tell your people that when they see the enemy you will be the foremost in the fight. Go now. Be not afraid. Look at me as I depart."

And the man saw him climbing the air backward, walking toward the morning. First he seemed to hide the sun, then to become a part of it. Mingled with its fires, he disappeared. At the same moment a tremor seemed to hold the limbs of the watcher, seemed to stop the whole earth for the length of a strong man's breath.

The man returned to his people and told them about the words of the strange spirit he had seen on the mountain. A few days later our enemy, the Blackfeet, were seen approaching us. We attacked them, both on foot and on horseback, the man leading as he had been directed. The Blackfeet horses fell, and in the holes of badger and fox they broke their legs. When the enemy bent their bows, they broke; and in surprising ways their spears and lances broke. We killed all of the Blackfeet except one. His life we saved so that he might tell his people how we had slain our enemies on the plains of *Sha-ka-how*.

On this same plain we slew also all of the Snake Indians that came to fight us—all but one. We spared him so that he might tell his people how all the Snakes and the Blackfeet who had come against us had fallen in battle.

"The old chief ceased talking and, lighting his pipe, looked so solemnly and thoughtfully out into the night that I could not but feel that this romance had probably been not altogether a fiction to his people, whatever it might be to us."

✳

Flathead and Kalispel Prophecies of the Black Robes

PIERRE PICHETTE classified Flathead stories in three groups: myths, legends (by which he meant fables), and true stories. The last are "tales handed down by the ancestors which everyone believes." Both this story and the following one about Little Mary, he said, are true stories.

YEARS AGO, before the Flatheads had seen any white people, and before the Iroquois came among them, they prayed to the Sun, the Moon, and the Stars. This story took place before the Iroquois came and told them about the Black Robes and about Christ.

One summer the tribe was camping somewhere, probably in the Bitterroot Mountains. Among them was a middle-aged couple. The wife became sick and after a short illness, she died. Her husband, poor fellow, loved her very much. They had married when very young and had been happy together. When he lost his wife, he worried and sorrowed very much. He did not know what to do without her.

One day he wandered away from his tribe, who lived near the high mountains, the Rockies. For a long time he kept always on the go, wandering from range to range. He kept himself alive with berries and roots. His moccasins became worn out. His feet blistered. He had to travel barefoot. The animals and reptiles and insects offered him medicine power, but he did not accept. He just kept wandering.

One day he came to the Rockies here—the Mission Range. He climbed up there east of Ronan. He went up and up. He struggled and he struggled. Finally he got on top of one peak. He thought to himself, "Here I am. On this spot I will stay and die."

Several days and nights went by. One night, about the beginning of the sign of dawn, he saw a light in the east. He looked and looked. Light was coming swiftly toward him—up in the air. All at once someone was standing right beside him. The being threw bright light.

The man heard a voice saying, "Here you are, wandering and mourning over the death of your wife. I am telling you that you will never find your wife anywhere in this world. She will not appear any more. Later on, you may see her again. From this spot here, when the break of day comes, go down the valley and out to the open prairie. Look over there—you see a little butte standing on the prairie. You are to go over there and stay. Stay for several days. During your stay there, someone will meet you and you will learn from him. Whatever he may tell you, believe him."

The figure of the man disappeared. When daylight came, the man struggled down to the bottom of the mountain. He saw the little butte, went to it, and stayed on top of it. It is a little rock butte close to Cold Creek. It has been dynamited, but it is still there.

One day, just before dawn, the man heard a voice. He was told, "You have been mourning over the death of your wife. You have been wandering around, searching for her. But you can not find her. Remember after this: go back to your tribe. Tell your tribe all that has happened to you during your sufferings on the high mountains. And tell your tribe: toward the east are men who are clothed differently from other men. They wear black gowns or robes. They are the ones that teach the right way of living, the right way of life. They teach that there is One. Everything in the world is under His care. If you ever see the Black Robes, believe whatever they teach you. And believe that the time will come when you will meet somewhere the wife you lost through death."

The man returned to his tribe and described what had occurred to him and what had been said to him in his visions. The man died before the Black Robes came, but his people were ready for them.

❧ THE KALISPEL INDIANS have essentially the same tradition. About two hundred years ago, said Nick Lassah, a sub-chief lost his son. He was so grief-stricken that he wanted to kill himself. As he climbed up to a sharp ridge on McDonald's Peak, animals and birds offered to give him spirit power, but he refused them. He wanted only to die.

Up on the ridge he made a little wall of stones in a circle. There he lay down, determined to die. But in a vision he saw two men and heard them say, "Your boy is happy where he is. If you take your own life, you will never see him again. But if you do what we tell you, you will see him."

The men in the vision told him that some day a man in a long black robe would come among them to teach them. "You must get your people ready to receive him." And they taught him what he should do.

In the version told by Eneas Conko, the man who had the vision was given a metal talisman of great strength. His name was Pierre. When the warriors were going out to fight, they would go into Pierre's lodge and bite his talisman, so that they would be kept from being hit by arrows or by bullets. One time, two men refused to bite it just before a battle with a great number of Blackfeet. These two were the only Salish warriors injured in a battle that lasted for four days.

When Pierre was dying, in the middle of a dark night, the place where he lay was covered with light. It was almost as bright as day.

Many years later, a priest came. When the people saw his long black dress, they said, "He is the one Pierre told us about."

�֎

Little Mary's Vision

I HEARD THIS STORY from the old people. Just as it was told to me, I will tell it to you. It happened before any white people arrived at Stevensville in the Bitterroot Valley.

A few Iroquois from way back East somewhere—I can't say how many of them—arrived among the Salish and stayed there quite a while. Before they came, our people knew nothing about Christianity; they had never heard of it. But the Iroquois had been taught by the priests and knew a good deal about it. They told the Salish in the Bitterroot Valley what they knew, and our people became very much interested. The Iroquois taught them how to pray, how to make the sign of the cross, and this and that. They taught the Salish to say a few prayers and even baptized some who had a strong belief in God.

A little girl about nine or ten years old was one of those baptized. The baptismal name given her was Mary. She and her parents were living in their own tipi. In those days there were no houses, just tipis.

After she was baptized, she became ill—very ill and weak. One day while she was lying in bed, her family noticed a sudden great change in her. Thinking that she was feeling much better, they asked her, "What has made you feel better so suddenly?"

"Someone just came into our tipi. Didn't you see the one that came in, wearing a dress?"

"No, we didn't see anyone," her father and mother answered.

"It was a lady that came," said Little Mary. "And as soon as she stepped in, the inside of the tipi was brightened up. The lady came and stood by my bed. She stood right by me. She had a baby in her arms. The baby was very bright and gave more brightness to the tipi."

That was why she felt better, she said. "The lady called me by name.

'Mary,' she said to me, 'I am coming after you and I want you to be with me where I came from.'"

Then the lady said to her, "This little child I am holding in my arms is my son, who is called the Son of God. I am going to tell you, Mary, that where you are lying at present, suffering, is the spot where you will die. Later on, the time will come when a house will be built over your grave. Right where you are lying is the spot where your grave is to be. The house that will be built here will be called the House of God, which means the church."

After the Blessed Virgin had spoken these things, she disappeared. But the girl's father and mother had not seen or heard her speak. In a short time, Little Mary passed away.

The old folks say that this did happen. They didn't say how many years later it was that the church was built at Stevensville, and we don't know whether it is on the spot where Little Mary died.

This was told me by the old folks, and this is the end of the story.

✽

Lewis and Clark Among the Flatheads

OF THE COMING of the Lewis and Clark Expedition among the Flatheads, Private Joseph Whitehouse wrote on September 4, 1805: "Two of our men who were a hunting came to their lodges first. The natives spread a white robe over them and put their arms around their necks as a great token of friendship. Then they smoked with them. When Captain Lewis and Captain Clark Arrived, they spread white robes over their shoulders and smoked with them. . . . But we could not talk with them as much as we wish, for all that we say has to go through six languages before it gets to them."

Pierre Pichette related the first of the following Flathead traditions of the event.

O UR PEOPLE WERE CAMPED in a kind of prairie along the Bitterroot River, a few miles upstream from the Medicine Tree. The place is called Ross's Hole now; the Indians then called it *Cutl-ḳḳh-pooh*. They kept close watch over their camps in those days and always had scouts out because they feared an attack by an enemy tribe. One day two scouts came back to report that they had seen some human beings who were very different from any they had known. Most of the strangers had pale skins, and their clothing was altogether different from anything the Indians wore.

"There were seven of them," the scouts told Chief Three Eagles (*Tchliska-e-mee*). "They have little packs on their backs, maybe provisions or clothing."

The chief immediately sent his warriors to meet the strange men and to bring them to camp safely.

"Do no harm to them," he warned his men. "Do no harm to them at all. Bring them to me safely."

So the strangers were brought into the camp. All the tipis were arranged in a circle in our camps, with an open space in the center. The people gathered there in the middle of the camping place, and so, when the warriors brought the strange men in, they were seen by the whole tribe. The Indians could not understand who the seven men were, but they knew they were human beings.

Chief Three Eagles ordered buffalo robes to be brought and to be spread in the gathering place. By signs, he told the strangers to sit on the robes. The men were a puzzling sight to all the Indians surrounding them.

After the white men had sat down, they took their little packs off their backs. The chief looked through their packs and then began to explain to the people.

"I think they have had a narrow escape from their enemies. All their belongings were taken away by the enemy. That's why there is so little in their packs. Maybe the rest of the tribe were killed. Maybe that is why there are only seven of them. These men must be very hungry, perhaps starving. And see how poor and torn their clothes are."

The chief ordered food to be brought to them—dried buffalo meat and dried roots. He ordered clothing also to be brought to them—buckskins and light buffalo robes that were used for clothing.

One of the strange men was black. He had painted himself in

charcoal, my people thought. In those days it was the custom for warriors, when returning home from battle, to prepare themselves before reaching camp. Those who had been brave and fearless, the victorious ones in battle, painted themselves in charcoal. When the warriors returned to their camp, people knew at once which ones had been brave on the warpath. So the black man, they thought, had been the bravest of this party.

All the men had short hair. So our people thought that the seven were in mourning for the rest of the party who had been slaughtered. It was the custom for mourners to cut their hair.

By signs, Chief Three Eagles and his counselors came to a little understanding with the white men. Then the chief said to his people, "This party is the first of this kind of people we have ever seen. They have been brought in safely. I want them taken out safely. I want you warriors to go with them part of the way to make sure that they leave our country without harm."

So by the chief's orders, a group of young warriors accompanied the white men to the edge of the Salish country. They went with the strangers down the river from Ross's Hole and up to Lolo Pass. The white men went on from there.

They did not take with them the robes and clothing Chief Three Eagles had given them. Perhaps the white men did not understand that they were gifts.[1]

THE FOLLOWING ACCOUNT of the coming of the first white men into the Flatheads' country was written in 1899 by Father D'Aste of St. Ignatius Mission, Montana. He recorded it from a reliable old Indian who had heard it from the widow of Chief Victor, the famous chief

[1] Sophie Moiese, interpreted by Louis Pierre, told essentially the same story. She added a few details: When the dried meat was brought to the men, they just looked at it and put it back. It was really good to eat, but they seemed to think it was bark or wood. Also, they didn't know that camas roots are good to eat. . . . Chief Three Eagles told his people that they must not harm the strangers in any way. Since then, no one has ever heard of the Salish tribe and whites getting into battle. During the Nez Percé War, the Nez Percés went through the Bitterroot Valley, but the Salish people stood by the whites at Fort Missoula. They would have fought their own Indian friends to keep them from harming the white people.

with whom Governor Stevens negotiated the reservation treaty of 1855. Chief Victor was the son of Chief Three Eagles.

～ ONE TIME WHEN the Flatheads were camping at Ross's Hole, Chief Three Eagles left the camp to do his own scouting. He feared that some enemy Indians might be sneaking near the camp, intending to steal horses. At a distance he saw a party of about twenty men traveling toward his camp. Except for two chiefs riding ahead, each man was leading two pack horses. Chief Three Eagles was puzzled by the appearance of the strangers, for never before had he seen men not wearing blankets. Perhaps they have been robbed, he thought.

Returning to his people, he told them about the strange beings. He gave orders that all the horses should be driven in near camp and watched. Then he went back toward the party, hid himself in the forest, and watched them approach.

He saw that they were traveling slowly, without any suspicious behavior. The two leaders would ride ahead, seeming to survey the country, and then would go back and consult with their men.

"They must be two chiefs," Three Eagles thought. "But what are they after? And why does one of their men have a black face? Who can he be?"

The Chief puzzled about the black man. Among his own people it was the custom to have a war dance if, on a buffalo hunt, they should see any sign of their enemies hiding around. For this dance, the warriors painted themselves—some with red, others with yellow, others with black. While dancing, they would encourage each other to fight bravely. This black man, thought Chief Three Eagles, must have painted his face black as a sign of war. The party must have fought with their enemies and have escaped, losing only their blankets.

Once more the chief returned to his camp and reported to his people.

"They are traveling in our direction," he said. "Let us keep quiet and wait for them. They seem to have no intentions of fighting us or of harming us."

So he and his people watched and waited. The strangers approached slowly, still showing no hostile intentions. When they came near the camp, the two leaders got off their horses and walked toward the people, making signs of friendship. They shook hands with Chief Three Eagles. Then all the Indian men shook hands with all the white men.

"Bring the best buffalo skins," said the chief, "one for each man to sit on. Bring the best buffalo robes, and put them over the men's shoulders."

The two leaders saw that the Indians were smoking a strange plant. They asked for some and filled their pipes. But they did not like it. "It is no good," they said.

Cutting some of their own tobacco, they asked the Indians to fill their pipes with it. But the Indians did not like it. It made all of them cough, and everybody laughed. Then the two leaders, making signs, asked for some kinnikinnick. They mixed the leaves with their own tobacco and gave the mixture to the Indians. The Indians liked it. So the people smoked together.

Seeing that everybody was friendly, the white men decided to camp there near the Indians. As they unpacked their horses, they explained with signs that they had blankets in their packs, used only for sleeping. So they gave back the robes.

The white men were very strong. Some of them carried on their shoulders very large logs to use for their campfires.

Our people and the white men continued to be friendly. On the third day they started off. We showed them how to get to the Lolo fork trail, which is the best way to get to the Nez Percé country on the west side of the mountains.

⌘

The Black Robes and the Coeur d'Alênes

THIS TRADITION concerning the first Jesuit missionaries among the Coeur d'Alênes was recorded from Julia Antelope Nicodemus, November 26, 1954. She had learned it from her mother-in-law, who was well acquainted with the oral history of her people.

CHIEF WHIRLING BLACK CROW was elected chief of the Coeur d'Alênes because he was intelligent, and because he had initiative and other good qualities no other man in the tribe had.

One winter the snow was so deep that people could not hunt deer. They were on the brink of starvation. The chief had a song, a certain tune. It was his guardian spirit song. After he would sing a few minutes, deer would come running. So he told his people to be ready to shoot.

Chief Whirling Black Crow sang his song. The deer came running, and hunters shot them. People skinned the deer, quartered them, and piled up the pieces. Then everyone got a share. In those days people shared everything with the rest. After the chief sang his song, everybody had plenty of food.

One night the chief had a dream. A voice said to him, "Some day in the future you will have a teacher. You will know him because he will wear a black robe that comes to his ankles. He will wear a belt around his robe. Though his hair may be white, he will be like a boy in energy and strength."

Chief Whirling Black Crow thought that the teacher would come right away, but he didn't. Every time travelers came from a distance, the chief listened to their stories, always hoping to hear about the coming of the promised teacher. Many years passed, but he never forgot the dream and the promise. After he had grown old, he became ill with a lingering illness. One day he called to his bedside his son and his two daughters.

The son's name was *Silipstulew,* meaning "Earth-Going-Round-and-Round." To his son the dying chief said, "Keep on looking for the teacher. He will come, in time. When the Black Robe comes, you do exactly as he tells you."

The old chief died, and Earth-Going-Round-and-Round became chief in his stead.

One day the new chief heard that there was a teacher down at Lapwai, among the Nez Percés. He was teaching them something different from what they knew.

The chief said to his people living near Lake Coeur d'Alene, "Come with me, and we'll go to see this teacher. Perhaps he is the one my father said would come."

So they went to Lapwai, arriving late in the day. They exchanged food with the Nez Percés—camas for white camas, bitterroot for kouse—as was the custom in those days. Next morning Chief Earth-Going-Round-and-Round said, "I want to see the new teacher."

The Nez Percés took him to the teacher and introduced him to the white man. Then the leader who had introduced them pointed to a house with a veranda.

"There is where our teacher lives. Those are his children playing on the veranda."

Our chief was disappointed. The teacher did not wear a black robe. The teacher old Chief Whirling Black Crow had told him about did not have children. Chief Earth-Going-Round-and-Round knew that the dream had not come true yet.

"We will go home," he said to his people. "This is not the teacher my father told us about."

They waited a few more years.

One year, at the time for catching white fish, many Coeur d'Alêne bands were camped along Lake Coeur d'Alene. They made a screen of twigs across the bay. The white fish would be stopped by the screen, and the men would dip up the fish in their nets. Then they would divide the fish among all the people in the villages.

One evening a man said to the chief, "Some Flatheads are camping near here. There's a man with them that may be the teacher you're looking for. He's wearing a long black robe with a belt. And he has a book. He's walking back and forth near the camp."

The chief went to the other camp and shook hands with the Black Robe. Then he started to cry. "You are the man my father looked for, for many years, but did not see. A voice told him that you would come. Teach us what the voice said you would teach us."

The Black Robe was Father De Smet. He had with him a Cree who could speak Kalispel. The Coeur d'Alênes could understand Kalispel. Father De Smet taught the Coeur d'Alêne people for a few days. He taught them the Lord's Prayer, the Hail Mary, and the

Apostles Creed, in our language. He picked out some of the older boys and girls and taught each of them just a part of a prayer. And he told them that they should always stand in the same order when they repeated the prayer.

Then he said to them, "I must leave you now. If I do not come back, I will send somebody to teach you."

And he did. He sent two Black Robes from his mission among the Flatheads. They were Father Point and Father Huet. They started the mission among the Coeur d'Alênes.[1]

[1] Father De Smet's account, in brief, is as follows: In the fall of *1841*, the Coeur d'Alênes, having learned that Father De Smet and his assistants were among the Flatheads, sent three of their tribe across the mountains to invite the Black Robe to visit them. The following spring, when the Coeur d'Alênes learned that Father De Smet was on his way, the head chief sent messengers to all the villages to summon all the people to the outlet of the lake.

"I was conducted in triumph by this multitude to the lodge of the chief," wrote De Smet. After the pipe had gone round two or three times, the chief began an eloquent speech: "Black-robe, you are most welcome. . . . For a long time we have wished to see you and hear the words that will give us understanding." (De Smet, *Life, Letters and Travels of Father Jean de Smet, S. J., 1801–1873*, 367, 374–75).

IV. The Kutenais

⟡

THE KUTENAIS "are the remnant of a once brave and powerful
tribe," wrote Ross Cox, who spent five years (1812–17) as a
young fur trader along the Columbia River and its northern
tributaries. Their number had been greatly decreased by their con-
tinual warfare with the Blackfeet over the right to hunt on the buffalo
grounds immediately east of them across the Rockies. Cox found them
strictly honest, remarkably truthful, clean and neat "about their
persons and their lodges . . . [and] devotedly attached to each other
and their country."

Father De Smet reported of the Kutenais a few decades later: "They
are the admiration of all the travelers who visit them, for their dili-
gence in all religious practices, their hospitality and love of justice.
Theft is unknown among them." Their honesty was so well known,
he wrote, that the trader among them often left his storehouse un-
locked during his absence of several weeks, and "had never lost the
value of a pin."

Today, members of the tribe live in northern Idaho, in northwestern Montana (at the north end of the Flathead Reservation), and in
southern British Columbia. In Canada, their name is spelled *Kootenay,* as are a lake and a river along which they have lived for generations. After interviewing tribal elders on both sides of the Canadian
border, the anthropologist H. H. Turney-High came to the conclusion that "the whole body of the Kutenai originated on the Great
Plains." At some time very ancient to his informants, they gradually
moved westward. Most of the Kutenais he consulted, however, had

no migration story and insisted that their people had always lived where they were found by the first white men.

They have long been proud that their language is different from all other languages they have heard, and that it is difficult for members of other tribes to learn. The origin and meaning of the word *Kutenai* have been explained in so many ways that no conclusion can be drawn. Their neighbors the Flatheads and the Nez Percés called them by names that mean "Water People"; some of the Plains Indians, using the sign language, referred to them as "Fish Eaters."

Each term suggests an important feature in their pattern of living. They were formerly noted for their pointed canoes made of tough pine bark on cedar frames, of excellent design for their rough water. "Unlike any other craft known to American tribes," these canoes are said to be similar to ones used in Amur, Siberia. The Kutenais used them to transport families and gear from place to place during the fishing season. Even after the days of horses and buffalo hunts, the Lower Kutenais (those on the lower part of the Kootenay River) depended more on fish than on bison.

In addition to deer and elk, which the Lower Kutenais in particular hunted, both the Upper and the Lower Kutenais hunted caribou; its tough hide was good for moccasins and leggings, its fur good for blankets. Sometimes they hunted moose, but these animals were too difficult to get to be of vital importance. Buffalo were so close that the Upper Kutenais had three brief hunts each year: in mid-June, September, and January. The midwinter hunt was made on snowshoes, men only in the party.

As among the Plains Indians, societies or lodges played an important part in Kutenai life. The Shamans' Society consisted of the village medicine men banded together for mutual assistance and service to their people. The Crazy Owl Society was formed when the spirits told Kutenai women to organize for the purpose of warding off epidemics; epidemics were thought to be the result of disobeying the spirits. Members of the Crazy Dog Society—warriors—were held back during a battle; if defeat seemed ahead, their chief led them in furious charge against the enemy. The Crazy Dogs had a role in the

Sun Dance also. Both they and their horses were painted alike for war and for ceremonies.

The Sun Dance, probably adapted from the Blackfeet or from the Crees, was the most important of their religious ceremonies. It was of social importance, also, for it brought together both groups—the Upper Kutenais and the Lower Kutenais—at the time and place directed by the Sun Dance spirit. Some details about their ceremonial are revealed in the story, "Why the Indians Have No Metal Tools."

Next to the Sun Dance in religious or emotional significance was the Grizzly Bear Dance. It was a prayer for plenty, held at the beginning of the berrypicking season. The spirit of the Grizzly Bear was prayed to because bears like berries and because huckleberries, serviceberries, and chokeberries were important foods among the Kutenais. The bear spirit told his people where to find the berries and how to keep out of trouble. Songs to the Grizzly Bear were accompanied by a rattle made from deer hide and claws. During the ceremony the medicine men related their dream-experiences.

The Fir Tree Ceremony was considered very powerful. When venison was scarce, it was thought that deer had been hidden by some hostile medicine man. So the Shamans' Society had a fir tree set up in the middle of the long house; the people hung gifts upon the tree, and the medicine men danced around it and directed prayers to it. At the proper time, the head shaman sent certain men out to hunt for deer. A Health Ceremony, originating in a vision, was held in early spring, to keep away disease and to promote the health and prosperity of the tribe.

The Midwinter Festival of the Plateau tribes, the Kutenais held in very simple form. At sunrise the chief prayed for the welfare of the band during the next year, and the people asked for help from the spirits and from their relatives and friends who had died. For three days there were feasting, singing, and dancing, both religious and social.

Daily prayers were a simple ceremony with the Kutenais. Leaving the children asleep, adults went forth every morning to pray to the

Dawn for the little ones of the family. Then they prayed to the Sun for children who were not related to them.

Tobacco they planted with ceremony and smoked with ceremony. They never smoked it for pleasure, but as a sacrifice to the spirits. Long ago, when the first Kutenais occupied the land, the spirits taught them how to grow tobacco and gave them the first seeds. Because the spirits must have tobacco, the people planted it for them and gave it to them in ceremonies. At every sunrise, a religious man filled his pipe, sang, and then held his pipe toward the east, for good luck. At night, he held his pipe toward the west, to ward off ill luck, and then toward the ground, in appreciation of the spirits' having given the earth to the people.

As long as there were Indians to pray to the spirits and to give tobacco to them, the Kutenais long believed, the United States and Canada could never be defeated by any foreign country.

The Kutenais used to hold tribal ceremonies, at irregular intervals, along Lake Pend Oreille (in present-day northern Idaho), where they made offerings to the spirits. The dead went to the sun, they believed, and at some future time all the dead would return to the shores of this lake. All the bands came, even those living in what is now Canada; on their journey they danced every night around a fire, going in the direction of the sun. The festival at the lake, which consisted principally of dances, lasted many days.

On the painted rocks high above Lake Pend Oreille were the figures of men and animals, believed by the Indians to have been painted by a race of men who lived in the area before them. Indians feared to pass that point, reported Governor Isaac Stevens in 1853–55, because their legends warned them that if they should attempt to pass, the spirits would create a disturbance in the water and would cause them to be swallowed by the waves.

Kutenai mythology bears many resemblances to that of their neighbors. Coyote, in his experiences with other animal persons—chiefly Grizzly Bear, Fox, Wolf, Cricket, and Chicken Hawk—often seems like Old Man of Blackfeet mythology. There used to be also a number of tales about giants. My principal Kutenai informant, William

Gingrass, said that the giants followed the big streams and that whenever Indians went to a big stream, giants killed them and ate them. So the Indians lived around little streams near the mountains.

"My great-grandmother's uncle," continued Gingrass, "once found the skeleton of a giant, buried in a sitting position, in a grave near Superior."

Another group of stories, told in great detail, concern a culture-hero who went to the one place in the world where serviceberries grew, gathered the shoots to make his arrows, and then planted serviceberries in many places so that there would be enough for arrows when people came into the world. From ducks, he obtained feathers for his arrows; from the horn of a mountain sheep, he made an arrow straightener. From a bull moose, he obtained sinew with which to put the feathers on his arrows.

From a stone that had supernatural powers, he obtained flint and then scattered it over all the world so that the new people who were to come could make arrow points. He took a cedar tree from those who protected it and declared that it should "grow all over this world" so that people could make bows from cedar wood.

"This is all that I know about what Chief Yankekam did among the people of ancient times," said the narrator at the end of his story about this culture-hero.

Because most of the few Kutenai tales that have been published are variants of tales published from other tribes, I was very fortunate in finding William Gingrass. He had variety in his repertoire. An intelligent, middle-aged Kutenai, he remembered vividly stories which he had learned from his great-grandmother. During our long session, it was interesting to detect in his voice a change of attitude toward the old tales that his great-grandmother had believed. At first, his voice suggested the amused disbelief to be expected from a man who had attended Chemawa Indian School and whose daily work for years had been with white men. But as he "warmed into his stories," his tone changed; he was temporarily believing them, as he no doubt had believed them when a boy in the family circle around the winter fires.

The Animals and the Sun

LONG AGO, when the animals were the people of the world, a chief asked, "Who will be the Sun?" All the animal people talked among themselves and decided that Raven should be the Sun. The chief agreed and told him what he should do.

When Raven started on his journey, it became dark. Next morning the people watched for him to come up. But he was not bright enough, and the whole day was like evening. When Raven returned, the people said to him, "We do not want you for the Sun. You made everything black."

Chicken Hawk was told that he should be the Sun. When he started on his journey, it became dark. The following morning the people watched him come up. As he went higher and higher in the sky, the world looked yellow. It was yellow all day. So when Chicken Hawk returned, the people said, "You can not be the Sun. You make everything look like bad weather."

The animal people held another council and talked the matter over again. Coyote said to them, "Let me be the Sun."

The people were willing. So when Coyote started on his journey, they slept. But next morning when he rose in the sky, it began to be hot. The higher he went, the hotter the day became. At noon when the women were cooking their food, Coyote called down from the sky, "Will there be any food left for me?"

So they set aside some food for Coyote to eat at the end of the day.

All the people were very hot. Even when they went into the shade, they were warm. The children began to cry, for the Sun burned them. Their mothers put them into the river, thinking they would be cool there. But the water was so hot it burned them. Water and air became warmer and warmer until sunset. When darkness came, the people felt well. They had almost been burned to death.

When Coyote returned to camp, he was told, "You can not be the Sun. You are bad. You were too hot."

Not far away lived a woman and her two sons. One of them said, "Let us go over there where the people are playing Sun."

When the two reached the camp, they were asked, "Why do you come here?"

"We heard that you are playing Sun."

"That is good," the people said. "One of you shall be the Sun."

The older one started, and the people slept. The next day he went up into the sky. In the morning it was rather cool, and the people were pleased. Even when he was high up in the sky, they felt comfortable. At noon it was warm, but when they went into the shade in the afternoon, they were comfortable. The water was always cool. When the people went swimming in the river, they felt cool and happy.

When the Sun came down and returned to the camp, all the people thought that he was the one who should be the Sun. "You are the best. You shall be the Sun," they said to him.

To his younger brother they said, "You shall go up in the evening. You shall be the Moon."

So he went off. Before it had been dark long, they saw him going up into the sky. He made it light all through the night. On the following morning, when he returned, he was told, "Your elder brother shall be the Sun during the day. You shall be the Moon during the night."

These two youths became the heavenly balls, the day Sun and the night Sun. They were thought to be good, and everyone was happy —everyone except Coyote.

Coyote was angry. "I will kill the Sun," he said to himself.

He made a bow and two arrows, and then went to the place where the Sun was to come up. He went in the night and found a good seat. When morning came he lay on his stomach and aimed his arrow at the right place.

The Sun rose. Coyote took good aim and was about to shoot. But his arrow caught fire. It was burning so fast that Coyote threw it away. Then everything around him caught fire. There was fire on all sides of him. Coyote ran and jumped into the river. He was almost burned. Then he saw a trail and lay on it. When the fire reached the trail, it turned back because there was no grass on the trail. So Coyote was saved.

Then he said, "Later generations will do this: when there is a fire, they will lie down on a trail. In that way they will be saved."

✖

The Great Flood in the Kutenai Country

COLUMBIA LAKE, in southeastern British Columbia, is the first of several mountain lakes through which the Columbia River flows in Canada. Some Kootenay bands lived near the lake and the upper course of the river.

IN THE DAYS when all the animal people lived on the east side of Columbia Lake, they used to cross the water for huckleberries. One day as they were returning, Duck and his wife were swallowed by a great monster named Deep Water Dweller. Duck's brother, Redheaded Woodpecker, decided to call all the fish together in order to find out where this monster could be found. So he sent Dipper up every stream, to invite all the fish to the council. He sent Snipe around the lake with the same message. Wherever they stopped, Dipper and Snipe called out, "You fish are all invited to come. If you do not, we will dry this lake and you will die."

When the fish arrived at the council meeting, Woodpecker explained to them, "I have lost my brother. Deep Water Dweller has swallowed him. You fish must know where this monster lives. Where can I find him?"

Sucker answered, "I have seen him at the bottom of the deep water, where I like to stay."

Woodpecker sent Long Legs, a kind of duck, to find the monster, but the water was too deep, and so he had to turn back.

At that moment there appeared in the council a very tall person, so tall that if he had stood upright his head would have touched the sky. He was a person, not an animal. He had been traveling from north to south, stopping at each place to give it a name. Redheaded Woodpecker asked him to drive the monster out of the water, and so the stranger waded into the lake. He kicked at the Deep Water Dweller, but missed him. The monster fled into the river, up a small creek, and into the very source of the stream under the mountains.

After him crawled the Tall Person. He built a dam at the place where the monster had gone under the mountain. Woodpecker now placed his brother Sapsucker beside the dam and told him what to do. "When the monster comes out," he said to Sapsucker, "tell him that Woodpecker is going to spear him. Then he will stop, and I will come round and kill him."

Woodpecker then went to the other side of the mountain and kicked, and the monster started to come out. When he reached the dam, Sapsucker became excited and so confused that he called out, "Sapsucker is going to kill you!"

The monster broke through the dam grunting, "Sapsucker! I am not afraid of your spear. I am going to swallow you."

Sapsucker turned and ran. Just at that moment, Redheaded Woodpecker appeared and pierced the monster with his bill. But as the monster had already started to enter the stream below the dam, he was wounded only in a foot. Leaving a trail of blood, he hurried down the stream.

Woodpecker sent Beaver ahead to build a dam. When the monster got that far, he could go no farther. Woodpecker came up and killed him. He ripped the monster open and released Duck and his wife.

Blood, which was really water, began to flow from the monster's wounds. Gradually, it spread over the earth until the people had to flee to the mountains. Chicken Hawk pulled out one of his spotted tail feathers and stuck it into the ground at the edge of the rising water.

"Watch!" said Chicken Hawk. "If the water goes above that first stripe, we shall be drowned."

The water stopped at the last stripe and then began to go down. The animal people were saved.

After the flood was gone, not all the animal people came down to the earth. At that time some of the birds began to live in the mountains, where they live to this day.

A Visit to the Sky World

THE THEME OF A JOURNEY of the ancient people to the Sky World along a chain of arrows is found in stories once related by several tribes of the Plateau and of the Northwest Coast. Here is a composite, somewhat abbreviated, of three versions of a myth recorded from the Kutenais. Fragments of it were known in 1954 by members of the tribe living near Windermere Lake in southeastern British Columbia.

ONE TIME Muskrat wished to marry the widow of his brother. When she refused him, he shot her with an arrow different from other arrows used by his people. Finding the woman dead, her friends asked about the owner of the arrow. Muskrat smelled it and then said, "It must have come from the sky."

The Earth People thought that Sky People had killed the woman and so decided to go up and make war upon them. First there would have to be a chain of arrows to make a trail to the sky. Coyote shot at a cloud but did not reach it. Other animal people shot their arrows, but they, too, failed to reach the sky.

At last, two hawks tried their skill. Their first arrow, after flying one day and one night, struck the sky. The Earth People heard the noise as the point struck. The second arrow hit the notch of the first arrow. One after another the people shot upward, each arrow hitting the notch of the one previously shot. But the last of their arrows did not quite reach the ground. So Raven put his beak in the notch of the bottom arrow and made the chain touch the earth.

When the people were ready to climb to the sky, Wolverine said, "Wait for me. It will take me two days to put away my things. Don't start for two days."

But the animals did not wait for him. Wolverine was still putting away his things when the others reached the sky. Finding that he had been left behind, he became so angry that he took hold of the bottom arrows and pulled the whole chain down. It was transformed into a mountain not far from Kootenay Lake.

Up in the sky, Muskrat made a large lake and put up many tipis around it. When the people attacked what they thought was a lake village, he shot from the houses, passing quickly under the ground from one house to the next. Soon Woodpecker discovered that there was really only one person in the village—Muskrat. So they killed him and decided to return to the earth.

When they came back to the place where the top of the arrow chain had been, they found that it was gone. They went to the drinking place of Thunderbird, snared him, plucked his feathers, and distributed them among the people. But there were not enough for everyone. Those who received feathers were transformed into birds; the others, into fish and land animals.

Two bats expected to be given the best feathers, but the best ones were given to two friends, Golden Eagle and Young Golden Eagle. When the bats saw that no feathers were left for them, they spread out their blankets and used them for wings. Flying Squirrel pulled out his skin and used it for wings. Coyote sailed down, steering himself with his tail. Sucker threw himself down so hard that he broke all his bones. He was given new ones; that is why sucker's body today is full of bones.

Flicker, the Woodpecker brothers, and the Woodpeckers' sister— a bird with yellow breast and gray feathers—were left in the sky. They walked to the place where the sky and earth meet. There, where the city of Nelson is now, they met supernatural beings who told them never to touch fish and never to stay overnight in the woods. On the shore of a lake they found a char, a kind of trout. Just as Flicker was about to touch it, a wave rolled in and without the others knowing what was happening, Flicker was swallowed by Water Monster.

Then Woodpecker sent Water Ouzel and another small water bird out to invite all the fish to a feast. "Tell them," he said, "that if they do not come, the lake will be dried up."

The water birds danced at every bay, inviting the fish. When the chief of the fish, the last to arrive, reached Woodpecker and his brothers, they gave him a pipe, and they all smoked together. "Where is my grandson?" asked the Fish Chief. He referred to Flicker as his grandson. Then Fish Chief moved his eyebrows, first this way and then that way, indicating that Flicker was in the lake.

As a reward for Fish Chief's telling them, the Woodpecker brothers gave the Fish Chief some of their food. When he went back into the water, he wore on each side of his body a red spot, because of the meat he had eaten. This fish still wears the two red spots.

Then the Woodpecker brothers made ready to kill the Water Monster. The first who tried to attack him was Long Legs, but he was swallowed. Woodpecker tried to kick the monster, but the blow glanced off. He and his brothers chased it along the Kootenay River and back by way of Lake Windermere. At Long-Water Bay the monster hid in a cave under the water.

Soon the Woodpecker brothers saw the old grandfather of the Kutenais crawling over the country, giving names to places. Wherever he crawled, a river flowed. "Dam up the end of the lake," Woodpecker told him, "so that the monster cannot escape."

So old Grandfather broke off a piece of a mountain, solidified it with his knees, and thus made the portage between the Kootenay and Columbia rivers. When Woodpecker at last got close enough to Water Monster to kill it, it looked at him and made him so afraid that he could do nothing.

At last Fox took a tomahawk, killed the monster, and cut it up. Flicker and Duck came out of its stomach. Both of them were white on their sides, and Flicker, who had been a large creature, had been worn down to his present size.

The animal people cut off the ribs of the monster and threw them down the river, where they became a cliff. They cut up the body and scattered the parts here and there, to become food for the new people. They forgot the Kutenais until only a little of the monster's blood was left. This they scattered over the land where they had killed the Water Monster. For this reason the Kutenai tribe has always been small.[1]

⌘

The Painted Rocks Along Flathead Lake

Flathead Lake is a large lake in western Montana. Along its west shore, accessible only by boat, are the Painted Rocks, with signs and characters in vivid colors. This myth about them was recorded from William Gingrass. His Kutenai name, given him by his great-grandmother, means "Grizzly Bear War Paint."

After the great flood long ago, no human beings were left in this country. But the spirits were left. Some of them were in the form of animals. They gathered together on a bench of land above where Flathead Lake is now. At that time there was no lake—just a big river coming down from the north. It wound around and flowed down through where the Hot Springs are now. All that country was under water; you can see the water marks yet on the east side of the Lone Pine country. A little stream flowed at the south end of the present lake. A long time after this story, Yawonick, something that lives down below the water, came up from the bottom of the river and changed its course. Then the lake was formed.

When the great flood went down, the spirits held a council there on the shelf above the old river. They had heard that new people were coming, and they knew they should decide what to do when the Indians arrived. While they talked, one spirit kept watch.

"The people will come in canoes from the north," said the chief of the spirits. "We must have everything decided when they come,

[1] In a partly forgotten version of the story related in the summer of 1955 by Mary Susan Finley, a Kutenai living at the north end of Flathead Lake, certain other details are localized. Her story begins in "a big camp of the spirits" between Libby and Rexburg (northwestern Montana). After the animal persons returned from the Sky World, they found the Great-Grandfather Creator near Nelson (southeastern British Columbia).

His footprint is still there, on a rock. Near it, another rock, shaped like a heart, was made by the Great-Grandfather from the heart of a young goat. Below Nelson, the four brothers cooked their meat in a pot between two rivers that are parallel but flow in different directions (probably the Columbia and its tributary the Kootenay). "That pot became hot springs. All hot springs are from the pot up there between the two rivers. Veins from it go to all parts of the world," said Mrs. Finley.

as to how we can help them. Each of you will have to have a special song that will help people. You will sing it and then put your picture or your name on these big rocks."

"But why should we put them up here?" asked one spirit. "They will be so high that they will be hard for people to get to or even to see."

"That is what we want," replied Nupeeka, the chief of the spirits. *Nupeeka* means "spirit"; in the old days he was a kind of teacher also. "We want the people to go to the high places when they seek spirit power. Seeking power will be too easy if they can find it in the low places. They will have to climb to get to the spirit pictures and the writing in the high places."

So the spirits sang their songs and painted their names in pictures on the rocks. The First Dawn of the Morning sang the first song and put his sign highest up on the rock; that spirit gave the strongest power. The spirits of Grizzly Bear and Cougar and Eagle—they sang their songs and painted their pictures. Each of them gives strong power. All the other spirits sang their songs and put their writing on the rocks—all except Rabbit. He just hopped around.

At last the lookout called, "We must end our meeting. I see the new people coming around the bend."

"But I haven't made up my song yet!" exclaimed Rabbit. "I haven't a song yet and I haven't painted my picture."

"It's too late now," the other spirits told him. "The people are landing below the Painted Rock."

So Rabbit was left out entirely. He has no power song. He gives no power to people seeking spirit power. He can do nothing but hop around.

The new people landed below the Painted Rocks, near where Rollins is now, in the Big Lodge country.

It is called the Big Lodge country because of a vision two men had many years ago. Each of them saw in a vision where he should put up a lodge for a Sun Dance, for a sacrifice to the spirits. When they followed their dream, they came to the same place; each had seen the same spot in his vision. So they put one big lodge there for the two groups of people.

That was a good place for the Medicine Lodge, because it was near the spirit writings on the rocks. All over the country there are picture writings painted on the rocks by the spirits or left as records by the people who got their spirit power there. Near Kerr Dam on the Flathead River is a cave where people used to go in search of power, and they left their records on the rocks. Up near Kamloops, in Canada, is another cave near a big waterfall. People went there for power; if they were successful, they were high in power, for the place was difficult to get to.

The harder a person had to work to get to the place for the power quest, the higher the spirit power he obtained. The spirit who appeared to a person in a vision recorded on the rocks how many days and nights he had been there and what power had been given him.

✽

The Mysteries in Flathead Lake

MADELINE LEFTHAND, interpreted by Adeline Matthias, related this Kutenai tradition about Flathead Lake in 1955. The Blackfeet and the Sarcees related a similar story about crossing on ice in Buffalo Lake in Canada. A Snake River band of Nez Percés used to tell essentially the same story about crossing the frozen Snake River. The Arapahos had a similar tradition about crossing the Missouri River.

LONG AGO a herd of buffalo used to graze on the shores of Flathead Lake. Whenever they saw people, they would run into the water and hide themselves. Only one of them was ever killed; the Indians cooked him but found his meat too tough to eat.

The first Indians lived on an island in Flathead Lake, not far from Elmo. One winter they decided to move camp. They crossed on the ice, carrying packs on their backs.

As two girls got about half way across the lake, they saw the antler of some animal sticking up out of the ice. The antlers were about two feet long.

"I'll chop it off," said one girl. "I might need it."

"Don't touch it," said the older girl. "It is a kind of mystery, an antler growing in ice. We mustn't cut it."

Her friend was determined, although she did realize the danger.

"If anything should happen in the ice," she asked, "do you have any power to escape?"

"Yes, I'd become a ball," replied the older girl. "That's my special power. Have you any power?"

"Yes, I'd become a round buckskin target. I'd get to land that way."

The girls waited until the other people had almost reached the shore. Then with sharp-edged rocks they began cutting the antler. When they had cut through to the middle, the antler began shaking. Then the ice around them began shaking. Soon it split into chunks and pieces. As the ice between the girls and the shore broke, the head of a monster appeared, shaking its huge antlers.

Quickly the girls called on their powers. One became a ball, the other a round buckskin target. They reached the shore safely, but one half of their people were drowned. That is why there are few Kutenai Indians.

The monster was never seen again, but our people never again went out very far on the lake. Not many years ago, some white men who were fishing on Flathead Lake said that they had seen a strange animal in the water.

⌘

The Origin of Flathead River

FLATHEAD RIVER, which flows southward from Flathead Lake, is the outlet of that long lake. "Its outlet during the glacial age was westward through the Big Draw," near Big Arm. A band of Kutenais now live along the west shore of the upper lake. Whether the following myth is Kutenai or Salish is now uncertain. A half blood related it in 1900 to Major R. H. Chapman.

LONG, LONG AGO, before Indians came to this valley, a big, big beaver lived in Flathead Lake. I don't know how large he was, but he was so large that no man could have killed him.

At that time the water did not run out of the south end of the lake as it does now. Instead, it ran out at the west, near Big Arm, where there is now a flat, long valley. If you go over there, you can see where the river used to be.

The big beaver built dams on that river and made the water in the lake deeper and deeper. As he grew bigger and got older, he wanted more and more water. But after a while he decided that he could not build his dams bigger and higher. If he did, the water would run out the south end of the lake.

So he swam down to the south end of the lake and there built a dam. He built it slowly and made it wide and high and strong. It went a long way, from the mountains on the east to the mountains on the west. He made it very strong, except in one place. Then the beaver went back and built on the river again. So the water in the lake became deeper and deeper.

By and by, a hard winter came with much snow and deep snow. Then one night a big chinook wind blew, and a warm spring came in a hurry. The snows on the mountains melted fast, the streams rushed into the lake, the water became bigger and bigger. It was bigger water than the Indians have ever known.

The dam at the south end of the lake, high and long and wide, held the water for a while. But at last it broke in that weak place, and the water poured out. As it ran out, it made the hole in the dam wider and deeper. That's the way the Flathead River was made. The beaver built no more, and the river did not change.

If you will go up on a hill above the lake and look, you will see where the water and the land came together long ago before the dam broke. Then go around the lake. At the south end you will see the big dam, from mountain to mountain, except where the water broke through. And near Big Arm you will see the dams, not broken, but washed down by water.

The big beaver? I will tell you about him someday. Not now.

❈

The First Blacktail Deer Dance

THE BLACKTAIL DEER DANCE reported by Clark Wissler and D. C. Duvall seems to have been the same as the Horned Animal Ceremony reported by Edward Curtis. It was performed either in the late autumn or in late winter when game was difficult to find and food was scarce. The Kutenai name for the ceremony has been translated as "Making the Deer Song." It was last performed among the Lower Kutenais in 1875. The Blackfeet also held the ceremony, having learned it from the Kutenais.

L ONG AGO in the camp of the Kutenais, one of the men died. He was a true and good man. After he died, his spirit went away to the land of the dead to find out what was there. After a while the spirit chief told him to return to his people and tell them what he had seen and what he had learned.

The man had been dead for seven days, and so his body was badly decayed. But the spirit chief of the dead took his spirit down to his body and it came to life. The man came to life in the midst of his friends.

Now it was this way: the watchers around the body heard a noise inside the corpse, but all the time the spirit of the dead man was sitting nearby, saying that he was trying to sing. So they quickly unwrapped his body. The man opened his eyes, looked at them, and said, "I have come from the land of the dead. I have come to teach you more songs and prayers."

Then he arose and picked up a small bell. All the people were very hungry, for they had had nothing to eat for a long time. "Now we will all dance," the man said to them.

He led the dancers around in a circle and, keeping time with the bell, he sang the songs he had learned in the land of the dead. When the dance was over, the people rested while he prayed for them. Then they danced again. When they awoke the next morning, the man who had been dead said to them, "I know all about power. I saw it in my dream. You can believe that there is such a place as the one I saw."

Then the men went out to hunt and brought home a great deal of deer meat. Thereafter, this dance was called the Blacktail Deer Dance.

After that, everyone took part in the dance before going out to hunt. They danced in the evening, and at night the hunters saw in dreams where game was to be found.

✖

Why the Indians Had No Metal Tools

WILLIAM GINGRASS prefaced the following legend, which he had learned from his great-grandmother, with some facts about the ceremony of the Sun Dance or the Medicine Lodge as the Kutenais used to hold it. Neither term, he said, is an accurate translation of the name of the ceremony. The Kutenai term for it really means "someone who has to make a smudge in order to make a sacrifice to the spirits." This person became the head man of the ceremony. He was purified by the smoke so that he was able to stay in the lodge, where he had to remain for three days and three nights. During that time he ate very little, and his food had to be a special kind. He went through certain movements when he entered the lodge and the same movements in reverse when he left it. After the coming of the missionaries, the Sun Dance ceremony was dropped for a number of years. After it was revived, it was held almost every year until 1949 or 1950, by the Kutenais along upper Flathead Lake.

ONE TIME, two boys in the Sun Dance Lodge asked one another, "Where did the spirit of the Sun Dance come from?" They knew that Kukluknam, the spirit of the Sun Dance,[1] had come into the lodge. The spirit had entered the image or doll that the Sun Dance chief had been singing to and drumming to for many days and nights. The boys knew that Kikum had come with the spirit of the Sun Dance and that he was seated behind the blanket. Kikum was the spirit from the water and the interpreter[2] for Kukluknam. (*Kukluknam* means "where you worship.") Kikum could speak any language in the world plainly, just like a human being.

---

[1] The images of Kukluknam and of two other spirits can be seen near Elko, British Columbia, on a cliff on top of a mountain. They are the three top spirits. First Dawn of Morning is the highest spirit one can obtain and the most difficult spirit to obtain.

[2] In the Sun Dance, the Interpreter sits beside the suppliant and corrects him. Each movement must be correct, according to ritual.

"People say that Kukluknam and Kikum come from the east," the boys remembered. "How can we find out where in the east they came from? Do we have enough power to trace them? Let's watch where they go."

They began to watch very closely just before dawn of the last night of the Sun Dance. Both of them used all of their power to find out where the Spirit of the Sun Dance and his interpreter went. The spirit knew that the boys were following him, and so he stayed just in sight of them. At last they got to the ocean. There the boys did not know what to do. The spirit, walking on the water, looked back at them.

"I know you really want to know where I go," he said to them. "You want to know how I perform my ceremonies. Follow me."

He gave each boy a bunch of feathers—small feathers. "Follow me," repeated the spirit. "Drop these as you walk. They give you power to walk on water."

The boys did as the Spirit of the Sun Dance directed, and they walked along after him on the water. At last, they got across the ocean to a big rock that juts out in the water.

There the boys saw the interpreter, Kikum, for the first time, and noticed that he was an old man.

"How did he get here?" they wondered.

The Interpreter did not explain, but he did speak to them. "This is where we live, Kukluknam and I. From here we can read the minds of all your people. Come in and see our lodge."

Inside, the boys saw a room full of buckskin costumes and strings of pipes—many different kinds of pipes.

"Each tribe has a pipe," explained the Interpreter. "This is the pipe of your people. When they have the Sun Dance ceremony, we can see in the pipe whether your people are in earnest. Some of these pipes, you see, are not burning. That means that the people are not in earnest in their ceremonies."

As the boys walked around looking at the costumes and the pipes, the Interpreter spoke again: "You will stay here until about the time your people will put up the Sun Dance next year. I'm going to make a present to give you then."

Every day the Interpreter was very busy, and the boys wondered what he was doing. They noticed that he would go out and get some clay and put it into two small boxes. But they were never allowed to look into the boxes, and Kikum never explained why he wanted the clay.

One day he told them about big boats that often passed by the big rock. "People in some big boat may capture you some day, because you are human beings. But they will not see Kukluknam and me."

Sometimes the boys heard the Interpreter talk to the pipes. Every once in a while the pipes would brighten up and smoke would come out of them. "The tribes are performing their ceremonies," explained Kikum. Then he would pick up a pipe and say to it, "Yes, we will grant your request," or "No, you are not making a big enough sacrifice." Then he would lay the pipe down again.

When the time approached for the boys to return to their home country, the old man had a small box ready for each of them. They were the boxes he had been putting the clay in.

"Now I am ready to take you back across the water. Here are two boxes for you to take with you. When you get to the other side of the ocean, wait until morning to start. You will walk for three days. Your box will seem heavy, but you must keep on carrying it. It has in it something important for your people.

"On the third day, watch the sun. When it gets to the middle of the sky, open the box. Not until then must you see what I have given you for your people."

So the boys got ready and joined the old man standing beside his canoe at the water's edge.

"Take your box and lie down in the canoe," he told them. "Lie face down and don't peek. If you hear a noise, don't get up. Lie still on the bottom of the canoe."

The Interpreter gave them other presents, also, probably more power of some kind. The boys obeyed him, lay down in the canoe, and pulled a skin over them.

They heard one oar strike the water. The boat started. They could feel themselves moving very swiftly, but they were surprised when they heard the Interpreter say, "Well, we're here." He had used only one oar for the entire journey.

When the boys threw off the cover, they saw they had landed exactly where they had begun to drop the feathers.

"Now you know where the Spirit of the Sun Dance and I live— east across the ocean beside the big rock. Go on home now. Don't forget anything I told you about the boxes."

Next morning the boys started walking toward the west. At first the boxes felt light and small, but during the day they became heavy and large. The boys camped at night and started out again the second morning. All that day the boxes kept getting heavier and heavier. One boy lagged behind with his box, and the other had to wait for him again and again.

"It's heavy," complained the one who lagged behind. "I can't walk any faster with it."

"We can't leave it," the other replied. "And we can't open it until tomorrow at midday."

They pushed on and camped another night. The third morning the boxes seemed heavier yet, and again one boy kept lagging behind.

Before the sun had climbed high in the sky, the laggard heard a tempting voice: "You don't need to wait until the sun reaches the middle of the sky. Open it now. Find out what is in the box."

So the boy lagged further behind and let a hill rise up between him and his partner. "I'm going to see what is in here," he said to himself. "I'm going to rip the top off."

He sat down on the ground and opened his little box. At first he did not see anything he recognized. There were just pieces of things. He emptied them on the ground and then found one complete object —a knife, made of ore. He picked it up—it was very light—and ran on to catch up with the other boy.

"I've opened my box!" he called out. "See this knife. It was the only thing in the box. Why was it so heavy?"

"You should not have opened your box," scolded the other boy. "It isn't time yet."

"It's almost time," said his partner. "See—the sun is almost overhead. Open yours. It won't hurt to be a little ahead of time."

So the second boy opened his little box. In it he found nothing complete, just pieces of things. Some of the pieces seemed to belong together, but the boys did not know what they were or how to put them together.

"We'll go home and put up a screen,"[3] they decided. "We'll ask the Spirit what we had in our boxes."

As soon as they reached home, they called a meeting of all the men of the village and told them their story—about the journey across the ocean to the place where the sun comes up, about the lodge on the big rock with its many costumes and pipes, where they had lived with the old man, the Interpreter for the Spirit of the Sun Dance. They told about the boxes.

"We've done something wrong," they confessed. "We disobeyed the orders of Kikum. So we do not know what was in the second box, and only one thing that was in the first box. Let us have a ceremony and ask the Spirit of the Sun Dance."

They passed the boxes around so that the people could see and handle the contents. In them were pieces of metal, a mystery of some kind.

That night they put up the screen in the lodge of the Sun Dance chief. All the spirits came, for all of them knew that the screen had been put up.

"No, we don't want you," the boys said to one spirit after another.

At last the Spirit of the Sun Dance came in, with his Interpreter. The boys explained and asked their question.

---

[3] The screen may be called at any time. It is not necessarily a part of the Sun Dance. It might be used to find out where a person is if he is lost. There is singing when the screen is called. Drums only are used for the Sun Dance. (William Gingrass)

"Yes, we know all about it," replied the Interpreter. "Everything we gave you came right back and hit us in the face as soon as you opened the boxes. Those things were of metal. They were patterns for all kinds of things you were to make in the future. Now you can make only the knife, for it is the only thing you have complete. You've lost the chance to make all the other things we gave you."

So they lost out on their chance to make tools and guns and other things from metal. That's why the Indians had only knives when the white people came.

That's how my great-grandmother explained it when she was an old woman and I was a young boy.

❦

Chief Cliff

PAT SHEA, United States Forest Service employee on the Flathead Reservation, told this Kutenai legend in 1953. He had heard the Indians tell it many times. Chief Cliff, about five miles west of Flathead Lake and directly north of the Indian village of Elmo, is at the end of a ridge which extends for about ten miles. At the east end, the ridge breaks off abruptly with an almost perpendicular cliff about 150 feet high. At the bottom of the cliff is a semicircle of loose and broken rock.

YEARS AGO, an aged chief of the Kutenais felt that he no longer had control of his band. In his younger years he had done many deeds of bravery and many acts of generosity, but now the young men in his band did not care to hear about them. He had laid down rules of conduct which were for the betterment of his people, but the young men and women now gave no heed to them.

They were fast departing from the ways of their elders and were following the wishes and the orders of a sub-chief. Much younger than the old chief, this man would probably be head man when the chief died. But he, too, was not in sympathy with the old ways, and he seldom counseled with his elders.

The old chief was sick at heart because of the changing ways and because of the young people's neglect of him. What could he do to regain the respect of his band? What could he do to remind them of his former bravery and prowess?

One summer when his people were camped at the base of the high, steep cliff north of Elmo, he thought of the answer to his questions. While the others were making merry with games and dancing, he planned how he would once more prove his worth. He dressed himself in his finest buckskin and in the headdress which showed his deeds in war. He arrayed his favorite horse in a richly decorated saddle blanket and put on him his best buckskin saddle.

Then he mounted his horse and, sitting erect and proud, rode to the top of the ridge and along its crest to the edge of the cliff. Seeing him up there, everyone in the camp stopped his work or his play and watched in wonder. Why was he dressed in ceremonial garb? What had caused the change in his bearing?

When all were looking up at him in silence, the old man began to address them in the strong tones of his younger years: "Hear me, my people. My heart is heavy with grief because you have forgotten the teachings of your elders. You have forgotten their brave deeds and their generous acts. The stories about them—stories which have been handed down for generations as examples for young people to follow—you now pay no attention to. Soon they will be forgotten.

"Only ill luck and misery will come to those who forsake the laws and the teachings of the elders of the tribe. Knowing that, I will make one last effort to remind you of the bravery and the wisdom of your grandfathers."

When he had finished speaking, he turned his horse and rode slowly back along the ridge. Suddenly he wheeled round, tightened the reins, and urged the horse at full speed back toward the cliff. In wonder and then in horror, the people below watched him, noting that he was singing the death chant. Still chanting, he rode on beyond the edge of the cliff. Horse and rider turned over and over among the rocks at the foot of the ridge.

All the people hurried to the spot. The women began the death wail. Sadly the men disentangled the body from the saddle and the horse's trappings. Some prepared it for burial, while others looked for the best place for the grave of the old chief. As it was already late afternoon, burial would not be until morning.

That evening there were no games or gambling or laughter around the camp fires. All spoke in subdued tones or listened in silence to the old men of the tribe. One after another they arose and paid tribute to their dead leader. Some spoke about his prowess in war, when they had been attacked by the enemy and he had led them as a war-chief.

Some spoke of his kindness to the poor of the tribe. "When there was food," they recalled, "he always saw to it that no one was hungry. The good of all his people was near and dear to his heart. Like a good chief, he was generous as well as brave. And he always obeyed the laws of the tribe."

The young men and young women, the boys and girls, all listened with pride in their hearts. "He was a greater chief than we knew," they said among themselves.

"It is well for us to respect the old people for what they have done," the young people said. "We must not overlook any of the old ones. We, too, will be old some day. We will remember the brave deed and the wise counsel of the good chief. The cliff will always remind us of him."

That is why the cliff is called Chief Cliff. And that is why the Kutenais, ever since, have remembered to treat their old people with kindness and with honor.

✳

"Things Are Changing"

THIS STORY William Gingrass also learned from his great grand-mother.

ONE TIME when the Kutenais were having their usual troubles with the Blackfeet, a band of our people were camping in the mountains. The leader of the band was named Sowatts.

Sowatts decided one morning that he would go out and get some fresh meat. He was warned that he might run into Grizzly Bear and was reminded that someone in the band had disobeyed the bear's instructions.

Grizzly Bear had charge of all plants, roots, and berries, and he forbade people to eat certain of them. "Some plants belong to animals," he said. "Human beings are forbidden to eat them." The first thing a boy or girl was taught was to avoid eating certain plants. Grizzly Bear had also taught the women how to cook plants—for example, how to steam camas roots.

Not long before this, some person had eaten a plant that belonged to the animals. So when Grizzly Bear met Sowatts alone in the mountains, he tore the man's hair out, pulled his arms off—tore him to pieces.

Three days later his people found him dead. They carried his body back to camp, planning to bury it in the shale the next morning. But he came back to life. He had no hair and no lips. It was difficult for him to talk, but people could see that he had something he wanted to say to them. "Tomorrow I will tell you," he managed to make clear.

After sunrise the next morning, he said to them, "Things are changing. While I was with the spirits, after Grizzly Bear killed me, they took me to the top of a mountain. When we looked toward the place where the sun rises, we saw many people. They were not dressed like us. One man I noticed in particular was dressed in a black robe.

"The spirit chief said to me, 'See that man? He is the one who will take over when we spirits are gone. We have done all we can for you and your people. That man will come some time in the next ten snows. Before he comes other people will come with the same words but not dressed like him. Let them pass through.'

"Today," continued Sowatts, "you must turn back and go forth to make peace with the Blackfeet. The spirits can no longer help us."

But some people in the camp did not want to believe Sowatts.

"Give us proof," they said to him. "Give us some proof that what you say is right."

"Prove it by killing Grizzly Bear," said another. "He is now near

163

our camp. He runs in, scares the children, and then hides in the brush where we can not see him and kill him."

Sowatts called his dog. Then he opened his medicine bag, took out some red paint, and painted marks on the dog's face and front feet. He said to the dog, "Now go over to that brush and get that bear out so that the men can kill him."

The dog rolled over three times and then jumped into the brush. Soon the bear ran out and the men killed him. All the people then believed Sowatts. They made peace with the Blackfeet, and the following year the Kutenais went to their country and exchanged gifts with them.

A few snows later a missionary and his wife came among the Kutenais, stopping at Nyack. They had some message, but the Indians paid no attention to them. Later Father De Smet came and started a mission.

From that time on, the Indians began to lose their power. The spirits had deserted them.

V. Shoshonean Tribes: The Shoshonis and the Bannocks

T HE SHOSHONIS, so Lewis and Clark learned in the winter of 1804–1805, were the Indians living nearest the Rocky Mountains on the route the captains planned to follow to the Pacific Coast. It was absolutely necessary that the expedition obtain a guide and horses for the journey over the mountains, from the headwaters of the Missouri River to the headwaters of the Columbia River.

The explorers found at Fort Mandan (Dakota) that one of the wives of the French-Canadian interpreter Charbonneau was Sacajawea, a young Shoshoni who had been captured by the Minnetarees about five years earlier. So they asked him to take her with them to assist in interpreting. In April they set forth, Sacajawea carrying her two-months-old baby on his cradleboard. No one could have foreseen her storybook reunion with her own band of Shoshonis in the Rockies and with their chief—her brother.

Before any of her tribe saw Sacajawea, and while they were still afraid of the strangers with guns, they had shared with the four hungry men of the scouting party the little food they had—dried chokecherries and cakes made of serviceberries. Next day the half-starved Indians ate even the intestines of two deer killed by one of the white men. Both salmon and roots, the chief foods of these people from mid-May until early September, had become scarce unusually early. But, with great skill, Captain Lewis persuaded the chief to delay the annual buffalo hunt with a party of Flatheads until the Shoshonis and their horses had helped the explorers get their cargo over the mountains.

This small band were some of the Indians whom anthropologists call the Northern Shoshonis, the most northern members of the Shoshonean branch of a very large linguistic family. During much of the nineteenth century, the Northern Shoshonis occupied eastern and southern Idaho, northeastern Utah, and western Wyoming. Other Indians most closely related to them by language include the Comanches, the Hopis, and the Paiutes. Some neighboring tribes gave the Northern Shoshonis names meaning "Grass Lodges" and "Grass-Thatch Dwellers"; others, names meaning "Serpents" and "Snake men." Early white men also called them "Snakes" or "Snake Indians," probably because of a misinterpretation of the sign language. The sign for them was "a serpentine gesture," say Virginia C. Trenholm and Maurine Carley, "—in reality the in-and-out motion used in weaving their shelters."

Within their own memories, the Shoshoni chief told Captain Lewis, they had lived on the plains, but the Blackfeet (the Shoshonis called them "Pahkees") had driven them into the mountains. In 1805 they were still without guns, and the Crows, Minnetarees, and other armed tribes of the plains helped the Blackfeet keep them in the mountains about two-thirds of the year. Before they reached the plains, anthropologists believe, the Northern Shoshonis had inhabited the Great Basin, the arid country southwest of the Salmon and the Snake rivers.

The Western Shoshonis lived in central and western Idaho, adjacent Nevada, northwestern Utah, and a small area near Death Valley, California. They depended so much upon roots for food that explorers often called them "Diggers" or "Digger Indians"—as they called bands of other tribes for the same reason. Their tales are not represented in this volume.

Concerning the Bannock Indians, there are two conflicting opinions. The one commonly held and recently presented again in a historical study by Brigham Madsen of Utah State University is that the Bannocks were an independent tribal unit, culturally and politically distinct, as well as linguistically. The other opinion, formulated by Sven Liljeblad of Idaho State College after years of studying the languages, is that although the Bannocks spoke a dialect of the Northern Paiute language, there has never been any cultural or political difference between the Bannocks and the Northern Shoshonis. For several generations, families and individuals among the Northern Paiutes of Oregon and Nevada moved into present-day Idaho and joined the Shoshonis. No independent tribal unit of Bannocks has ever existed, Professor Liljeblad believes: "The word *Bannock* itself comes from terms in the Shoshoni and Northern Paiute languages that mean 'the Northern Paiute side of the mixed speech community.'"

By the middle of the nineteenth century, when the first Mormon missionaries came among Sacajawea's band of Shoshonis (along the Lemhi River in eastern Idaho), some Bannocks were living with them. There were intermarriages, and soon the newcomers were integrated into Shoshoni life. Larger numbers of Shoshoni-Bannocks, in historic times, spent their winters in the valleys of southeastern Idaho, in the vicinity of old Fort Hall and present-day Pocatello. Many of them spoke both languages. Most of the descendants of these mixed bands, from both areas, now live on the Fort Hall Reservation.

The Idaho Shoshonis were the first Indians in the northern Rockies to own horses, having obtained them from Southwest tribes about 1700. Directly or indirectly, many Indians obtained their first horses from the Shoshonis—the Nez Percés, Flatheads, Coeur d'Alênes, and other Plateau tribes, the Blackfeet and the Crows of the Plains.

Horses enabled the Fort Hall Indians to improve their living, for they had to wander far from their semi-arid country to get food. Salmon, roots, and berries were the staples, supplemented by buffalo and other game. In the spring, groups of related families traveled from their winter quarters to the Snake River below Shoshone Falls and to its nearby tributaries to catch and dry salmon. Annually, large numbers of the Shoshoni-Bannocks went west to where the Boise, Payette, and Weiser rivers join the Snake, to fish and barter with other tribes. Some families went on as far as the fishing territory of the Walla Walla Indians, some even to the Willamette River in western Oregon.

After the fishing season, all traveled to the best places for choke-cherries, berries, and sunflower seeds. These foods the women preserved for the winter. While traveling and while wintering, families lived chiefly in tipis made of seven to twenty buffalo hides stitched together.

Until about 1840, buffalo were plentiful in the neighborhood of Fort Hall. After that, the Fort Hall Shoshoni-Bannocks made a hunting trip each autumn into the buffalo country east of them, traveling in bands under the direction of chiefs. Often they were accompanied by Nez Percés, sometimes by Flatheads, the Lemhi Shoshonis, and the Wyoming Shoshonis. This co-operation with the others was necessary for protection of themselves and their horses against the Blackfeet and other Plains tribes. After the return from the buffalo hunt, groups of Shoshoni-Bannocks went to nearby areas for smaller game animals—deer, elk, antelope, mountain sheep, beaver, and bear.

The Shoshoni Indians of Wyoming are reported by some writers to have lived, in the nineteenth century, a way of life very much like that described for the Plains Indians. But on the Wind River Reservation, Wyoming, said Alice Nash, who was a missionary there in the early twentieth century, Shoshoni traditions were "full of references to a period when they had no horses, when small game took the place of buffalo and the people lacked the skin-covered tepees of more recent times . . . . Old men and women remembered the grass lodges of their early childhood, with willow frames walled with grass."

Late in obtaining firearms, the Wyoming Shoshonis were frequently attacked by most of the Plains tribes and were robbed of their horses. They welcomed the whites, and when they were reduced to scarcely more than one thousand individuals, their noble Chief Washakie asked for a reservation and for protection by the United States government. A number of Idaho Shoshonis had previously joined his band. He and his followers were placed on the Wind River Reservation after the signing of the peace treaties at Fort Bridger in 1868. Chief Washakie refused to join the Nez Percé War in 1877.

When the government completed a school building on the reservation, the agent gave full charge of it to the Reverend John Roberts. In 1883 the Protestant Episcopal church had sent him there as a missionary. Roberts remained on the reservation for sixty-six years, a greatly loved missionary, teacher, and, even after his retirement, a counselor and friend.

Apparently the Shoshonis had little ceremonial life until they adopted customs from the Plains Indians. The Sun Dance, which Robert H. Lowie thinks the Wyoming Shoshonis borrowed from the Arapahos and the Fort Hall Shoshonis adopted from their kinsmen, is still performed on both reservations. Among the Wyoming Shoshonis, a thanksgiving dance, seemingly native with them, took place in the autumn of the year, around a great cedar or hemlock set in the ground for the occasion. Men, women, and children formed a circle around the tree and moved slowly to the rhythms of their chant. Hundreds of times they repeated, "Send rain on the mountains." Then they thanked the Creator or the "Great Father" for their food and asked him to send rain upon their land and into the rivers.

The Idaho Shoshonis, in early historic times, celebrated the first catch of salmon. All members of the band painted themselves, said prayers and made signs over the first fish, and then ate their small share of it before beginning the salmon feast. Failure to observe this ceremony, they believed, would bring bad luck to the fishermen. The Fort Hall Shoshoni-Bannocks held several kinds of dances. Most common was the Circle Dance, usually held in the spring and in the summer, in order to bring rain and to make seeds grow. Individuals offered prayers at their meals, and at other times they prayed to the Sun, to "Father," or to Nature.

Shoshoni mythology seems to have been more like that of the Plateau and California tribes than like the mythology of the Plains tribes. Coyote was the culture-hero and trickster in several tales similar to some referred to or related in detail in the second and third sections. Wolf, his elder and benevolent brother, tried to make life pleasant and easy for people, but Coyote thought that they should work hard for their living—details found in myths of tribes in northern California. Because of Coyote's impudence toward the Creator, death was brought into the world.

The Lemhi Shoshonis related no important stories about buffalo because, said an old medicine man in 1906, "the buffalo was never an Indian." They did relate stories about a race of gigantic ogres that lived in stone houses and about a giant who slept on rocks in the water. He was so afraid of Indians that if one approached he immediately dived below the surface. Other supernatural beings were the water buffalo and a water baby, which Indians could never see but would hear crying in the night.

In the origin myth recorded from Idaho Shoshonis, Coyote was the father of all the Indians and the special guardian of this tribe. When he washed the first Shoshonis, his new-born babies, he said to them, "You are my children. I am going to stay with you. Be brave and do not be afraid of the other Indians." But because their mothers had washed the babies that became the other Indians, the other tribes were always fighting the Shoshonis.

According to a creation myth recorded from the Wind River Shoshonis, "our own Father made us." From the top of a high mountain—the only dry spot when the earth was covered with water—our Father sent Chickadee to bring some dirt from the bottom of the flood, saying, "I will once more create the drowned people." From this dirt he made earth, sky, and people.

An origin myth was related, years ago, by an old Bannock chief to John Rees, who, beginning in 1877, knew well the Indians of his area. Gray Wolf had the power to change all animal and plant life into other forms, the Bannock chief said. When animals were bad, he changed them into other, smaller beings—sometimes into fish, sometimes into plants. When they were very bad, he changed them into skunks. Some that were very good he made into birds with beautiful feathers; to some of them he gave the power to sing. From the song birds with the most beautiful feathers, Gray Wolf created the first Bannock Indians, the first people.

"At that time," continued the old Bannock chief, "all living things spoke the same language. When a person dies, he is taken to the Sun. On the Sun, there is no night, only day, and all people are happy."

Other Bannocks, wrote Rees, believed that after death the soul goes west along the Milky Way to the Father. Another Bannock creation myth is among the stories that follow.

Fragments of traditions about landscape features were recalled in 1953 by Ralph Dixey, a Shoshoni in southern Idaho. His wife, a Bannock, had heard most of them also, in the old days of storytelling. In a lake north of Jenny Lake in the Grand Tetons, Dixey's people once saw a huge monster. When they were camping there, the monster came out of the water, moved around the tipis, and swept them into the lake. The Shoshonis never camped there again.

In his boyhood, Dixey heard about a great flood that had occurred before people were created; the water marks can still be seen on the Ogden Hills, and the bones of big animals that were drowned by the flood have been uncovered. His elders told him also about a time when the whole country was burned; then were formed the lava rocks and the caves in the Snake River country. (See the legend "The Lava Beds of the Snake River.")

Another legend of the Idaho Shoshonis is about the giant cataract of the Snake River known as Shoshone Falls. The Shoshonis called the falls *Pahchulaka,* which means "hurling waters leaping." Quishin-demi of the Fort Hall Reservation told J. A. Harrington that, long ago, a young warrior and the girl he loved used to slip away from their families to meet on a cliff above the falls. Just before he left for war, they came here together for the last time. Every day during his absence she stood in the wild but familiar place, fully expecting that her sweetheart would return. Moons came and went, and still the girl waited in solitude. One day while she stood there, another warrior came to her, whispered something, and then disappeared. For a long time the girl remained there, looking down upon the cataract and upon the white foam and spray below it. Then she lifted her arms slowly above her head, stood on tiptoe, and dived into the leaping waters.

Of the traditions that follow, the first is Bannock. About half of

the others are from the Idaho Shoshonis or Shoshoni-Bannocks; about
half are from the Wyoming Shoshonis.

✖

The Fire, the Flood, and the Creation of the World

SUNNI WHITE BEAR NAVO related this myth to Sven Liljeblad in 1941,
in the Bannock language, and Professor Liljeblad translated it. An
old Chehalis Indian, near the Washington coast, told me a variant
of this story in 1953. The Algonquian tribes and the Siouan tribes,
represented in the next two sections, also related origin myths about
the "earth-diver," as did the Hurons, the Iroquois, and other North
American Indians. Toad, Turtle, Muskrat, Beaver, Duck, and Mink
are among the successful earth-divers. Other animals tried but failed.

A LONG TIME AGO this earth was made. Nobody knows when, but
there is a story about it. Our Father was on this earth. When
he was here, the earth got on fire. He had a wife, who stood at his
left side. Their son stood at his right side. When the earth was burning, they walked among the flames.

As they were walking, the Father said to his wife and to his son,
"Don't look back at the fire. No matter if it is burning your heels,
don't look back."

Right behind them the flames made a roaring, and the fire was
ready to catch in their skirts. The woman felt it. She looked behind
her and was immediately turned into stone. She was turned into
stone because she had done what the Father told her not to do.

He had a walking stick. Wherever he and his son walked, he put
his walking stick on the ground ahead of them. There the flames
went out, and so the Father and his son could pass through the fire.
Everything around them was burning, the whole earth. But because
of the walking stick, they could travel around.

Behind the fire came the water. Soon it flooded the whole earth.
Everything was covered by water, even the mountains. The Father
and his son made themselves very small, so that they could ride on

the foam on top of the water. There they remained for a long time, on the water-foam.

Thinking about the earth where he had lived, the Father knew he would like to have it back again. He used to wonder, "How can I get the earth back again?"

For many years the water stayed like that. At last the Father knew that it would not go down or dry up. He stayed there on the water-foam another winter. During the time they lived on the water, the Father made his son part of himself. Now they could get the earth back again.

"How can I get help?" he wondered.

He thought of the water-people. "I could ask them to help me get earth," he said to himself. "They must be somewhere around here."

Then he called out, "Water-people, where are you? Come. Let us smoke and hold council."

Beaver came when he heard the call. "Are you good at diving in the water?" asked the Father.

"I am not a good diver. This water is too much for me. I have a younger brother. He could. He is a good diver."

So the Father called out again. "Where are you, water-people? Come. Let us smoke and hold council."

Muskrat came, and the three smoked. Then the Father said, "We will call for more people."

Once again he called out, "Where are you, water-people? Come. Let us smoke and hold council."

Otter came and the four smoked together. They held council. Then they said to Muskrat, "You dive to the bottom of the water and bring up earth."

"I will," he replied. "I will go now, at once."

And then he dived off from the water-foam, where they all were sitting. The three waited for Muskrat to come up. They waited, and they waited. When they were just about to give up, they saw his body coming up to the top of the water. He was bloated with water. He had drowned.

They pulled him up on the foam, and the Father made him come to life again. Under Muskrat's fingernails, they found bits of mud. The Father took these bits of mud and formed them into a little ball.

"You did get earth," he said to Muskrat.

Then the Father began to roll the ball of earth in his hands, to and fro. Then he would stretch it, and then roll it into a ball again. Then he would flatten it between his hands. He did that again and again, and the earth-ball got bigger and bigger. The bigger it got, the harder it was for him to work with it. He would stop and look at it and would say, "It is too small yet."

So he would work at it again. He stretched it, he rolled it, he flattened it between his hands. When it got very large, and he had flattened it out, he spread it over the top of the water. Then he began to make hills and mountains on his earth. Later he made springs and rivers beside these mountains. Later he made different kinds of trees and flowers to grow around the springs and on the mountains. Then he made different kinds of animals and birds.

After the Father had finished making all this, he made the earth so that it would turn. He made it turn to the shady side, and it got winter. He made it turn to the sunny side, and it got summer.

※

Origin of the Snake and Yellowstone Rivers

RALPH DIXEY, a Shoshoni in southeastern Idaho, related this traditional tale in 1953. His wife, a Bannock, also had heard it in her family. The myth has two interesting parallels with geological theory, said the former chief naturalist of Yellowstone National Park, after he had heard a summary of the story: (1) Yellowstone Lake is thought to be older than Yellowstone Canyon; (2) more than once in the geological past the lake is thought to have drained into the Pacific Ocean by way of the Snake River. Now about two miles of ridges separate the lake from the source streams of the Snake. Black-spotted trout, a native of Pacific coast waters, were the only fish found in Yellowstone Lake, said the naturalist, when white men first came to this area. Jim Bridger, famous wilderness scout and trapper who discovered Two Ocean Pass in 1830, used to talk about a "Two-World Lake," which he thought was Yellowstone Lake.

Long ago there was no river in this part of the country. No Snake River ran through the land. During that time a man came up from the south. No one knows what kind of person he was, except that among his people he was always nosing around, always sticking his nose into everything.

He came through this valley, traveled north past Teton, and then went up on a mountain in what is now called the Yellowstone country. He looked around there and soon found an old lady's camp. She had a big basket of fish in water—all kinds of fish—and the man was hungry. So he said to her, "I am hungry. Will you boil some fish for me?"

"Yes, I will cook some for you," the old lady answered. "But don't bother my fish," she warned, as she saw him looking into the basket.

But he did not obey her. While she was busy cooking, he kept nosing around, kept monkeying around. At last he stepped on the edge of the basket and spilled the fish. The water spread all over.

The man ran fast, ahead of the water, and tried to stop it. He piled some rocks up high, in order to hold the water back. But the water broke his dam and rushed over the rocks. That's where Upper Yellowstone Falls are now. The man ran ahead of the water again, and again he tried to stop it. Four or five miles below Yellowstone Falls he built another pile of rocks. But that didn't hold the water back either. The rush of water broke that dam, too. That's where Lower Yellowstone Falls are today. The water kept on rushing and formed the Yellowstone River.

Then the man ran to the opposite side of the fish basket, to the other side of the water emptying from it. He built another dam down the valley where Idaho Falls are now. By the time he got there, the flood had become bigger and swifter. And so, though the man built a big dam, the water broke it and rushed on down the valley.

Again he ran, overtook the water, and built another dam. "Here's where I'm going to stop it," he said to himself. But the water had

175

become bigger and bigger, swifter and swifter. So it broke that dam and left American Falls where they are today.

The man rushed ahead and built two piles of rocks in the form of a half-circle, one pile where Shoshone Falls are now and one where Twin Falls are now. "I'll really stop the water this time," he said to himself. But the water filled the dam, broke it, and rushed over the rocks in giant waterfalls.

The man ran ahead, down to near where Huntington, Oregon, is today. There the valley narrows into a canyon. "Here's where I'll stop the water," he said, "here between these high hills."

So he built a dam and walked along on top of it, singing and whistling. He was sure he had stopped the water this time. He watched it coming toward him, sure that he would soon see it stop. It filled the dam, broke it, and rushed on down the canyon. With the rocks and the great flood of water, it gouged a deeper canyon. Hell's Canyon, it is called today.

Just before the dam broke, the man climbed up on top of the canyon wall.

"I give up," he said, as he watched the water rush through the gorge. "I won't build any more dams. They don't stop that water."

After the river left Hell's Canyon, it became wide again and very swift. The water went on down to Big River and then on down to the ocean, taking with it the big fish that had spilled out of the old lady's basket. That's why we have only small fish up here. Salmon and sturgeon were carried on down to the ocean, and they have never been able to get back up here because of the waterfalls. Salmon used to come up as far as Twin Falls, a long time ago, but they don't come now.

The big fish basket that the man tipped over is Yellowstone Lake. The water that he spilled ran off in two directions. Some of it made the Snake River, as I have told you, and finally reached the Columbia and the Pacific. Some of it ran the other way and made the Yellowstone River and then reached the Missouri River.

Who was the old lady with the basket of water and fish? She was Mother Earth. Who was the man who wanted to see everything, who was always sticking his nose into everything? He was *Ezeppa,* or Coyote.

※

The Theft of Fire

ONE WINTER EVENING Coyote noticed a fire far down the mountain. He asked his powers, "Who owns that fire?" To him they answered, "Some other people own it. Crane is their chief. Go down and get their fire for yourself."

Coyote did not tell anyone that night. After he woke up the next morning, he painted all his body and then talked to his people. "I saw something strange last night—a fire down the mountain. Shall we go and get it?"

All his people held a council and debated whether or not they should go. Mice, Rats, and all the other men decided to go, but the women stayed at home. Coyote and his men went down toward the fire, the first they had ever seen.

When they reached the people who had the fire, Crane told them to receive their guests hospitably. After a feast, the Coyote people gambled, and the Crane people held a *nuakin* dance. The purpose of the *nuakin* dance was to make sure that they would have a big supply of food, especially of salmon and berries.

Crane told the Coyote people to go on enjoying themselves at gambling and later to come to the *nuakin.* When Coyote joined the dance, he wore a headdress that reached to the ground. The old women said to him, "You are not watching your headdress. See—you are dragging it along the ground and are burning its edge in the fire."

But Coyote was doing what he intended to do. When the women were not watching him, he spread the fire. Toward morning he summoned a council of his people. "As soon as we can get their food and their fire," said Coyote, "we shall all run away."

Crane's people kept all their food in a large bag high up in a tree, and Crane kept the fire in his own lodge. Just before dawn there was another dance. While it was going on, Coyote danced around the lodge until his headdress caught fire. He seized the fire, hid it under his blanket, and sneaked out of the lodge.

Jack Rabbit had already been told to play his flute outside the houses of the Crane people, so that all of them would fall asleep. As he went around from lodge to lodge, playing, they listened and soon were sleeping. Then the Coyote people tried to steal the food. Coyote jumped and jumped, but could not reach the bag of food. All of his followers jumped and jumped, one after the other, but no one could jump high enough. At last the woodpeckers were asked to fly up, put their bills together, and pierce the bag. When they did, the food fell through the hole—pine nut food. Coyote and his people ate some, and then ran away with the rest of it and with the fire.

In the morning, when the Crane people got up, they could not start a fire. Then they looked for their food bag and found it empty.

"Where are those visitors?" they asked.

"They are all gone," said Crane. "Let us run after them and get our food and our fire."

They started at once and kept running until they saw Coyote and his people. Coyote was in war dress, the last in line and nearest the enemy. They shot at him but could not kill him. They kept on shooting at him until they had shot off all his hair. By that time Coyote was so tired he had to stop running. At first he did not know what to do, but when he came to an old track, he hid himself in it.

Twice he hid from the Crane people, but each time they found him and threw rocks at him. When he was too exhausted to run again, he gave the food and the fire to his people in front of him. The enemy then overtook him and killed him. After skinning him, they looked over all his body, but they could not find the food or the fire.

Crane and his people ran on after the Coyote people and killed them, one by one. Only three escaped. Jack Rabbit jumped aside and hid in a hole. Rock Squirrel, carrying the fire, and Hai, carrying the food, were stoned by the enemy pursuing them. Hai was a black bird. When the Crane people almost caught Hai, he wished that his leg would rot. One leg did rot, and he put the food inside it. Then he fell down exhausted.

Crane said to the black bird, "You are a great chief," and then kicked him. When Hai screeched, his leg with the food in it fell off, and ran away by itself. But Crane and his followers did not notice, so busy were they searching Hai, cutting him up, and looking for the food and the fire. When they found that one leg was missing, they looked for it, saw its track, and followed it.

Hai made another wish: he wished that rain and snow would fall behind his leg. When rain and snow covered the footprints, the Crane people had a council.

"There is no use following the leg up the mountains," they said. "It is too far away. Let us go after Rock Squirrel, who must have the fire."

Hai's leg went westward, scattering pine nuts all the way. That is why the people living there have pine nuts now. When the Crane people got near Rock Squirrel, he hid the fire by his breast. That is why he has a spot there now, as if he had been burnt. Several times they nearly caught him. At last he jumped down from a steep cliff and threw his fire sticks all over the mountains. He said to the fire, "Everybody is going to use you hereafter. Go and burn everywhere."

That is how the Shoshoni people got fire.

When Crane came to the cliff and saw the fire burning everywhere, he was too tired to do anything more. So he said to his people, "I give up the chase. I am going down to the river."

Then he turned into the bird he is now and went to the river, where he belonged.

Jack Rabbit came out of the hole he had hidden in, found Coyote's body, and hit it with his whistle. Coyote woke up and asked, "Why did you wake me up? I was having a nice dream."

Jack Rabbit went around and hit every one of the Coyote people with his whistle. He brought all of them back to life.

✸

Rabbit and the Sun

WHEN I WAS gathering stories on the Wind River Reservation, I was directed to the Wind River Community School, to read some mimeographed pamphlets which Shoshoni children had written in the 1930's.

Under the supervision of their teacher, Miss Helen Overholt, they had recorded their elders' recollections of old customs, tales, and traditions. Among them was this little story.

Several Northwest tribes told slightly different versions of it.

ONCE THERE WAS a rabbit with only three legs. So he made a wooden leg for himself and was able to move fast. At that time the Sun was very hot. Rabbit said to himself, "I will go and see what makes Sun so hot."

As he hopped off toward Sun, he found it getting hotter every day. "The only thing on earth that doesn't burn," said Rabbit, "is cactus."

So he made a house of cactus and stayed in it during the day. He traveled at night. When he came closer to Sun, he arose early one morning and ran toward the place where it should come up. When he saw the ground boiling, he knew that Sun was ready to come up. Rabbit stopped, sat down, and took out his bow and arrows.

When Sun was about halfway out of the earth, Rabbit shot at it. His first arrow hit the heart and killed Sun. Rabbit stood over it and began to cry. "The white part of your eye will be clouds." And it was.

"The black part of your eye will be the sky."

And it was.

"Your kidney will be a star, your liver the moon, and your heart the dark."

And they were.

Then Rabbit said to Sun, "You will never be too hot again, for now you are only a big star."

Sun has never been too hot since then. Ever since that day, rabbits have had brown spots behind their ears and on their legs. There Rabbit's fur was scorched during his journey, long, long ago, to see why the sun was so hot.

The Little People

A PIONEER in the Wind River country, Wyoming, once came upon several ancient dwellings made of sticks and stones held together with mud, high up in the rocks near the sources of Muddy Creek. Talking about them with a number of old Indians, he was told that the structures had been made before the Indians came into the region. They were the homes of the Ninnimbe, the Little Demons or Little People. Here are some former beliefs about them.

THE LITTLE PEOPLE were two or three feet high, strong and fearless. They wore clothing of goatskin and always carried a large quiver of arrows on their backs. They were stealthy stalkers, expert hunters, and good fighters, also, but they sometimes fell prey to eagles. Their poisoned arrows, shot with deadly aim, picked off many of the early Shoshonis. Their arrows were invisible.

Usually, the Little People themselves were invisible, deep in the woods or in the deep shade of a canyon. But one time a Shoshoni actually saw one of the Ninnimbe. Walking along the edge of a high cliff, the Indian heard a cry like the cry of a child. Looking down, he saw one of the Little People on a ledge, being attacked by an eagle. The Shoshoni climbed down to him and drove the eagle away. The little fellow expressed deep gratitude to the Indian for saving his life.

The Little People made the drawings on the rocks in the Wind River country. Sometimes these carvings talk at night. If you should look at the rock pictures, you would anger the Little People. To protect yourself from them, put on lots of paint, for the Little People are afraid of paint.

One of the Little People is still living. He, too, is called Ninnimbe. Some say that he is a little boy about two feet tall, who runs through the mountains, shooting game with his bow and arrows. Others say that he is an old man, sturdily built, dressed in the skins of mountain sheep that are painted with bright colors. His nose is red. He lives in the mountains, from where he appears and disappears at will. Old stone darts that have been picked up here and there are evidence that he has shot his arrows.

People do not often call a relative or friend by his true name because of their fear of Ninnimbe. If he should hear anyone's name, he might cause some misfortune to come upon that person or even kill him with invisible arrows. Some people will not say their own names aloud lest Ninnimbe overhear them and shoot his arrows.

If a Shoshoni becomes ill, if his horse becomes lame, if his wife runs away with another man, or if his horses get loose—each of these misfortunes is the result of Ninnimbe's shooting his invisible arrows. If even a trifling accident occurs when a Shoshoni is starting out on a journey, he will turn back, afraid of Ninnimbe. Every sudden death is due to his arrows, and to meet him anywhere means sudden death.

Sometimes in the middle of the night, a Shoshoni may become fearful that Ninnimbe is after him. So the man will leave his tipi and wander off into the mountains, seeking out lonely places in crags and canyons, hoping to hide from the little creature. When he returns, he sneaks back with light tread, so that Ninnimbe will not hear him.

Ninnimbe is always malicious, always on the watch for a Shoshoni to do him harm.

꒰ IN CAVES in certain parts of the Owyhee Range of Idaho and in the mountains of the Salmon River country, both the Shoshonis and Bannocks used to say, lived a race of cannibal dwarfs. Although only about two feet high, they could carry home on their backs the deer, elk, and mountain sheep they had killed with their bows and arrows. The women dressed the skins and made clothing for themselves, but the men wore no clothing, even in winter.

If these little ogres were near an Indian camp, a woman did not dare to get out of sight of her baby. If she did, one of the dwarfs would seize the child and devour it. Then he would cry just like the baby, the mother would rush back, and the ogre would begin to eat her. Her screams would make him take flight, but the poor woman would die before morning.

When one of these ogres would see a group of children playing a little way from camp, he would conceal his tail by winding it around his body and then ask the children if he might play with them. Soon he would run off with one of them astride his tail. The child was never seen again.

But the ogres never ate the men. Whenever they met an Indian man near their caves, they would invite him in and give him something to eat. They would urge him to stay all night, but he always refused, saying that he had killed some game and should get it home before the wolves found it.

These dwarfs were seldom seen or heard except in the evening. Then they would often gather together on high rocks and cliffs and there would sing most boisterously.

Another kind of dwarf lived in streams. They were called *Pahonah,* which means "water infants." They devoured women and children in the same way the land dwarfs did.

⌗

What the Five Brothers-in-Law Learned

THIS STORY, related by Ralph Dixey in 1953, may possibly have some connection with a tradition of the Northern Shoshonis that their ancestors came from the south.

L ONG AGO, a man from the north country wanted to go somewhere to look for other kinds of people. He went south and found a tribe down there somewhere. He married a woman of that tribe.

Some years later, he decided to return to the north. His young brothers-in-law, all five of them, wanted to go with him. So he let them. They had never seen deer or rabbits or buffalo. They had eaten almost nothing but fish, frogs, roots, seeds, and berries. They did not have bows and arrows, but their brother-in-law made bows and arrows for them and tried to teach the boys how to use them.

The men traveled north, up to this country. The man from the north country killed a rabbit and cooked it for his supper. His brothers-in-law were afraid of the rabbit and would not come near it. But while the man was eating it, one of them, a little braver than the others, said to him, "Will you give me a taste of it?"

The man gave him a taste and the young brother-in-law liked it. "That is good!" he exclaimed.

Then the second brother-in-law tasted it. "That is good!" he said. So they all had a taste and all liked it.

The men traveled farther north. When the man from the north country saw a deer, he killed it for food for all of them.

"Skin this deer," he said to the young brothers, "and we will cook some of it for supper."

But the men were afraid to touch the deer. So their brother-in-law skinned it, cooked some of it, and ate. The young men stood around camp and watched him eating. They smelled the meat, and it smelled good to all of them.

"Will you give me a little taste of it?" asked the boldest of the young men.

So the brother-in-law gave him a piece of deer meat. "Oh, that tastes good!" he exclaimed.

Then the second brother tasted it, and the third brother, and the fourth brother, and the fifth brother. "That is good!" they each exclaimed.

"You can use the skin of the deer also," explained the man from the north country.

And he showed them how to make moccasins from the hide. The young brothers-in-law had never worn anything on their feet before.

Next morning they broke camp and traveled north again. Soon the man from the north country saw a herd of buffalo standing on top of a hill.

"See the buffalo up there?" he asked his brothers-in-law.

"I don't see any buffalo," they answered. "I see only some cedars on top of that hill."

"Those aren't cedars," said their brother-in-law. "Those are buffalo. Their meat is good to eat. You go around on the other side of the hill and make them run toward me. I will kill one."

So the young men went round the hill. When the buffalo started moving, the brothers-in-law were scared and ran. The man from the north country aimed carefully with his bow and arrow and shot a buffalo. But the other men would not help him skin it, for they were afraid to get near the animal. "He looks dangerous," they said.

When the man had finished skinning the buffalo, he said to the brothers, "Cut some pieces from it and roast them for your supper."

But again they would not touch the flesh until they were made hungry by the odor of roasting meat.

"Will you give me a piece of it?" the braver brother asked again. And again he exclaimed, "That tastes good!"

Again the four brothers tasted the meat, and each said as before, "That is very good."

"We will cut up the rest of it and carry it with us," the man from the north said next morning. "We will carry the skin with us, too. It is good to sleep under when it is dry. From buffalo hides my people make robes and tipis also."

But the young men would not help him cut the meat. They were still afraid of the big animal.

They left the camp and traveled farther north. In those days every tribe was an enemy of every other tribe. Soon the brothers-in-law ran into a band of Indians.

"Shoot them with your bows and arrows," the man from the north called to his brothers-in-law. "Those people are dangerous. They will kill us if we do not kill them."

But the young men would not use their bows and arrows. Instead, they plunged into the band and fought with their hands. They fought a hand-to-hand battle and killed many warriors. So the enemy ran away.

The men traveled north again until they came to the brother-in-law's people. They gathered around the chief's place where the Indians were smoking pipes. The brothers-in-law from the south had never seen people smoking before. Their eyes smarted and tears ran down their cheeks. Finally, they stood up and left the lodge.

Then their brother-in-law told his people about the young men. "They do not know how to use bows and arrows," he explained, "but they can run faster than a rabbit. They fought the enemy with their bare hands. The enemy shot bows and arrows at them but could not kill them. It is good that they stay with us."

The five brothers-in-law stayed in the north country for many snows. By the time they wanted to return to their people in the south, they could shoot with bows and arrows; they could kill rabbits and deer and buffalo; they knew how to cook the flesh of the animals. They had learned how to tan deer hides and to make moccasins, how to make robes and tipis from buffalo hides.

They taught their people in the south all those things. Every year after that, the people traveled north to hunt deer and buffalo for their meat and for many other things that they needed.

✳

The Shoshoni Sun Dance

THE FOLLOWING ACCOUNT of the Shoshoni Sun Dance is abbreviated from a manuscript written in 1926 by Lynn St. Clair, a prominent tribal leader on the Wind River Reservation. He had gathered the details from his elders over a period of years.

"This has been a secret," wrote St. Clair. "The Indian is afraid to tell because he has been made fun of so much. The writer wishes his white friends to understand this Indian way of worship and to understand the symbols."

The Shoshonis call the dance *Dagoo Winode,* "Thirst Stand," which will be explained in the legend. "They do not worship the sun. They worship through the symbolic 'Thirst Stand' Dance."

Unable now to follow the first step in the traditional preparations, the Shoshonis use a mounted buffalo head. Into its nostrils they stuff sweet sage, symbol of vapor or clouds. A special forked pole ceremonially cut for the Sun Dance Lodge symbolizes the Milky Way, "a great path over which travel the people who have passed to the great beyond."

The three stripes painted around the pole in the center of the lodge used to "stand for something good," when only four men danced. Now a Christian interpretation is given to parts of the lodge: the center pole symbolizes "Our Brother"; the three stripes represent "the three days He died and rose again from the dead"; the twelve poles that form the framework of the lodge symbolize the twelve apostles.

Four days are spent in ritualistic preparation, three in the ceremony itself. "The dancer's motion is a prayer that he may be active as only a live person is active."

Both St. Clair and R. L. Lowie, who was able to get a little information about the dance on the Wind River Reservation in 1912, wrote that the Shoshonis did not practice torture at the dance, as did some men in some other tribes. Informants told Lowie that the dance is the oldest and foremost of Shoshoni ceremonies. It was not held every year but only when someone had had a dream. "A man would dream of the Sun Dance and if he failed to perform it as described in his dream, he would die; accordingly he told the chief, who gave his permission. . . . All the participants expect to get good luck and increase their prospects of long life by the ceremony."

Some danced, Lowie was told, in order that they or a friend or a relative might recover from illness—a statement that was true in 1953 among the Idaho Shoshonis. That friend might be white.

All that follows is from Lynn St. Clair.

I N DAYS GONE BY, the older men would give a party and invite the young men. While they were sitting around in a circle, one man would fill a pipe and light it with a burning stick from the campfire. He would take a few puffs and pass it on until all had smoked from this pipe. One man would tell stories. One story would explain how the Sun Dance was given to the Shoshonis through a man's dream.

One night when this man was asleep, he saw a vision of himself sitting on a hill. Looking toward the place of the rising sun, he thought he saw a little, black, moving speck, and he wondered what it was that was moving toward him so rapidly. When the object came near, he saw that it was a buffalo. The man got scared and was about to leave, but the buffalo spoke to him. "Do not be scared of me," it said. "Do not be afraid. I will not harm you. I only bring you a message."

The man was mystified. He was so astonished that he sat very still. The buffalo came up to him and said, "I am sent to tell you about a dance. You will call it *Dagoo Winode*. It is a dance in which you will not eat or drink for three days and three nights. You will do nothing but worship during those three days and nights. If you will pray for your people, the sick ones in this dance and the others who are brought to you will get well."

Then he told the man that from time to time the Sun Dance would change. The buffalo showed him, in a vision, a brush structure like a windbreak. Near it four men were dancing. As they danced up to the center pole of the brush structure, they passed two old women on each side of the entrance. They sat there holding willows tied in bunches. With these willow branches the old women brushed out the footprints the dancers made in the dirt. The reason for rubbing out the tracks is not known.

Later, another Shoshoni saw the same vision. He saw a large structure made of brush, and noticed that it had a forked center pole. He saw many people dancing, all of them men. In the man's vision, the buffalo called his attention to the twelve long poles and said, "Those twelve poles mean something good. Everything in the Sun Dance Lodge is a prayer. Each part of it is a symbol, a symbol of something good."

Then the buffalo told this man, in his vision, the first step he should take before he put up the Sun Dance Lodge.

"You must go out and kill a buffalo," it said. "You will take only the hide and the head. They will remind you that the Great Mystery came to the Shoshonis in the form of a buffalo and that the buffalo brought them this message that is called the Sun Dance. Tell your people that this dance was given to you and to them by their Father, the Great Mystery."

Then the buffalo taught the man four prayer songs to be used in the Sun Dance, saying, "All four songs are to be sung sixteen times."

During the preparation of the Sun Dance Lodge, seven prayers are made. After the poles have been selected, but before they have been cut, before the twelve forked poles are cut, before the tree for the center pole is felled, before it is placed in the center hole of the lodge area, and before the buffalo head is fastened over the bunch of willows tied to the center pole—at each of these times, an old man or the Sun Dance leader prays. Then there are prayers with songs as men and women fasten strips of blue and green cloth to the center pole and raise it. There is a prayer after the people have bathed in the river and are assembled in the Sun Dance place. The green cloth stands for the green things of the spring and summer months; the blue stands for the clean, fresh air we breathe and for the blue skies, where the Great Mystery, our Father, lives.

When the dancers are in place, the leader stands under the center pole and makes this prayer: "Our Father, bless me now that my people and I have built this place, a gift from you, our Father, a gift which you have given to our forefathers, which through them you gave to us. Bless us, that all of these men who came in to dance with me may be well, that the sick ones may be made well through this Sun Dance. Bless us, even though we may become dry and weak from thirst and hunger. Protect us through these days and nights, so that at the end of three days, when we get out, with your blessing, we may take of your precious gifts, water and food, and receive our strength back. Grant that we may become healthy, the sick and weak become strong, both old and young be protected from diseases.

"Bless us, I pray to you, our Father, that my people who are sick may be made well through you, our Father. Amen."

�֍

Legend of the Old Indian Hunter

ALONG THE SALMON RIVER, not far from the village of Clayton, Idaho, is a cluster of rocks on a low hill. If one uses his imagination, he can see the likeness of a face on the outline of the rocks against the sky. On a hilltop nearby is a rocky cliff which looks, from a distance, like an Indian's headdress.

AN OLD SHOSHONI who had been one of the best hunters in his band went alone one day into the mountains to hunt. His people never saw him again.

Years later some of his tribe traveled that way, saw the rock that resembled the headdress, and recognized it as the property of the old hunter. The other hill with the outline of a person told them that the hunter had become tired, put his headdress on a cliff, and fallen asleep.

Years have passed. The old man has been asleep so long that a growth of mountain mahogany shows he has grown a beard. Every season, Indians camp at the foot of the hill and watch for the sleeping hunter to stir. Some people say they have seen him make a slight movement. But this is only a trick effect of moonlight and shadows.

When the Indians leave there, they always say: "Goodbye, tired old hunter. Rest and dream until the time when you are awakened to go to your last Happy Hunting Ground."

⌘

The Indian Spirit at Mesa Falls

A FEW MILES WEST of Yellowstone National Park, the North Fork of the Snake River plunges over wide escarpments in two cascades about a mile apart—Upper Mesa Falls and Lower Mesa Falls. The picturesqueness of the waterfalls is enhanced by a thick growth of spruce and by a high mountainous background.

ONE DAY an Indian mother and her son went to see Mesa Falls. As they stood near the lower falls and looked up at the mist over the upper falls, the mother spoke earnestly to the boy.

"My son," she said, "soon you will be a big man like your father. Every year you will come here to camp and fish. In these beautiful falls is the spirit of a maiden. I'll tell you her story.

"Once, many, many moons ago, when the tribes came to fish at the falls, a pretty girl was helping her lover fish. He skillfully threw his spear; she gathered the fish as he threw them out on the bank. Becoming bold, he waded out into the deeper water. But he lost his footing and the swift stream swept him down. The girl went into the deep water after him. She, too, was carried away by the rushing river.

"Ever since, Indians who come here watch for the girl in the falls and in the mist. At times she appears to them dressed in white, her long hair floating with the wind and spray, her face beaming with smiles. Sometimes when the wind is blowing softly, her sweet voice can be heard calling:

" 'Do not long for me, for I am happy here, guarding these falls and watching over you. I must stay here to warn my people of the dangerous water below the falls. I want no one to be lost in the swirling current. I can see you and hear you, and all who are good can see and hear me. The breezes are my blessings. The rushing waters remind you that if I were not here to warn people, many might fall in and drown.' "

The boy looked intently at the falling water and up at the mist. Some times he thought he could see the Indian maiden, but she stayed in his sight not more than a moment at a time. When he thought he was going to see her, the spray would veil the beauty of the girl.

Many Indian youths have shouted with joy when, gazing at the falls, they have thought that they saw the spirit of the Indian girl.

The Great Medicine Man and the Spring

An old Shoshoni named Quishindemi, meaning "Bob-tail-horse," told the following legend to J. A. Harrington in 1925. It is the story of one of the greatest medicine men of the Shoshonis. The place of the story is probably the ebbing-and-flowing spring near the Wyoming-Idaho border. Imagine a bottomless bottle lying on its side, facing downstream, said Mr. Harrington. At times the water enters the bottle faster than it can run out; it stops, but pressure from above forces it out the small end of the bottle. Hence the term "ebbing-and-flowing stream."

Long years ago, a great sickness fell upon the Indians throughout the Snake River Valley. The Shoshoni chiefs and sub-chiefs called upon a medicine man to tell them what to do for their people. The medicine man's name was *Tenupah Dome-up,* which means "Man-from-the-Sky."

Man-from-the-Sky went into his lodge alone, opened his medicine bundle, and performed his sacred ceremonies. Then he returned to the chiefs and said to them, "Bring all those who are ill to my tipi tomorrow morning, very early. I will take them on a journey of five suns."

Then he led the chiefs up the trail along the Snake River toward the Three Tetons. After five suns, the medicine man called a halt. At the place he chose, he made his sacred tipi and stayed in it for several hours. When he came out, he advised those who were sick to follow him next day at sunrise to a place which the spirit had shown him.

The next morning, just as the stars were disappearing, all who were ill started from their tipis. They were helped by their friends and relatives. All followed the medicine man to a place in the hills not far from where they had made camp the night before. Here Man-from-the-Sky told them all to stop; he ordered the sick people to remove their clothes.

Then, dressed in his ceremonial robe and carrying in his hand his medicine bundle, he led the people to a creek.

"Healing waters," he said, "will soon flow from a rock that is up on the side of the hill. They will soon reach the place where your sick people are. When the healing waters reach you, drink from them and bathe in them. They will not flow long. I will soon stop them."

So he went up to the rock on the hillside above the place where the Indians were waiting. With something from his sacred bundle he tapped the rock. Then he spoke secret, mystic words. Instantly the water flowed from the rock in great quantities. Soon it reached the part of the creek where the sick people waited. They drank from it and they bathed in it. Then the medicine man tapped the rock again and the water soon ceased to flow.

After a while, he told them that he could cause the healing waters to flow again. Again he took something from his sacred bundle, tapped the rock, and spoke the mystic words. Again a great quantity of water flowed from the rock into the creek. The Indians drank from it and bathed in it. Then the medicine man caused it to stop.

All day the ceremony continued at intervals. When the stars came out, Man-from-the-Sky stopped the ceremony and the healing waters for the night. All the people returned to their camp, as the medicine man directed.

By the next morning most of them had been cured of their illness. Those who were still sick were again taken to the spot in the creek where they had been the previous day. Again the waters flowed and ceased to flow in obedience to the tapping and the words of the medicine man.

When the people awoke the next morning, every sickness was gone. All had been healed by the healing waters. On the third day the Indians returned to their homes entirely cured.

"Do not visit the healing waters alone," the medicine man warned them. "Never go there without me. Those are sacred waters. Only I control them. Anyone who goes there alone is sure to die."

Forever after, the Indians held the place in reverence and in awe. No one is known to have visited it again. And Tenupah Dome-up became known as one who could control the forces of nature. He was henceforth the greatest medicine man of the Shoshoni people.

�֍

The Craters of the Moon

THE CRATERS OF THE MOON National Monument in southern Idaho is part of a vast lava field. Its name comes from the fact that "its caves and natural bridges, cones and terraces and weird piles of stone resemble the surface of the moon as seen through a telescope." The Idaho Shoshonis have handed down this myth about the origin of the weird formation.

LONG, LONG AGO, a huge serpent, miles and miles in length, lay where the channel of the Snake River is now. Though the serpent was never known to harm anyone, people were terrified by it.

One spring, after it had lain asleep all winter, it left its bed and went to a large mountain in what is now the Craters of the Moon. There it coiled its immense body around the mountain and sunned itself.

After several days, thunder and lightning passed over the mountain and aroused the wrath of the serpent. A second time flashes of lightning played on the mountain, and this time the lightning struck nearby. Angered, the serpent began to tighten its coils around the mountain. Soon the pressure caused the rocks to begin to crumble.

Still the serpent tightened its coils. The pressure became so great that the stones began to melt. Fire came from the cracks. Soon liquid rock flowed down the sides of the mountain.

The huge serpent, slow in its movements, could not get away from the fire. So it was killed by the heat, and its body was roasted in the hot rock. At last the fire burned itself out; the rocks cooled off; the liquid rock became solid again.

Today if one visits the spot, he will see ashes and charred bones where the mountain used to be. If he will look closely at the solidified rock, he will see the ribs and bones of the huge serpent, charred and lifeless.

�֍

The Lava Beds of the Snake River

FOR A LONG DISTANCE, the upper Snake River flows through the Lava Beds of southeastern Idaho. They are a weird assortment of small caves, buttes, fissures, and solidified rock flows. Not far away is the Craters of the Moon National Monument. Because many arrowheads and other Indian relics have been found in the Lava Beds, it is supposed that an ancient village was buried by the eruption.

The Idaho Shoshonis and Bannocks have the following tradition about the origin of the Lava Beds.

LONG AGO the valley of the Snake River here was covered with forests, and many streams flowed into the big river. In the forest roamed many game animals of all kinds. In the clear streams were many fish. So the Indians were well fed and happy.

But strange people, in great numbers, came into the valley to hunt and to fish. Soon they crowded out the Shoshonis and forced them to give up forest after forest and stream after stream. These strangers lived in caves and in huts made of stones. They were skillful with bow and arrows, and they were cruel warriors.

When they had killed a good many people, the head chiefs of the Shoshonis and of the Bannocks called a council. They gathered in a large group on the top of a high mountain overlooking the river. There they talked and talked about what they should do to get rid of the strangers and to possess again their lands along the Snake River.

In the council was a great medicine man, the only one of them who could receive messages from the Great Mystery. After chanting and praying a long time for wisdom, he made a speech to the assembly. He advised the warriors to be patient and not stir up further trouble.

"I will go into the deep forest," he told them at the end of a long and eloquent speech. "There I will pray for more knowledge and more wisdom. Then I will be able to tell you how to drive the strangers from our country."

His listeners gave their approval, and the medicine man departed alone. As he walked through the deep forest, he occasionally saw a bright star and traveled toward it. Sometimes he was frightened by the cry of a cougar and by the mournful sounds of other animals. for the safety of his people.
But he kept on traveling, always praying to the spirits to protect him

At last he entered an opening where there was light. In it he saw a large number of wolves, foxes, bobcats, and cougars. One very large cougar had hands instead of front feet, and he had a head like an Indian's. The medicine man realized that he was in the land of spirits, that the animals were spirits, and that the manlike cougar was their chief.

Trembling, the medicine man approached the large cougar. To his surprise, the animal greeted him kindly, speaking in the Shoshoni language. "I have been told that you were coming," he said. "You may tell all of us why you have come."

With a loud voice, the cougar called the animals to come near and to listen to the visitor. "They are all good spirits," he said to the medicine man, "and they are ready to hear what you have to say."

The man told them about the coming of the brutal strangers into the country of the Shoshonis and Bannocks and about the suffering of the people. "They have seized our lands and they are killing our people. We do not know who they are or where they came from. But I beg you to send them back to their own country."

"The strangers are great warriors," replied the spirits, "and they do not fear us. If they are sent away, they will not heed the warnings of the spirits but will surely return to your land."

Their words made the medicine man very sad, but the chief spoke encouraging words.

"The spirits will get rid of your enemies if all your people will make a solemn promise, for all time to come. These animals that you see—cougars, foxes, wolves, bobcats—are spirits. Your people must promise never to kill any of them. If any one of you should ever kill or eat of the flesh of any of them, he will be considered a rebel against the spirits. Then the spirits will appear in the form of animals and will devour every Shoshoni and Bannock in the land. Go home now and return as soon as possible with all your people. Then we will hold another council, a great council."

Again the medicine man entered the dark forest and followed the star as he had done before. Before the dawning of another day, he reached the council still gathered on the mountain. There he told about his meeting with the spirits, and about the promise their chief had asked of him. "Go now," ordered the medicine man, "and bring here as soon as possible all your people—all the warriors, the old men, the women, and the children. Together we will go to see the spirits and their chief."

Some of the warriors laughed at their medicine man, saying that no Indian could see the chief of the spirits and talk with him. But the man gave them proof: when he touched a stone, it took fire, melted, and ran like water.

Believing him, the members of the council started forth to bring all the people together. Several suns later, all the people of the Shoshoni and Bannock country had gathered on the mountain. Their journey to the land of the spirits was made during the night. When they reached the opening in the forest, they could see nothing but animals sitting around on their haunches.

Again the warriors doubted the medicine man and began preparations to put him to death. He begged the chief of the spirits, the Great Mystery, to help him. The Great Chief appeared before the people and spoke to them in words of wisdom and caution. "Do not go to war any more," he said, "without first obtaining the advice of the spirits. It will be given to the great medicine man and his successors for all time. In return for your promise to obey this caution, your prayers to be restored to your country will be answered."

When all the members of the great council had given their promise to the Great Chief of the spirits, the medicine man was lifted high into the air. So high was he taken that his companions lost sight of him in the darkness. The spirits carried him above the treetops to a tall and rocky mountain. There they ordered him to touch the topmost point with his finger. When he did, the peak instantly ignited and burned fiercely.

Then the spirits carried him back to the opening in the forest and told him to depart immediately with his people. "Go back to the mountain on which you hold your councils."

As they journeyed, they saw a bright light gleaming through occasional openings in the forest, and they reached their mountain quickly. From it they saw another mountain burning and melted rock running down its sides like red water. The fire grew bigger and bigger. Nearby hills and cliffs melted and flowed into the valley.

All the trees were rapidly consumed by the fire. In a short time the valley was a lake of fire as far as the eye could see. All the strangers who had invaded the land of the Indians were destroyed.

After many moons the hot rocks cooled, but it was many snows before trees began to appear again on the foothills. More snows came and went before there was plenty of game and fish once more.

The valley burned by the fire was left bare. When other members of the strange race came and saw what had happened to those who had been there before them, they hurried back to the land they had come from. They feared the lava beds.

197

The Shoshonis and Bannocks have always kept their promise to the Spirit Chief. Remembering the lava beds, they remembered his order not to kill or eat of the flesh of wolves, cougars, and kindred animals.

✳

The Mysteries in Bull Lake

BULL LAKE, on the Wind River Reservation, has a Shoshoni name that means "Buffalo Bellowing Lake" or the "Lake That Roars." It is situated in a deep canyon; when the wind rushes through this gorge, it sounds like a buffalo bellowing. Although some Indians were afraid to pass the lake, the medicine men used to spend a night there, hoping for a vision in which they would be given more supernatural power. Here are three of several traditions about the lake.

MANY YEARS AGO in the area around Bull Lake there lived a great herd of buffalo, the leader of which was an enormous white bull. Indians have always held the white buffalo in reverence; any man who killed one was thought to be superhuman, almost a god.

The Shoshonis hunted this herd again and again, hoping to kill the great white leader. Always the buffalo escaped. At last, in fear and desperation, the herd tried to get away from their pursuers by crossing the lake on the ice. But the ice was not strong enough. The animals broke through and went down to their death with a great plunging and roaring. Above all the others could be heard the cry of the big white leader as he went down into the icy water.

To this day, a roar often comes up from the depth of the lake. It comes from the spirit of the old white bull, roaring on and on forever in protest against the fate that befell him and his herd. And so it is called "the Lake That Roars."

☙ ONE DAY when my grandmother was a little girl, wrote a child at the Wind River School, she and her father and mother and some friends were traveling near Bull Lake. Hearing a baby crying, they looked and saw a water baby out on the lake, combing its hair. Every time it brought the comb through its hair, it would give a loud cry. As soon as it saw or heard the people, it went down into the water.

The people were so scared that they turned around and went in the other direction. They would not pass the lake. In order to get as far from it as possible, they traveled quite late that night. They camped at a little creek near the road, but they could not sleep. The next morning they found that their horses were gone.

They had felt sure they would have some kind of bad luck because they had seen the water baby.

In the days of my great-great-grandfathers, wrote another Indian child, some Indians camped at Bull Lake while they were on a hunting trip. Two men out hunting by themselves had been having such bad luck that they had not killed any game for several days.

At that time two white buffalo bulls lived in Bull Lake. The Indians often heard them and saw them, for water buffalo come out on the land now and then to get fresh air or to eat grass. As the two unlucky hunters were walking along, they saw the two white buffalo come up out of the lake.

The men sneaked up on them and killed one of them. They skinned it and cooked some of the meat. Soon after they started eating it, their feet began to feel queer. They kept on eating, for they had had no food for two days. Their feet kept feeling strange, and soon the men noticed the beginning of hoofs. Then horns began to grow under their ears, and tails appeared. When they stood up, they found that each had turned into a buffalo. Then they plunged into the water and disappeared.

Bull Lake is haunted by these men who were turned into buffalo.

✖

Origin of the Big Horn River

The Big Horn River has its source in the Big Horn Mountains of Wyoming and flows northward into the Yellowstone River. François Larocque of the Northwest Fur Company, who camped along the Big Horn in August, 1805, wrote that in the river thirty or forty miles above where he camped was a wolf-man. The Indians said that he lived in a waterfall and went out to devour every animal or person that approached; they claimed that it was impossible to kill him because he was "ball-proof."

LONG, LONG AGO, the Big Horn Basin was a great sea. Round it roamed the animals who like water and green grass. To the south and the west was the land of the people of the Moon, the ancestors of the Shoshonis. To the shores of this inland sea they came one time to hunt and to fish. But the animals were intelligent in those days and refused to be killed. The fish refused to be caught.

So the Indians became hungry and then thin. They said among themselves, "If the Creator made the fish and animals so wary, he should provide other food for his people. Surely he cares as much for us as he does for them." The whole tribe prayed for food.

Suddenly the waters of the great inland sea began to lower. Down they went, the Indians following, until the water was so low that fish were piled on top of each other. Quickly the men took the fish, the women cooked them, and all ate as much as they wished. Then they caught more and dried plenty for the future.

At last the great sea disappeared completely, but there was left behind a river that roared through a crack in the mountains. From its banks the people could see that it was full of fish. The river was crooked, and its canyon was lined with trees and brush where hunters could hide and wait for the animals to come to the stream to drink.

Because there was less shore line than the sea had had, hunting became easier. Fish were easily caught. The people were no longer hungry and thin, but plump and happy. They stayed that way until the white men came.

Origin of Big Horn Hot Springs

BIG HORN HOT SPRINGS, now in Hot Springs State Park, Wyoming, was thought by the Indians to have supernatural powers. By bathing in that water, they would gain health and long life. Before a battle, warriors hurried there, believing that the first to bathe in the spring would be the most enduring fighter. A granddaughter of the famous Chief Washakie of the Wind River Shoshonis dipped her baby into the hot water of the shrine to make him as great as her grandfather. The area "abounds in legends," wrote a pioneer.

A SMALL BAND of Shoshonis were greatly loved by Our Own Father, the Great Mystery, because they faithfully performed all the tribal rituals. He had given them many favors, from the beginning.

Greatly loved by all the band were a young chieftain, whose father had recently died, and his sweetheart. She was the loveliest girl in the whole Big Horn Basin. The couple planned to give some special feasts honoring the Great Mystery for his goodness to their people.

One day, as they were walking at the head of the Wind River Canyon, a strong wind blew an eagle feather from the girl's hair. Both she and her lover started in pursuit. Down the steep walls the feather floated, just out of their reach, until they had passed through the entire canyon. Near where Thermopolis now stands the feather drifted to the ground, and they picked it up.

Immediately they saw steam issuing from the ground, but they were not afraid. They knew that the Great Mystery had led them there. The water of the spring was hot and smelled clean. They bathed there and later told their people about the good qualities of the water.

Soon their entire band of Shoshonis moved to the spring, and in time its members became famous for their strength and endurance.

To this day, if a weary traveler will loose a feather at the head of the canyon and follow it, as the Indian lovers did, it will guide him to the hot spring. There he can bathe and lose his weariness.

THERE WAS ONCE bitter war among all the people in the region of the Big Horn and Wind rivers. A neighboring tribe had stolen the daughter of a Shoshoni chief and had not offered to pay her father with horses or robes or anything else of value. The chief was very angry, and his warriors were very angry.

They fought battle after battle with the tribe that stole the girl. Suns rose and set, moons waned, and still the war went on. The Chief-with-No-Daughter saw that his band had thinned terribly, but he did not stop. Of course the other tribe thinned also, but he did not seem to notice.

One spring morning the two groups of fighters met on a high hill. The sun was red with anger because of so much fighting among his children. As the Chief-with-No-Daughter saw how small his band had become, his conscience hurt him. Suddenly he noticed at the base of a hill a swirl of white smoke curling upward. First he drew the attention of his own warriors to what looked like smoke west of them. Then he called across to the Chief-Who-Stole-a-Maiden, "Look down below you."

The other chief looked and was awed. Soon he called back, "It is a sign from the Great Mystery. He is telling us to smoke the pipe of peace."

Both bands of warriors then started down the hill toward what they thought was white smoke. At first the odor seemed unpleasant. "This is not peace pipe smoke," said the Chief-with-No-Daughter. But he did not order his men to start fighting again, and he walked on down beside the Chief-Who-Stole-a-Maiden.

After a while the odor became less unpleasant. Then the smoke became a great cloud and was not unpleasant at all. The men soon learned that it came from a spring. All the warriors and the two chiefs sat down beside the smoking spring and passed the pipe of peace from one to another.

⌘

Legend of the Sweet and Bitter Springs

BECAUSE OF THE SIMILARITIES between the dialects of the Shoshonis and the Comanches, it is thought that they were once one nation. The following Shoshoni tradition of the separation of the two tribes was recorded in the first half of the nineteenth century by George Ruxton, a traveler in the Rocky Mountains.

Pike's Peak towers above these springs. Both the Shoshonis and the Comanches roamed over parts of Colorado, hunting and warring.

At the spring of pure water, Ruxton found gifts that the Indians had left for the spirit of the water: in the basin were beadwork, knives, and pieces of cloth; hanging from the surrounding trees were moccasins and strips of cloth and of deerskin.

LONG AGO, when the cottonwood trees along Big River were no higher than arrows, all the people who hunted buffalo on the nearby plains spoke the same language. Game of every kind was so plentiful then that there was no quarreling, no fighting between people of different nations and tribes.

One day during that peaceful time, two hunters met at a tiny stream to quench their thirst. This little stream came from a spring in a rock within a few feet of the bank and fell splashing into the river. One hunter, tired and cross from his unsuccessful efforts to find game, lay on the ground and buried his face in the running water. The other man went to the spring itself. He had with him a fat buck, which he threw from his back to the ground before he stooped to drink from the spring. Before drinking, he took some water in the cup of his hand, lifted it toward the sun, and then reversed his hand to let the water fall upon the ground. In this way he expressed his thanks to the Great Power for success in hunting and for the refreshing drink he was about to have.

When the other man looked up from the stream where he had dipped his face, he felt jealous and then angry. He saw the fat buck, and perhaps he realized that he had not thanked the Great Power for the water. An evil spirit entered his body and mind, and his temper flared into angry speech. He rose from the ground, wanting to provoke a quarrel with the stranger.

"Why does a stranger drink at the spring," he asked, "while one it belongs to contents himself with the water that runs from it?"

"The Great Power, the Creator, placed the cool water in the spring," answered the other hunter, "so that his children may drink it pure. The running water is for the animals. I am Ausaqua, a chief of the Shoshonis. I drink at the spring."

"The Shoshonis are only a tribe of the Comanches," replied the angry hunter. "I am Wacomish, chief of the Comanches. Does a Shoshoni dare to drink above one of the leaders of the grand nation?"

"The Comanches and Shoshonis are brothers," said Ausaqua. "Let them both drink of the same water."

"The Shoshonis pay tribute to the Comanches," replied Wacomish, the quarrelsome man. "Wacomish is chief of the Shoshonis, as he is of his own people. He leads the Shoshonis also."

"Wacomish lies," retorted Ausaqua. "His tongue is forked, like the rattlesnake's. His heart is as black as the evil spirit. When the Creator made His children, he gave them the buffalo to eat and the pure water of the spring to quench their thirst. He gave them to all His children—to the Shoshonis, the Arapahos, the Cheyennes, and the Paiutes, as well as to the Comanches. He did not say to one nation, 'Drink here' and to another, 'Drink here.' He gave this clear spring to all, that all might drink and be refreshed."

Wacomish almost burst with anger as the other spoke. Only his cowardly heart kept him from striking at the Shoshoni. Ausaqua, made thirsty by the words he had said, once again knelt beside the spring to drink. While he stooped, the Comanche suddenly threw himself upon the kneeling hunter, forcing his head into the water, and held it there with all his strength. When his victim no longer struggled, Wacomish loosened his grasp. Ausaqua's limbs relaxed, and his body fell forward over the spring, drowned.

As the murderer stood over the body, bitter remorse quickly took the place of his anger and hatred. Clasping his hands to his forehead, he stood horrified, staring at the dead man. Mechanically, he dragged the body a few feet out of the water. To his amazement, the spring was suddenly and strangely disturbed. Bubbles sprang up from the bottom and, rising to the surface, escaped in hissing gas. A thin, vapory cloud arose and gradually dissolved. The murderer trembled as he watched.

Slowly a figure emerged from the dissolving cloud—the figure of an aged man, with long, snowy hair and beard. Wacomish knew that he was seeing the great Wankanaga, the father of both the Comanche and the Shoshoni tribes. His elders had told him about the great Wankanaga, who was reverenced by all for his bravery and for his good deeds.

Stretching out a war club of elk's horn toward the trembling Wacomish, the old man spoke sharply: "Accursed member of my tribe! Today you have broken the bond between two of the mightiest peoples in the world. The blood of the brave Shoshoni hunter cries to the Great Power for vengeance. May the water of the Comanches be bitter in their throats!"

Swinging his war club around his head, Wankanaga struck Wacomish and dashed out his brains. The dead body fell into the spring. From that moment until the present day, the water of that spring has been bitter and nauseous. Not even when half dead from thirst can anyone drink from that foul water.

But Wankanaga wanted to keep alive the memory of Ausaqua, the Shoshoni hunter, who was well known for his bravery and for his noble heart. So with the same club he struck a hard, flat rock which hung over the little stream, just out of sight of the bitter spring. At once the rock opened into a round, clear basin, which instantly filled with sparkling water. No thirsty hunter ever drank a sweeter or cooler draught than comes from this spring.

A long and bloody war followed the murder of Ausaqua, in which many a Comanche lost his life. From that day to this, the two tribes have remained apart. The two springs, the bitter one and the sweet one, remain there in the mountains, an everlasting reminder of the murder of the noble Shoshoni and of the stern justice of Wankanaga.

✳

Lewis and Clark among the Shoshonis

THE FOLLOWING STORY was related to Warren A. Ferris of the American Fur Company in 1831. He wrote that it was told by a Flathead Indian, but a comparison with the journal of Captain Lewis reveals that Ferris was in error about the tribe. Most of the details in the story parallel Lewis's account of a band of Shoshonis whom he found in August, 1805. They were then living along a little river on the west slope of the Rocky Mountains and were the people of Sacajawea.

There were four men in the explorers' scouting party, not just two. Lewis found the Shoshonis poverty-stricken but cheerful, even gay.

A GREAT MANY SNOWS past, when I was a child, our people were always in fear of the Blackfeet. They had firearms, and we had none. We knew nothing about guns except their effects. Often they attacked us when we went on the plains to hunt buffalo. With their thunder and lightning they killed many of our bravest warriors, but they never came in reach of our arrows. Sometimes their young warriors closed in with us and were defeated, but their friends never failed to repay us fourfold, from a safe distance.

One time when we were in the buffalo country, we saw our best warriors falling around us almost daily for several moons. But we were never able to avenge their deaths. Goaded by thirst for revenge, we often rushed forth upon our enemies. They retreated as we advanced, and so remained at the same distance, where our arrows could not reach them.

At last Big Foot, the head chief of our tribe, gathered his warriors in a council and made a speech to them. He reminded them of their helplessness before their enemies, and he persuaded them to leave the country and to find a safe retreat in the mountains.

Next morning, the sun shone upon a deserted camp. Our people were leaving the beautiful plains. For one whole moon we traveled southwestward, over winding trails and over mountain areas where there were no trails. We went through a gap in the mountains and down to a river that flows toward the setting sun.

There we pitched our camp. The women found plenty of roots and berries. Our hunters went out in safety and came back with plenty of game. Others found that the river was alive with salmon, which the women dried for use in winter. Our fears were forgotten. We smoked in peace around our council fires and heard the stories of long ago.

But after several snows—I don't know how many—our fears returned. Two strangers appeared suddenly. They were unlike any people we had ever seen and wore clothing unknown to us. They gave us things like solid water, which were sometimes as brilliant as the sun and which showed us our own faces. At first we were delighted by the men's appearance, for we thought that they must be the children of the Great Power Above. But soon we were afraid. We learned that they also knew how to make thunder and lightning. We learned that a party of beings like themselves were but a day's march behind them, on the east side of the mountains. They were coming up the Beaverhead River.

Many of our people were terrified. They felt sure that the strangers were in league with our enemies and that together they were coming to attack us. When the white men asked us to go with them to meet their friends, our people at first refused. But our chief believed that they might possibly protect us from our enemies. "Our retreat has been found," he said in a speech to the council. "Let us make friends with these strangers who are so terribly armed."

Some of his warriors decided to follow him, but the women were still afraid. As their men disappeared over a hill near the camp, the women set up a doleful wail. They felt that they were saying farewell forever, and the spirits of the men sank within them as they went.

But when they reached the Beaverhead River, they found only a small party of men like the ones with them. All treated them with great kindness and gave them many things they had never dreamed existed.

Our chief noticed that the strangers were careless about their belongings. They did not seem to know about theft. So he warned his men that they must not steal anything, not even a small thing, from the white men. His men obeyed.

Then the strangers went back over the mountains with the chief and his men. They were made welcome in our camp, and there was joy among our people. They stayed with us for several days. Ever since, my people have been friends of the white men.

❈

The Story of Sacajawea

MY MOST INTERESTING DISCOVERY in those booklets written by Shoshoni school children was the story of Sacajawea. She was the girl-mother who accompanied Lewis and Clark in 1805–1806 as one of the interpreters, and I knew that for several years there had been a controversy over the date and place of her death.

In 1920, the century-old journal of the fur trader John Luttig was published. In it he recorded the death, in 1812, of the Shoshoni wife of Charbonneau, aged twenty-five years. Though Luttig did not indicate which of Charbonneau's two Shoshoni wives had died, several people have been positive that the one buried in what is now South Dakota was Sacajawea.

But on the Wind River Reservation from 1871 until her death in 1884 lived an old woman who had an intimate knowledge of the Lewis and Clark Expedition. She was the mother of Bazil, an important sub-chief when Chief Washakie made a treaty with the government in 1868 and important also during the Shoshonis' early years on the reservation.

Legally witnessed testimonials recorded by Dr. Charles Eastman, an educated Sioux Indian sent to investigate for the Commissioner of Indian Affairs in 1925, and independent studies made by Grace Hebard, convinced the two investigators (and others later) that Bazil's aged mother was Sacajawea of the Lewis and Clark Expedition. Chief Washakie's great-grandson was told by his elders that the young woman who died in 1812 was Charbonneau's other Shoshoni wife, Otter Woman. A recent addition to the puzzle, not published until 1962, is in a list of the members of the expedition written by General Clark, seemingly between 1825 and 1828. Beside Sacajawea's name, in his handwriting, is the word "Dead."

Bazil's mother "was known among the Shoshonis as *Wadze-wipe,* meaning 'Lost Woman,' evidently with reference to her disappearance and long absence from her kinfolk," wrote Finn Burnett, agricultural supervisor on the reservation all the years she lived there. "She was also called *Porivo* or 'Chief Woman,' " said Bazil's grandson in 1925, "because the white people looked up to her as big woman and respected her." White people on the reservation, after hearing her reminiscences, knew her as Sacajawea of the Lewis and Clark Expedition. The wife of the agent recorded the story of her life, wrote Burnett in 1925, but the manuscript was destroyed in a fire at the agency.

Bazil's mother died in 1884. The Reverend John Roberts, who conducted her funeral service, wrote later that she had been "wonderfully active and intelligent, considering her great age. She walked alone and was bright to the last." Bazil had told the missionary the previous year that his mother was about one hundred years old. The day after the young Welsh missionary arrived, the agent took him to see Sacajawea, who lived about one hundred yards from the office. "He alluded to her connection with the Lewis and Clark Expedition," wrote Roberts, "and seemed keenly interested in that fact."

With their elders' recollections written by Shoshoni school children are woven here a few details from the reminiscences of Finn Burnett, written for Charles Eastman in 1925. He knew Sacajawea and Bazil very well, learned the Shoshoni language from them, and heard the old woman's stories many times. A few other details are from John Rees, who lived among Sacajawea's band of Shoshonis for many years, beginning in 1877.

Her name is usually pronounced *Săc-à-já-wē'à,* the accent being on *we.* In the Dakotas, her name is spelled *Sakakawea* and is pronounced *Să-ḵă'ḵà-wē-à.* On the Wind River Reservation, it is pronounced *Săc-à-jä'wa.* When or why she was given that name is not known. A Shoshoni child was seldom named, wrote John Rees, until something occurred to designate him particularly—perhaps not until he was ten to fifteen years old. An expert in the Shoshoni language, Professor Sven Liljeblad, says that *Sacajawea* is not a Shoshoni word. Four months before the explorers reached the Rocky Mountains and the Shoshonis, they named a stream Sacajawea, wrote Lewis, "or Bird Woman's River after our interpreter, the [Shoshoni] woman." So it is thought that her name means Bird Woman. (*Bazil* is pronounced *Bazeel'* on the reservation. *Cameahwait* is accented on the first syllable—*Cam.*)

WHEN SACAJAWEA WAS A GIRL, she lived with her people in valleys of the Rocky Mountains. In the summers, they often made camp at the Three Forks of the Missouri River. One time when they were there, Sacajawea, with other girls and women, was picking berries at a little distance from the main camp. Suddenly their village was attacked by their enemies the Minnetarees. Hearing the war whoops, the women and girls ran. Sacajawea tripped and fell. A Minnetaree warrior picked her up, threw her on his horse, and carried her off to his camp.

When the Minnetarees left the buffalo country along the upper Missouri, they took with them the Shoshoni girls they had captured. One of them jumped through the water of a stream like a fish and so escaped. When she reached home and told her people about her escape, they named her Pop-pank, which means "Jumping Fish." Because Sacajawea had not succeeded in escaping with her, she was given a name that means "Lost Woman."

Sacajawea lived with the Minnetarees a few years, as their slave. In their village she used to see white traders when they came to trade knickknacks for beaver skins. Sacajawea was a very pretty girl. One day a French-Canadian trapper and interpreter named Charbonneau noticed her.

"Who is she?" he asked the chief.

"A Shoshoni captive," replied the chief. "And she *eats* too much!"

"I want to buy her," said Charbonneau. "How much do you want for her?"

"We will gamble for her," replied the Minnetaree chief.

Charbonneau won. He made Sacajawea his slave, but her life was no harder than it had been with the Minnetarees. Later she became his wife, and so did Otter Woman, a friend who had been captured at the same time.

When Lewis and Clark and their soldiers were building their winter quarters near some Indian villages along the Missouri River, Charbonneau asked to be their interpreter. One day Sacajawea and Otter Woman went to see the white men. The army officers hired Charbonneau as their interpreter among the Minnetarees and Mandans near them. When they found out that Sacajawea could speak Shoshoni, they asked that she go with them in the spring. They would travel up the Missouri as far as they could go. Then they would need horses to carry their baggage over the Rocky Mountains to some stream that flows into the Columbia River. And they would need a guide. Lewis and Clark had learned that the Shoshonis lived near the Rocky Mountains. So they hoped that Sacajawea would help them get horses and a guide.

Sacajawea had a little baby named Baptiste, born that winter. She took the baby with her on the trip with the white men. Lewis and Clark, the captains, were always kind to her. They would let no one harm her, and they gave her medicine when she was sick. They helped her take care of the baby when he was sick.

Once, in a storm, Captain Clark saved her and Baptiste from drowning. And Sacajawea helped the white men. One day when a boat almost overturned in white water, she saved the papers and the compass and the medicines. The army officers were much pleased with her then.

When they reached Three Forks, Sacajawea remembered the place where her people had camped. As they came nearer the Rocky Mountains, she recognized a rock that is shaped like the head of a beaver.

"We will find my people along this river," she told the white men, "or along a river on the other side of the mountains."

Not very long after they saw Beaverhead Rock, they met an Indian who had horsehair braided into his scalp lock. Sacajawea began to dance up and down with joy, and she sucked her fingers.

"What is the matter with her?" Captain Clark asked Charbonneau.

"She sucks her fingers because she sees her own people."

A little farther, they met a group of Shoshonis. One of the girls rushed out and threw her arms around Sacajawea. She was Pop-pank. Sacajawea cried because she was happy.

While she was talking with her friends, the white men sent for her to interpret for them. So Sacajawea went to the circle of willow branches that had been made as shade for the council meeting. When she looked at the chief, she realized that he was her own brother.

Running up to him, she threw her arms about him. Then she threw her blanket over their heads and burst into tears again.

Her brother, now Chief Cameahwait, told her that he and their father had pursued the Minnetarees after she was captured, but had not been able to overtake them. In another battle, their father had been killed, and their mother was now dead. Recently their oldest sister had died, leaving a little boy about five years old. Sacajawea immediately adopted him as her own son, but left him with her brother. Later, her adopted son was called Bazil.[1]

Chief Cameahwait and his men brought their horses and took the white men's baggage over the mountains to the Shoshoni camp on the west side. Then the army officers bought horses from the chiefs. Cameahwait planned to steal the horses back, but Sacajawea overheard his plan and told Lewis and Clark. Some of the people were so afraid of the white men that they hid behind trees and bushes, planning to kill them. But the Indians did not shoot, because Sacajawea and the baby were with them.

After they crossed the mountains and left the Shoshonis, they could find no game for a while. Once they had to kill a horse for food, but Sacajawea would not eat any of it. One time they killed dogs and cooked them, but Sacajawea would eat no dog meat. "I would rather starve," she said. "Only dogs eat dogs." She ate berries and fish.

When the party came to the mouth of the Columbia, they saw a big lake. The water went clear out to the sky, and the waves were so big that the men could hardly keep their canoes on top of the water. Lying on the shore was a great big fish—"as high as this ceiling," Sacajawea would say, "and as long as from the door to the hitching rack." She carried part of the big fish on her back when they returned to camp.

They saw also strange brown people at the edge of the big water. Sacajawea wanted to talk with them, but when she and the men

---

[1] It seems doubtful that Bazil was really Sacajawea's nephew. Finn Burnett said that Bazil's complexion "was very fair for a half-breed." Charles Eastman, an educated Sioux, after research among both the Shoshonis and the Minnetarees in 1925, concluded that Bazil was the son of Charbonneau and of Otter Woman, his other Shoshoni wife.

tried to get near them, they dived into the ocean. She thought that seals were people who lived in caves underneath the water. Our people thought she was lying when she told about the whale, but they believed her story of the seals.

Somewhere along the Columbia, the white men met a war party of Indians. Sacajawea made signs with her blanket to tell the Indians that she was a friendly Shoshoni. So the white soldiers were not attacked.

When they got back to the Rocky Mountains, the party was divided. The army officer with the red hair asked Charbonneau and Sacajawea to go with him, so that she could show him the way through the country she had known as a child. She showed him the pass over the mountains, where her people crossed when they went to gather roots and to hunt for beaver. There the explorers crossed over the mountains to the Yellowstone River and then down that river to the Missouri.

Many years later, Sacajawea came back to her people and found her adopted son Bazil. When the Wind River Reservation was started, Bazil and his family came here from Fort Bridger. They lived in a house near the agency until Sacajawea died. Baptiste lived with them part of the time. When Bazil and his sons and Baptiste would go on a big buffalo hunt, they would leave Sacajawea in care of the agent. They knew that the old people and children would be safe near the agency and near the soldiers at Fort Washakie. When Sacajawea was a little girl, everybody had to go on the buffalo hunts.

Sacajawea had some papers the white men had given her, and she wore around her neck a medal they had given her or her brother. It was bigger than a dollar, and it had a gold rim around it. On it was a picture of Thomas Jefferson. After she died, Bazil wore the medal. Sacajawea lived to be very old. Bazil took good care of her. Both of them are buried in the cemetery not far from the agency.

VI. Algonquian Tribes: The Araphos, the Gros Ventres, and the Blackfeet

THE ARAPAHOS, their sub-tribe the Gros Ventres of the Plains, and the Blackfeet are western members of the Algonquian linguistic family that once occupied large areas of North America from the Atlantic Coast to the Rocky Mountains. Other Algonquian tribes are the Cree, the Cheyenne, the Chippewa (or Ojibway), and the Micmac of Nova Scotia.

The Arapahos and the Gros Ventres, according to their traditions, were once an agricultural people living in what is now northeastern Minnesota. Apparently they moved westward with the Cheyennes, with whom the Arapahos seem always to have been allied. The Gros Ventres (also called Atsina, Gros Ventres of the Plains, and Minnetarees of the Plains) seem to have moved westward up the north side of the Missouri and, according to some traditions, seem to have been separated from the larger groups by the breaking of the ice in the river. Later, the Gros Ventres drifted off toward the Blackfeet. Frequently thought of as a distinct tribe, they are now most closely associated with the Assiniboines on the Fort Belknap Reservation, Montana.

The Arapahos proper moved westward along the south side of the Missouri and then southward. In time they separated into two divisions. Those in the Northern or main division—the ones represented in this book—have been identified with Wyoming during most of the historic period. They became a typical Plains people, following the buffalo and living in skin tipis. Until placed on reservations, both divisions of Arapahos were almost constantly at war with the Crows, the Shoshonis, the Utes, and the Pawnees. But fur traders who wintered with them in the early 1830's spoke "highly of their integrity and generosity." "They consider hospitality a virtue second only to valor," wrote Warren A. Ferris. "They are brave, candid, and honest, for though [they are] good warriors they neither rob nor steal."

In 1876, the Northern Arapahos were placed on the Wind River Reservation, Wyoming, beside the Shoshonis, with whom they had signed a peace treaty only seven years earlier. (The Southern Arapahos had already been placed on a reservation in Oklahoma.) In Wyoming, the Arapahos have been described by their white neighbors as kindly, reflective, and deeply religious. They worshipped in prayer the Father ("the Great Power Above"), "the great mother" Earth, the Sun, and the Four Old Men. These Old Men represented the four "world quarters of the semi-cardinal points." The Arapahos addressed prayers also to the moon, the morning star and other stars, the winds and thunder, as well as to the spirits of animals and of birds.

Unlike other tribes, the Arapahos undertook their vigil for their supernatural helper in adulthood, not in childhood. They were devoted to their ritualistic observances, which included the Sun Dance and the ceremonies of the eight societies in which men were organized according to age. Even their robes and tipis had ceremonial decorations.

The three most sacred objects of the Arapahos have been carefully preserved by the northern division: the "flat-pipe," the stone turtle, and an ear of corn transformed to stone. Whenever a man smokes the flat-pipe, said an Arapaho chief in 1897, "he is obliged to tell the truth. We use it in the Sun Dance, the sweat house, and whenever we want to worship." The sacredness of the turtle is explained in the Gros Ventre creation myth which introduces this section of legends. The ear of corn is a relic of the agricultural background of the Arapahos: at the beginning of the world, said an ancient myth, their ancestors were given an ear of corn by Duck, "from which comes all the corn of the world."

In the traditions of the Arapahos there used to be many tales about Spider similar to Coyote tales in the traditions of other tribes. They told also long stories about the origin of ceremonial lodges and the origin of sacred objects.

The Blackfeet, or Siksika, were one of the largest of the Algonquian tribes and the most powerful on the northwestern Plains. They once held most of the vast territory extending from the North Saskatchewan River, Canada, to the southern headstreams of the Missouri and Yellowstone rivers, and from the Rocky Mountains to the eastern borders of the province of Saskatchewan and of the state of Minnesota. *Siksika* means "black foot." Some people believe that the name refers to the discoloring of their moccasins by the ashes of prairie fires; others, to the black-painted moccasins their people wore in ancient times.

The Blackfeet are really a confederacy of three sub-tribes: the Siksika or Blackfeet proper, the Blood, and the Piegan. Each of these had its independent organization, and each was subdivided into bands. Most of the Siksika and the Blood bands now live on three reserves in Alberta, Canada; most of the Piegans, about two-thirds of the confederacy, live on the Blackfeet Reservation in western Montana.

According to the traditions of the Blackfeet, they have always been roving hunters of buffalo and antelope, without permanent homes, without agriculture except for the planting and gathering of a species of native tobacco used in their ceremonies. Their traditions recorded by the fur trader David Thompson in 1787–88 went back to a time when they lived northwest of the Saskatchewan River, and when they had no canoes or horses and hunted with primitive weapons. They may have obtained horses shortly after 1730, when the Shoshonis began to use them in wars against the Piegans. Soon horse-stealing was considered a virtue among the Blackfeet (as it was among other tribes), and they became noted for their large herds of horses, which they called "elk-dogs."

A restless, daring, pillaging people, they made long expeditions to the north and to the south as far as Mexico. Sometimes, warriors were gone for several years and then, around the campfires, they told long tales about their adventures. The most aggressive and warlike of all the Plains tribes, the Blackfeet were nearly always at war with the Crees, Sioux, Assiniboines, Crows, Cheyennes, and Shoshonis. They fought the Kutenais and the Flatheads when the latter came to the plains to hunt buffalo, and they sometimes crossed the mountains to attack these nearer Plateau tribes. A band of two Blackfeet and six Gros Ventres were the only Indians against whom the Lewis and Clark Expedition had to use firearms (July 26, 1806).

The Blackfeet were hostile to the whites, massacring them "in the cruelest manner," wrote Father De Smet. Though his pages glow with affection for the other Rocky Mountain tribes he worked with, De Smet called them "the fearful Blackfeet . . . murderers, traitors, and all that is wicked." And Maximilian, a German scientist who studied the Indians of the Upper Missouri River in 1832–34, described the Blackfeet as "extremely dangerous, in whom no confidence could be placed, and whose perfidious, sanguinary and predatory character was sufficiently known."

But when Father De Smet was living among the Blackfeet in 1846, he discovered "them equal in hospitality with other Indian tribes." And John Stanley, artist with the Pacific Railway Expedition, wrote after an eleven-day journey among the Piegans in 1853: "During my sojourn among them I was treated with the greatest kindness and hospitality, my property guarded with vigilance, so that I did not lose the most trifling article."

In the mid-nineteenth century, the Blackfeet were at the height of their power—the most powerful tribe of the northwestern plains. Soon their vigor was undermined by white man's measles, smallpox, and alcohol, and they lost most of their land. The extermination of the last great herds of buffalo in 1883 ended the centuries-old life of nomadic hunters. During the following winter more than a fourth of the Piegans died of starvation. Had it not been for "the courage and unselfish character of their great chiefs," says John Ewers, "the Blackfeet might not have survived the discouraging years of readjustment to a new way of life."

The native religion of the Blackfeet was a form of Sun worship. "We believe that the Sun God is all powerful," said an old man puzzled by the white man's religion. "We can see that all life comes from him." They made daily prayers to the Sun and to *Napi* (Old

Man), and they undertook nothing of importance without first praying for divine aid. The Sun sent them dreams to tell them what was going to happen.

They had many sacred or medicine bundles, with each of which there was a ritual. These were opened ceremonially—to call the buffalo, to heal the sick, to bring success in war, to promote personal and tribal welfare. Oldest and largest of these was the "beaver bundle"; the most interesting of several myths about the origin of the beaver bundle is included in this section. So complex was the ritual connected with it, including hundreds of songs, that a man needed several years in which to learn it. Old and important also was the medicine pipe bundle. Very important among these "bundles" were the painted lodges, the handsomely decorated covers of which indicated the symbols of the owner's spirit power.

"The supreme expression of their religion, by the middle of the nineteenth century," was the annual Sun Dance, or the ceremony of the Medicine Lodge. In late summer, when the berries were ripe, the Blackfeet gave thanks to the Sun through this prolonged religious ceremony. It was prompted by the vow of a chaste woman, made to the Sun for the recovery of the sick. At the Sun Dance and on other occasions, sacrifices were made to the Sun, usually gifts of clothing. The Blackfoot ceremony of the Medicine Lodge was greatly influenced, both in symbolism and in sacred objects, by the older ritual of the beaver bundle.

In the mythology of the Blackfeet are hundreds of tales about *Napi*, or Old Man. Like Wisakedjak in Cree lore and like Coyote in the lore of many Western tribes, Old Man is an interesting combination of power and weakness, of goodness and maliciousness. Each of these mythological characters might be considered "an allegory of the human race." The serious stories, like "Old Man and the Beginning of the Blackfoot World" and "Old Man and Old Woman," make it easy to understand that, as late as the 1880's, Old Man was still reverenced and still addressed in prayer. In other stories he is selfish, mischievous, even cruel; playing tricks on animals and on people, Old Man got into many difficulties, at which the narrator and his audience used to laugh delightedly. To at least some modern Blackfeet, many of these humorous stories are obscene.

Chewing Blackbones, an elderly grandfather, recalled a fragment of one version of the end of Napi's days—spent in what is now Glacier National Park. (Because he could tell the old tales only in the old Blackfoot language, his fourteen-year-old grandson had to ask a middle-aged neighbor to interpret for us.) Napi, pursued by people who wanted to kill him, ran over a hill and up a deep coulee into the mountains. There he came to two lakes, now called Lower St. Mary Lake and Upper St. Mary Lake. At the Upper lake he said to himself, "I believe I will go up on that highest mountain and change myself into stone." In a crevice in the mountain he lay down, with just his face peeking out, and turned himself into a rock. He is still there. You can still see Napi's face on Going-to-the-Sun-Mountain. At times the face seems to be moving around, just as if Napi were peeking out and watching for people to come looking for him.

Besides the numerous tales about Old Man's adventures, the Blackfeet related an unusual number of star myths and many myths about the origin of sacred rituals, "the rituals themselves being in part dramatic interpretations of the narratives." There were also many adventurous, historical, and military narratives. Almost all of the stories collected by a Blackfoot woman for the Federal Writers' Project just prior to the outbreak of World War II are about warriors' conflicts, in the old days, with the many enemies of the tribe.

No tribe in the northern Rocky Mountain region has been so thoroughly described, in word and picture, as the Blackfeet. The explorer and fur trader David Thompson, Maximilian and the Swiss artist Karl Bodmer who accompanied him, the American artist and writer George Catlin in the 1830's, the Jesuit missionary Father De Smet in the 1840's—all these made studies of the Blackfeet when they were a dominant military power. Later, Walter McClintock and James Schultz, who lived among the Piegans for years, and George Grinnell, who spent considerable time with them, wrote about their customs and beliefs. In recent years, John C. Ewers, former curator of the Museum of the Plains Indian at Browning, Montana, has published both an illustrated pamphlet and a very interesting historical study of the Blackfeet, "raiders on the northwestern plains."

The Creation of the World

THIS CREATION MYTH of the Gros Ventres Indians is similar to the origin myths of at least two other Algonquian tribes (the Arapahos and the Crees), to myths handed down among the Huron and Iroquois tribes of eastern North America, and to one related in 1953 by the oldest Chehalis Indian near the Washington coast. The successful diving animal differs in the different tribes.

THE PEOPLE BEFORE the present people were wild and did not know how to do anything. Because the Creator did not like the way they lived, he thought, "I will make a new world." He had the chief pipe. He went outdoors, hung the pipe on three sticks, and picked up four buffalo chips. He put one under each of the three sticks supporting the pipe, and took the fourth chip for his own seat.

The Creator said to himself, "I will sing three times and shout three times. Then I will kick the earth. There will be a heavy rain, and soon water will cover the earth."

So he sang three times, he shouted three times, and he kicked the earth. The earth cracked, and water came out. Then it rained many days and many nights, until water was deep over the earth. Because of the buffalo chips, he and the pipe floated. Then the rain stopped. For days he drifted, floating where the wind and water took him. All the animals and birds had drowned except Crow.

Above the Creator, Crow flew around, crying. When it became tired, it cried, "My father, I am tired. I want to rest."

Three times Crow said these words. After the third time, the Creator replied, "Alight on the pipe and rest."

At last the Creator became tired from sitting in one position, and he cried. For a long time he did not know what to do. Then he remembered to unwrap the pipe. It contained all the animals. He took out all those that have a long breath and thus are able to dive through water. Large Loon, which he selected first, was not alive, but its body was wrapped up in the pipe. The Creator sang to it and then commanded it to dive and try to bring up some mud. Not half way down, Large Loon lost its breath and turned back. Almost drowned, it reached the place where the Creator sat.

The the Creator took Small Loon's body from the pipe, unwrapped it, sang, and commanded it to dive for mud. Small Loon nearly reached the bottom before it lost its breath and turned back. It was almost dead when it came back to the surface. Then the Creator took Turtle from the pipe, sang until it became alive, and sent it down after some mud.

Meanwhile, Crow flew about, crying for rest. The Creator paid no attention. After a long time Turtle came up from the water, nearly dead.

"Did you reach the mud?" asked the Creator.

"Yes," answered Turtle. "I had much of it in my feet and along my sides, but it was washed away before I reached you."

"Come to me." The Creator looked in the cracks along its sides and in its feet. There he found a little earth, which he scraped into his hand. Then he began to sing. Three times he sang, and three times he shouted.

"I will throw this little dust in my hand into the water," he said. "Little by little, let there be enough to make a strip of land large enough for me."

He began to drop it, little by little, opening and closing his hand carefully. When he had finished, there was a small strip of land, big enough for him to sit on. Then the Creator said to Crow, "Come down and rest. I have made a piece of land for myself and for you."

Crow came down and rested, and then flew up again. The Creator took from his pipe two long wing feathers, held one in each hand, and began to sing. Three times he sang, and three times he shouted, "Youh, hou, hou!" Then he spread out his arms, closed his eyes, and said to himself, "Let there be land as far as my eyes can see around me."

When he opened his eyes, the water was gone and there was land as far as he could see. He walked over the earth with his pipe and with

Crow. When he became thirsty, he did not know what to do to get water. Then he thought, "I will cry." So he closed his eyes and cried until his tears, dropping on the ground, formed a large spring in front of him. Soon a stream ran from out the spring. When the Creator stopped crying, a large river was flowing. In this way he made all the streams.

When he became tired of being alone with Crow and his pipe, he decided to make persons and animals. First he took earth and made it into the shape of a man. Then he took another piece of earth and made it into the shape of a woman. He molded more figures out of earth until he had created many men and women. People are dark because the earth is dark.

When the Creator thought he had enough people, he made animals of all kinds, in pairs. Then he gave names to the tribes of people and names to all kinds of animals. He sang three times, shouted three times, and kicked the ground. When he had finished, many pairs of living creatures stood before him, persons and animals.

He called the world "Turtle" because Turtle had helped him create it. Then he made bows and arrows, and he taught men how to use them. The pipe, he gave to a tribe called *Haa-ninin*. White people call them Gros Ventres.

He said to the people, "If you are good, there will be no more water and no more fire. Long before the flood came, the world had been burned. This now is the third life."

Then he showed people the rainbow and said, "This rainbow is the sign that the earth will not be covered with water again. Whenever you have had rain, you will see the rainbow. It will mean that the rain has gone. There will be another world after this one."

He told the people to go off in pairs and to find homes for themselves. That is why human beings are scattered.

❈

The Origin of the Flat-Pipe

THE SACRED PIPE, or "Flat-Pipe," is the most treasured possession of the Arapahos. Its wooden stem, about two feet long, is inserted in a cylindrical bowl of black soapstone inlaid with whitish stone. Wrapped in skins and cloth, and kept in a ceremonially painted lodge, it is the most sacred object at the Sun Dance of the Northern Arapahos and at other important gatherings.

"Only occasionally," wrote Edward S. Curtis, "was the sacred pipe revealed to a favored few who could afford the expense attendant upon the ceremony. On such occasions those who were present smoked the pipe, praying for health, prosperity, and any special boon desired, and the keeper related the history of the pipe."

This history "constitutes the unwritten bible of the Arapaho. It can be recited only when the pipe is exposed, and only by the pipe-keeper, and four nights must be consumed in the telling." It includes not only the origin of the Flat-Pipe but, apparently, the history of the first people, rules governing ceremonies, and precepts about moral living. Those who hear the story must not repeat it.

During Curtis' study of the Arapahos on the Wind River Reservation, he concluded that since 1908, when the keeper of the pipe died without a male heir, no one had known the entire tradition. Only fragments of the origin myth have been recorded, and these vary a great deal. The fragment given below was recorded from the Reverend John Roberts, one of the very few white people to have seen the pipe. A few details are from the Reverend Sherman Coolidge, a Northern Arapaho who was educated for the Christian ministry.

The Arapaho religion and priestly elders, Roberts thought, had several parallels with the Hebrew religion and the Levites.

THE FIRST ARAPAHO, long, long ago, sat on the highest peak of the highest mountain, weeping with loneliness. All he could see was sky and water, for the world was covered with a great flood. Looking up one time, he saw the Unknown-One-on-High descend from the sky and walk over the water.

"Why do you weep?" asked the Unknown-One-on-High.

"I weep because I am lonely," replied the first Arapaho. "I have no country to live in."

So the Unknown-One-on-High—the Creator—sent forth Dove, saying, "Go and find a country for this man."

But Dove returned without finding a country. "All the land is covered with water," reported Dove.

Just then Turtle swam by. The Creator said to Turtle, "Go and find a country for this man."

Turtle dived far down beneath the water and came back with a lump of mud in her mouth. "Under the water there is a country," reported Turtle.

The Unknown-One-on-High then commanded the waters to roll away into distant seas and commanded the dry land to arise. The waters obeyed. Almost immediately, a beautiful country unfolded before the eyes of the first Arapaho. It had forested mountains, green valleys, sparkling rivers, and blue lakes.

"This is your country," the Creator said to him. "To you and your children and your grandchildren I give it forever and forever."

Then the Unknown-One-on-High and the Arapaho walked together among the trees, until they came to a deep lake that was beautifully shaded. Near it they sat down and talked. During the conversation the Unknown One threw some pebbles into the lake. The Arapaho, seeing them sink into the water, cried out, "Oh, must my children die? Can they not be like this?" And he threw a stick into the water, which floated away on the surface of the lake.

The Unknown One shook his head. "No, they would be too numerous."

Seeing the anxiety of the Arapaho, the Creator gave him something to comfort him—a flat-pipe. "This sacred pipe I give to you," he said. "Guard it carefully. Throughout the ages it will guide your children and bless them. If they will gaze upon this pipe as they are dying, it will carry their spirits safely to Our Home. Very soon I shall go away, but before I go I will make other tribes of people near you. After that, I will cross the big water and make white people, a great many of them.

"In time, this sacred pipe will waste away. When it does, the people who have died will rise from the grave. Then I, the Deliverer, will come from the northwest to be chief over your people forever.

"Be kind to your friends. Fight your enemies bravely. Farewell."

Then the Creator, the Unknown-One-on-High, went away to the northwest.

At all times the pipe has worked wondrously for the Arapahos. Because it has always been too sacred to be carried on horseback, the one who kept it always walked and carried it in his arms, as was done before we had horses. When it moved, the people followed. Where it rested, there they camped. It led the warriors to victory in battle. It has carried the spirits of dying Arapahos safely to Our Home.

Hence it is called *Hodde Jevaneauthau,* or "Chariot of the Unknown-One-on-High."

⌘

The Origin of the Arapaho Sun Dance

THE NORTHERN ARAPAHOS hold annually one of the most elaborate of the Sun Dance rituals. It has long been their most important tribal ceremony.

Their Sun Dance on the Wind River Reservation in August, 1953, was carried out according to ancient ritual, but the pledge behind it had a modern touch: on a battlefield in Korea the previous year, a young Arapaho sergeant vowed that if he should reach home safely, he would "put on a Sun Dance in the old way." In the old days, Arapaho warriors made similar vows. Other people promise a performance if the Man-Above will grant their wish.

Among the Northern Arapahos, it has long been the custom for the keeper of the Flat-Pipe to direct the Sun Dance. Only he may relate the complete version of the tribal origin myth, and telling it requires four consecutive nights. The following story is greatly condensed from the "Origin Myth" recorded by the anthropologist George Dorsey from the Southern Arapahos. It follows his detailed account of the Sun Dance. When he observed the ceremony in 1901 and 1902, it lasted for eight days and was "performed with much religious fervor and happiness." Different bands of Arapahos had camped in a big circle in the place chosen for the Sun Dance. After the Crier had formally announced the opening of the ceremony, four days were spent in ritualistic construction of the "Offerings-lodge" and in secret rites inside the "Rabbit-tipi." The formal beginning of the Sun Dance itself was near midnight after the fourth day.

Some knowledge of the objects used in the ceremony is necessary for an appreciation of the myth. A cottonwood tree, carefully selected, becomes the center pole in the lodge. It symbolizes the Man-Above and carries the prayers of the people to heaven. In the fork of the pole is a painted buffalo robe. A painted buffalo skull is on the altar, which is made partly of a cedar tree. Throughout the four days of the Sun Dance, the Lodge-Maker wears a painted buffalo robe decorated with tufts of rabbit fur.

The Wheel, the most sacred object in the possession of the Southern Arapahos, is about eighteen inches in diameter and is made of wood. One end of it is shaped like a snake's head; the other, like a snake's tail. The snake (or the Wheel because of it), some informants said, represents the water which surrounds the earth. Blue beads around the head of the snake represent the sky.

At four opposite sides of the Wheel are designs representing the Four Old Men, who are frequently prayed to during the Sun Dance. Some people told Dorsey that these Four Old Men have control over the direction the wind blows; others, that they guard the people of the world; another, that they represent Summer and Winter, Day and Night. Attached to the Wheel by short buckskin thongs are four clusters of the tail feathers of eagles. They represent Thunderbird, which gives rain; they therefore symbolize a prayer for rain and thus for vegetation.

Because the Sun is regarded as the grandfather of the Four Old Men, the Wheel may be considered the emblem of the Sun. The Wheel and the additions to it "may be said to be symbolic of the creation of the world, for it represents the sun, the earth, the sky, the water, and the wind."

The first episode in Dorsey's twenty-one-page "Origin Myth" is the creation of the world, somewhat similar to the two myths which precede this one. So his first eight pages are summarized in the opening paragraph below.

AFTER ALL THE BIRDS, animals, and reptiles had dived into the great flood and had returned without finding earth, the man with the Flat-Pipe, the first Arapaho, turned himself into a redhead duck, and with Turtle he dived deep. Each brought back a small piece of clay. From these two pieces the man with the Flat-Pipe created the earth.

Then he sat down on the dry land, carefully laid the Flat-Pipe beside him, and faced the sunrise. He sat in silence, in deep thought. He was waiting to complete his creation. Among the animals and birds there was great rejoicing for some time, great thanksgiving for the new earth. All came up to see the sacred pipe.

After a while, Turtle stepped up before the man and spoke: "Please take and accept me. I am a harmless creature, slow to anger, and very charitable. I want to represent the earth with those qualities. I want my name to mean these things: to cleanse the sick, to comfort the sorrowing, and to paint."

The man replied so that all might hear: "Turtle has made a wise choice, and it is acceptable to me. His body shall represent the earth with all things. The markings on his back shall represent a path. His four legs shall represent the Four Old Men; his legs or feet shall be somewhat red. His shield will represent mountain ranges and rivers. Look closely. Turtle's desires shall be fulfilled."

So Turtle was placed beside the Flat-Pipe.

His offer started the other creatures to thinking. Kit-Fox offered her body, with its soft fur, as a sacrifice. Otter-Weed and Cat-Tail offered their services, and the man found them so acceptable that he placed them beside the Flat-Pipe and Kit-Fox. That is why there are two messengers at the Rabbit-tipi and at other lodges during the Sun Dance.

Then White Buffalo spoke: "Please accept my request that I may live long in happiness and in prosperity. I am quiet and peaceable, and I desire to be of service in every way. I want my skin to be used as a robe. It can be used also in making caps, belts, arm bands, knee bands, and moccasins. I wish to be used on all occasions."

"As far as I can see," replied the man, "the desires of White Buffalo are very good." So he placed the white buffalo robe beside the Flat-Pipe.

Eagle spoke next: "Well, I wish to be included. So I give to Flat-Pipe two of my wing-feathers—the very last one at each shoulder. I sincerely hope that they will be accepted."

And they were.

Then Garter-Snake, with tears in his eyes, looked up at the man and spoke at some length: "I am very low in spirit, and I wish to place myself away from harm and violence. In behalf of all people, I beg that the time of fasting and offering of prayers for an accomplishment be limited to four days instead of seven. And I repeat that I wish to be located away from harm and be a circumference of the earth."

This young man, Garter-Snake, had gone for four days in search of clay or mud and had failed to find it. Of course his request was granted.

"Now, my people," said the man with the Flat-Pipe, "I wish to tell you that I am ready to complete my work. Watch me." With a corner wing feather of the Eagle, he made motions in different directions and so formed the mountain ranges, the rivers flowing eastward, and the rivers flowing westward.

While the man rested, all the creatures upon the new earth talked with each other in one language. Soon the man with the Flat-Pipe was ready to make the sacred Wheel. One after another the creatures offered themselves. One young man, Long-Stick, a bush that has a slender, flexible body with dark red bark, said, "Since this is for good in the future, please use my entire body for the circumference of the Wheel."

So Long-Stick was made into a ring for the Wheel. After the man with the Flat-Pipe had shaped it nicely, he painted the inside black, to symbolize the earth. He painted the outside red, to symbolize Indians offering prayers to Man-Above. He carved a design to represent Morning Star, the messenger of the Four Old Men. He carved other designs to represent many other stars; on opposite sides of the wheel he carved designs of Thunderbird. When Eagle asked to be used at all sacred rituals, four bunches of eagle feathers were tied to four parts of the wheel. When the man with the Flat-Pipe had completed the Wheel, he gave it to Garter Snake, who was made happy by becoming an emblem to the people.

Then the other creatures came forward and offered to be useful in any ceremony with the Wheel: Rabbit, Badger, Cottonwood, Cedar-Tree, Willow, Red-Bush, Water-Grass, and all the Rabbit-Weeds. White Buffalo repeated his offer to be useful. These are used in the construction of the Offerings-lodge or in the preparation of the objects used in the Sun Dance ceremony.

When the earth was fully created and when the sacred Wheel was completed, the man with the Flat-Pipe made an image of a woman and breathed life into her. He wanted a companion. After they had lived together for some time, the man decided that they should have a child to live with them. So one day while they were out viewing the beautiful land, he again made a clay image and breathed life into it. This time he made a boy child.

For some reason the boy became ill. The father, being fond of him and not wanting to lose him, vowed that a Sun Dance Lodge should be erected for his recovery. The mother also wanted the lodge to be built. So one bright morning the man started off, stopped at four places, and with a loud cry called out to all the birds and beasts, "We are going to build a Sun Dance Lodge for the recovery of my son. Come and help us build it."

Pleased with the invitation and with the undertaking, all the birds and beasts of every kind gathered at the place decided upon. They helped the man and his wife construct the lodge and prepare for the ceremony. It lasted four days and four nights. The boy recovered and gave thanks for his recovery. All the birds and beasts were happy, too, as were the owner of the Flat-Pipe and his wife. They were the pledgers, the givers of the Sun Dance.

Years went by. The man and his wife and their boy multiplied, so that there was a big camp circle. One day a boy, an only child, suddenly became ill and gradually grew worse. His father went to the owner of the Flat-Pipe and said to him, "You have told me about the Sun Dance Lodge you erected when your son was ill. Will you put up one like it for my sick son?"

The owner of the sacred pipe gladly agreed to do so, and the whole camp moved to another place and formed a circle. There the man taught the people the proper way to conduct the ceremony. He had an old man paint himself with natural red paint, carry a pipe and a buffalo tail, and announce to the people: "Listen this day! May all our remaining days be brighter because of this ceremony. May there be an abundance of food. And may the Flat-Pipe protect us from sickness and the plague."

Then the old man called upon all the people to live in harmony together, that they might be prosperous forever. At four different places he stopped and made his announcement. Hearing him and seeing him, many people made their prayers also.

"May this cry of mercy be heard for me," one man said, "so that I may live to be an old man."

"May I overcome trials and hardships and follow a straight path!" prayed another.

"May I get well and be able to walk around," said a sick woman.

"May I live in peace and harmony hereafter" was the wish of another.

Then the Rabbit-tipi, in which all the things for the Offerings-lodge are made and painted, was placed within the camp circle. The owner of the Flat-Pipe made a shallow, circular hole and in it put some water. Immediately, a flock of geese came flying, cackling, circling. Descending in file, they came and drank four times. Then the people came to the hole and took a good drink for health and prosperity. Though many drank, there was a continuous flowing of sweet water, and plenty was left after all had quenched their thirst.

When everything in the Rabbit-tipi had been prepared in the proper way, the trees and birds and animals came up again and offered themselves for the materials of the Offerings-lodge. They were used according to their strength, purity, and height. Everything was done in the proper way. The Lodge-maker and the dancers wore paints alike during the entire ceremony. That is, they were painted in white clay decorated with dark circles at their wrists and ankles. They were also ornamented with diamond-shaped designs of black, green, pink, and yellow.

Throughout the ceremony the dancers danced to the beatings of drums and to the singing of the old men and old women.

Thus was the Sun Dance ceremony performed according to the instructions of the first Arapaho, the owner of the Flat-Pipe.

✖

The Beginning of Many Things

A MAN TRIED TO THINK how the Arapahos might kill buffalo. He was a hard thinker who would go off for several days to fast and think. At last he dreamed that a voice spoke to him and told him what to do.

Going back to his people, he made an enclosure of trees set in the ground with willows wound between them. At one side of the enclosure there was only a cliff with rocks at the bottom. Then four runners who never tired were sent out to the windward of a herd of buffalo, two of them on each side of the herd. They drove the animals toward the enclosure and into it. Then the people drove the buffalo around inside until a heavy cloud of dust rose. Unable to see in the dust, the animals ran over the cliff and were killed.

This man also secured horses for his people. There were many wild horses. The man made another enclosure, complete except for an an opening. Into this enclosure horses were driven, just as the buffalo had been, and then the opening was closed. After the horses had run around until they were tired, they were lassoed. At first it took a long time to break them, and only one horse was caught for each family. But this was not enough, so more were caught. After a few years, the horses had had so many colts that every Arapaho man had a herd. No longer did the dogs have to drag the meat and baggage, nor did the women have to carry heavy packs on their backs.

At that time the people had nothing to cut their meat with. Another man took a buffalo shoulder blade and cut out a narrow piece of it with flint. This he sharpened until it was a good knife. He also made a knife from flint by flaking it into shape. All the people learned how to make knives.

This man made the first bow and arrows also. He made the first arrow point from the short rib of a buffalo. With his bow and four arrows, he went off alone and waited in the woods at a buffalo path. When a buffalo came along the path, he shot; the arrow disappeared in the body and the animal fell dead. Then he killed three others. He went back to camp and told his people, "Harness the dogs; there are four dead buffalo in the woods." Thereafter the Arapahos were able to get meat without driving the buffalo into an enclosure.

In the early days, people used the fire drill. A man, another hard thinker, went off alone to think. He learned that certain stones, when struck, would give a spark and that this spark would light tinder. He gathered stones and filled a small horn with dry, soft wood. Then he went home.

His wife said to him, "Please make a fire." So he took out his horn and his flint stones, struck a spark, blew it, put grass on it, and soon, to the surprise of all who saw it, he had a fire. Making a fire in this way was so much easier than using a fire drill that soon all the people did it.

These three men—the one who made the first enclosure for buffalo and for horses, the one who made the first knife and the first bow and arrows, and the one who showed people how to make fire easily—they were the men who brought our people to the condition in which they live now.

✄

The Little People

THE LITTLE PEOPLE, old Arapahos say, were less than three feet high. They were dark-skinned, had big stomachs, and were powerfully built. They used the sign language, but not exactly as the

Indians did. In deep canyons in the mountains they carved houses out of rocks. Some of their houses can still be seen there, and some of their skeletons have been found also.

They were such swift runners that if one of them pursued an Arapaho, he had little chance of escaping. And they were so strong that one of them could carry an Indian home on his back. There they killed him and ate him, for the Little People were cannibals.

One time an Arapaho did escape. He was a big man, but one bright moonlight night one of the Little People chased him. When the Indian reached a narrow stream, he jumped over it. The dwarf looked at the stream, saw that it was too wide for him to jump over, and saw the moon and stars reflected in the water. "That creek is too deep for me to cross," he said to himself, and then returned to his home in the rocks. The Arapaho was unharmed that time.

They lost so many of their people, however, that they decided to kill off the Little People. The dwarfs were difficult to get rid of, for wounds from arrows had little effect on them. The Indians surrounded the Little People in a deep gorge, through which ran a rushing stream, and then set fire to the brush on the canyon walls. There seemed no way of escape.

As the fire was making its way toward the Little People, they gathered in a council to decide what they should do.

"Who knows most?" asked one dwarf. "Let him now stand forth and tell us how we can save our women and children from being devoured by the fire."

"We will dig a hole in the sand," answered a little wise one. "We will put our women and children in the hole and cover them with earth, so that the fire can not reach them."

"But do we want to roast our people?" asked another. "How do we cook our meat? We make a hole in the ground, cover it with a roof of earth, and light a fire on the roof. That's the way we roast our meat. Do we want to roast our women and children?"

So that plan was not accepted.

The tribal crier went through the gathering of Little People and called out, "Who knows most? Who knows most? Let him now stand forth and tell us how we can save our women and our children from the advancing fire."

"We will place them in the river," answered a wise one, "with their heads above the water. That is the way we will save our women and children."

After a short silence, a little fellow stood on a rock and made a speech to the council. "How do we boil buffalo meat? We make a hollow in the ground, we open out the buffalo hide, we fit it carefully in the hollow, fill it with water from the river, and put our meat in the cold water. Then we make a fire and heat some rocks. We drop the hot rocks into the water until it boils and cooks our buffalo meat.

"The fire is advancing upon us in the brush on each side of the creek. It is heating the rocks and the boulders. Do we want to boil our women and children?"

So that plan was not accepted.

In despair the tribal crier called out again, "Who knows most? Who knows most? Let him stand forth and tell us how we can save our women and children from the advancing fire."

Then an important little wise man, brown as a ripe pine nut, stood up and spoke. "I know how we can save our women and children. Do you see these tall trees around us? Let us quickly build nests in their highest branches. Let us place in them our women and children, so that they will be out of reach of the fire. That is what we will do."

"That is what we will do!" all the Little People shouted. "That is what we will do. He knows most! He knows most. He has shown us how to save our women and children."

So they built nests on the highest branches of the tallest trees and placed the women and children in them.

But, in the meantime, the fire had come down the canyon walls, burning the brush as it came. Then it burned the brush along the creek and roared up the canyon toward the trees. Soon it reached the tall trees and climbed up their trunks. It burned the trees and the nests and all the Little People in them.

The men, too, had no way of escape. So all the Little People were destroyed. That is why there are no dwarfs to trouble us today.

Old Man and the Beginning of the World

CHEWING BLACKBONES, a very old grandfather, related a fragment of this creation myth in 1953, in the old language of the Blackfeet. He began with the statement that the father of Napi (Old Man) was the Sun and his mother was the Moon. The Sun sent Napi to the earth to create people and to remain with them for a while. The Blackfeet call the white man *Napi-kwan*, meaning "Old Man Person," because they first thought of him as having wonder-working powers.

OLD MAN CAME from the south, making the mountains, the prairies, and the forests as he passed along, making the birds and the animals also. He traveled northward, making things as he went, putting red paint in the ground here and there—arranging the world as we see it today.

He made the Milk River and crossed it; being tired, he went up on a little hill and lay down to rest. As he lay on his back, stretched out on the grass with his arms extended, he marked his figure with stones. You can see those rocks today; they show the shape of his body, legs, arms, and head.

Going on north after he had rested, he stumbled over a knoll and fell down on his knees. He said aloud, "You are a bad thing to make me stumble so." Then he raised up two large buttes there and named them the Knees. They are called the Knees to this day. He went on farther north, and with some of the rocks he carried with him he built the Sweet Grass Hills.

Old Man covered the plains with grass for the animals to feed on. He marked off a piece of ground and in it made all kinds of roots and berries to grow—camas, carrots, turnips, bitterroot, serviceberries, bullberries, cherries, plums, and rosebuds. He planted trees, and he put all kinds of animals on the ground.

When he created the bighorn sheep with its big head and horns, he made it out on the prairie. But it did not travel easily on the prairie; it was awkward and could not go fast. So Old Man took it by its horns, led it up into the mountains, and turned it loose. There the bighorn skipped about among the rocks and went up fearful places with ease. So Old Man said to it, "This is the kind of place that suits you; this is what you are fitted for, the rocks and the mountains."

While he was in the mountains, he made the antelope out of dirt and turned it loose, to see how it would go. It ran so fast that it fell over some rocks and hurt itself. Seeing that the mountains were not the place for it, Old Man took the antelope down to the prairie and turned it loose. When he saw it running away fast and gracefully, he said, "This is what you are suited to, the broad prairie."

One day Old Man decided that he would make a woman and a child. So he formed them both of clay, the woman and the child, her son. After he had molded the clay in human shape, he said to it, "You must be people." And then he covered it up and went away. The next morning he went to the place, took off the covering, and saw that the shapes had changed a little. The second morning he saw more change, and the third morning he saw still more. The fourth morning he went to the place, took off the covering, looked at the images, and said, "Arise and walk." They did so. They walked down to the river with their maker, and then he told them that his name was *Napi*, Old Man.

That is how we came to be people. It is he who made us.

The first people were poor and naked, and they did not know how to do anything for themselves. Old Man showed them the roots and berries and said, "You can eat these." Then he pointed to certain trees. "When the bark of these trees is young and tender, it is good. Then you can peel it off and eat it."

He told the people that the animals also should be their food. "These are your herds," he said. "All these little animals that live on the ground—squirrels, rabbits, skunks, beavers—are good to eat. You need not fear to eat their flesh. All the birds that fly—these, too, I have made for you, so that you can eat of their flesh."

Old Man took the first people over the prairies and through the forests and the swamps, to show them the different plants he had created. He told them what herbs were good for sicknesses, saying often, "The root of this herb or the leaf of this herb, if gathered in a certain month of the year, is good for a certain sickness." In that way the people learned the power of all herbs.

Then he showed them how to make weapons with which to kill the animals for their food. First he went out and cut some service-berry shoots, brought them in, and peeled the bark off them. He took one of the larger shoots, flattened it, tied a string to it, and thus made a bow. Then he caught one of the birds he had made, took feathers from its wing, split them, and tied them to a shaft of wood.

At first he tied four feathers along the shaft, and with his bow sent the arrow toward its mark. But he found that it did not fly well. When he used only three feathers, it went straight to the mark. Then he went out and began to break sharp pieces off the stones. When he tried them at the ends of his arrows, he found that the black flint stones, and some white flint, made the best arrow points.

When the people had learned how to make bows and arrows, Old Man taught them how to shoot animals and birds. Because it is not healthful to eat animal flesh raw, he showed the first people how to make fire. He gathered soft, dry, rotten driftwood and made a punk of it. Then he found a piece of hard wood and drilled a hole in it with an arrow point. He gave the first man a pointed piece of hard wood and showed him how to roll it between his hands until sparks came out and the punk caught fire. Then he showed the people how to cook the meat of the animals they had killed and how to eat it.

He told them to get a certain kind of stone that was in the land, while he found a harder stone. With the harder stone he had them hollow out the softer one and so make a kettle. Thus they made their dishes.

Old Man told the first people how to get spirit power: "Go away by yourself and go to sleep. Something will come to you in your dream that will help you. It may be some animal. Whatever this animal tells you in your sleep, you must do. Obey it. Be guided by it. If later you want help, if you are traveling alone and cry aloud for help, your prayer will be answered. It may be by an eagle, perhaps by a buffalo, perhaps by a bear. Whatever animal hears your prayer, you must listen to it."

That was how the first people got along in the world, by the power given to them in their dreams.

After this, Old Man kept on traveling north. Many of the animals that he had created followed him. They understood when he spoke to them, and they were his servants. When he got to the north point of the Porcupine Mountains, he made some more mud images of people, blew his breath upon them, and they became people, men and women. They asked him, "What are we to eat?"

By way of answer, Old Man made many images of clay in the form of buffaloes. Then he blew breath upon them and they stood up. When he made signs to them, they started to run. Then he said to the people, "Those animals—buffalo—are your food."

"But how can we kill them?" the people asked.

"I will show you," he answered.

He took them to a cliff and told them to build rock piles: "Now hide behind these piles of rocks," he said. "I will lead the buffalo this way. When they are opposite you, rise up."

After telling them what to do, he started toward the herd of buffalo. When he called the animals, they started to run toward him, and they followed him until they were inside the piles of rock. Then Old Man dropped back. As the people rose up, the buffalo ran in a straight line and jumped over the cliff.

"Go down and take the flesh of those animals," said Old Man.

The people tried to tear the limbs apart, but they could not. Old Man went to the edge of the cliff, broke off some pieces with sharp edges, and told the people to cut the flesh with these rocks. They obeyed him. When they had skinned the buffalo, they set up some poles and put the hides on them. Thus they made a shelter to sleep under.

After Old Man had taught the people all these things, he started off again, traveling north until he came to where the Bow and the Elbow rivers meet. There he made some more people and taught them the same things. From there he went farther north. When he had gone almost to the Red Deer River, he was so tired that he lay down on a hill. The form of his body can be seen there yet, on the top of the hill where he rested.

When he awoke from this sleep, he traveled farther north until he came to a high hill. He climbed to the top of it and there sat down to rest. As he gazed over the country, he was greatly pleased by it. Looking at the steep hill below him, he said to himself, "This is a fine place for sliding. I will have some fun." And he began to slide down the hill. The marks where he slid are to be seen yet, and the place is known to all the Blackfeet tribes as "Old Man's Sliding Ground."

Old Man can never die. Long ago he left the Blackfeet and went away toward the west, disappearing in the mountains. Before he started, he said to the people, "I will always take care of you, and some day I will return."

Even today some people think that he spoke the truth and that when he comes back he will bring with him the buffalo, which they believe the white men have hidden. Others remember that before he left them he said that when he returned he would find them a different people. They would be living in a different world, he said, from that which he had created for them and had taught them to live in.

✻

Old Man and Old Woman

LONG, LONG AGO, there were only two persons in the world: Old Man and Old Woman. One time when they were traveling about the earth, Old Woman said to Old Man, "Now let us come to an agreement of some kind. Let us decide how the people shall live when they shall be on the earth."

"Well," replied Old Man, "I am to have the first say in everything."

"I agree with you," said Old Woman. "That is—if I may have the second say."

Then Old Man began his plans. "The women will have the duty of tanning the hides. They will rub animals' brains on the hides to make them soft, and scrape them with scraping tools. All this they will do very quickly, for it will not be hard work."

"No," said Old Woman, "I will not agree to this. They must tan hides in the way you say; but it must be very hard work, so that the good workers may be found out."

"Well," said Old Man, "we will let the people have eyes and mouths, straight up and down in their faces."

"No." replied Old Woman, "let us not have them that way. We will have the eyes and mouths in the faces, as you say, but they shall be set crosswise."

"Well," said Old Man, "the people shall have ten fingers on each hand."

"Oh, no!" replied Old Woman. "That will be too many. They will be in the way. There will be four fingers and one thumb on each hand."

So the two went on until they had provided for everything in the lives of the people who were to be.

"What shall we do about life and death?" asked Old Woman. "Should the people live forever, or should they die?"

Old Woman and Old Man had difficulty agreeing about this. Finally Old Man said, "I will tell you what we will do. I will throw a buffalo chip into the water. If it floats, the people will die for four days and then come to life again; if it sinks, they will die forever."

So he threw a buffalo chip into the water, and it floated.

"No," said Old Woman, "we will not decide in that way. I will throw this rock into the water. If it floats, the people will die for four days; if it sinks, they will die forever."

Then Old Woman threw the rock into the water, and it sank to the bottom.

"There," said she. "It is better for the people to die forever. If they did not, they would not feel sorry for each other, and there would be no sympathy in the world."

"Well," said Old Man, "let it be that way."

Old Man and the Roasted Squirrels

After a time, Old Woman had a daughter, who soon became sick and died. The mother was very sorry then that they had agreed that people should die forever. "Let us have our say over again," she said.

"No," replied Old Man. "Let us not change what we have agreed upon."

And so people have died ever since.

❄

Old Man and the Roasted Squirrels

ONE TIME as Old Man was walking along, he came to a place where many squirrels were playing in hot ashes. While some of them lay in the ashes, the others would cover them with more ashes. When the buried squirrels became so hot that they could not stand the heat any longer, they would call out to the others, who would take them out at once. After Old Man had watched them for a while, he asked that they allow him to play with them.

When the squirrels consented, he asked, "May I be baked first?"

"Oh, no," replied the squirrels. "We are afraid that you do not know how to play and that you will be burned. We will be baked first to show you how."

Old Man asked them again, but again they refused. At last Old Man agreed with them, on the condition that they would let him cover all of them at one time. "There are so many of you," he said, "that it will save time to bury all of you at once."

The squirrels consented. So he covered all of them with hot ashes except one squirrel that was about to become a mother. She begged so pitifully not to be put in the ashes that Old Man said, "Well, you may go. Run away, so that there may be other squirrels."

When all the other squirrels were well covered with ashes, some of them became too warm and called to Old Man to take them out. Instead, he heaped on more ashes and roasted them to death.

Then Old Man took some red willows and made a scaffold on which he laid his roasted squirrels. They made the willows greasy, and that is why the red willow is greasy even to this day. He ate as

241

many of the squirrels as he could. In fact, he ate so many that he lay down beside a tree and fell asleep.

While he was asleep, Lynx came along and ate all the other squirrels left on the scaffold. When Old Man awoke and found his roasted meat gone, he followed Lynx and after a while found him fast asleep. Old Man was so angry that he seized Lynx by the ears and shortened his head by hammering it against a stone. He pulled out the long tail and, breaking it in two, stuck the brush part on the rump. He stretched the legs and body of Lynx until they were long and slender. Then Old Man threw him on the ground and said to him, "You bobcats will always have a bobtail. You will always be so short-winded that you will never be able to run far."

Old Man then realized that he had been burned by the hot ashes. So he called upon the wind to blow. Because the cool air made him feel better, he continued calling upon it to blow harder and harder. Soon the wind was so fierce that he was blown away. Every tree that he caught hold of was torn up by the roots, and he could not stop himself until he grasped a birch tree. When the wind died down and Old Man rested, he spoke angrily to the birch tree: "Why have you such strong roots? Why can you not be pulled up like other trees? I was having a good time being blown around by the wind, until you spoiled my fun."

He was so angry that he drew his stone knife and gashed the birch bark all over. That is why the bark of a birch tree always has such a nicked appearance.

※

Scar Face and the Sun Dance of the Blackfeet

THE VERSION of this tradition recorded by McClintock from the Canadian Blackfeet begins with the widespread "Star-Husband" theme, part of a story later in this section. Scar Face, in the Canadian version, was the son of a mortal woman and Morning Star. (Morning Star is said to be Venus; Mistaken Morning Star, Jupiter.) Sun, Moon, Morning Star, the removal of the scar from the face of the hero—all are recognized in some way in the Blackfoot Sun Dance.

Scar Face and the Sun Dance of the Blackfeet

ONCE A VERY POOR YOUNG MAN lived with his sister. In the same camp with them lived a pretty girl, the daughter of a chief. All of the young warriors of the tribe wanted to marry her, including the poor young man. But he had a long, ugly scar on his cheek and so was afraid to speak to the girl. One day Scar Face asked his sister to go over to the chief's lodge and try to persuade the daughter to marry him.

When his sister returned, she said to her brother, "The girl laughed at you because of your ugliness, but she says that she is willing to marry you whenever you get rid of the scar."

Very much hurt, the young man decided to go away and seek someone who could remove his scar. Though he traveled long, no one could tell where to go for help. At last he determined to go to the Sun, and so traveled on and on and on. The farther he went, the blacker the people became. As he went along he asked for the Sun's house. Always he was told to go on until he came to a very high ridge, where some people lived who could tell him the whereabouts of the Sun's house.

At last Scar Face came to this ridge. There a man with black skin and curly hair told him that at the end of the ridge he would find Sun's lodge. As he traveled along, he saw a man standing alone.

"Where are you going?" he called to Scar Face.

"I am going to the Sun."

"Oh! the Sun is my father. There is his house," answered the other. "My name is Morning Star. My father is not a good man. He is not at home now, but when he comes in the morning he will surely kill you. However, I will talk with my mother, who is a good woman and will treat you kindly."

Then Morning Star took Scar Face up to his father's lodge and said to his mother, the Moon, "Mother, I have brought a strange young man here. I wish him for a companion. He has come a long way to find us, and I hope that you will take pity on him, so that I may enjoy his company."

"Bring him in," replied his mother. "We will talk to your father when he returns, but I fear we shall not be able to keep the young man."

243

When Scar Face was taken into the lodge, he saw on the ground a kind of earthen square, some cedar brush, and buffalo chips. This was the Sun's smudge place. After a time Moon asked Scar Face, "Is there anything you especially want?"

"Yes, I want this scar taken from my face."

When it was about time for her husband to return, Moon took Scar Face to one side of the lodge and covered him with cedar boughs. Soon he began to feel warm, because Sun was approaching. He began to shift about under the cedar, but Moon whispered that he must be quiet. So he lay very still, becoming hotter and hotter as the Sun came nearer. At last the woman whispered, "Now Sun is at the door."

Sun looked into the lodge and exclaimed, "Phew! My, this lodge smells bad!"

"Yes," said Moon. "Morning Star has a chum here."

"Well," said Sun, "make a smudge with cedar."

After Moon had made a smudge with cedar, Sun entered the lodge. Now Scar Face was very hot. Sun asked, "Where is that young man?"

"We covered him up," replied Moon.

"Come," called Sun. "Get up."

Then Scar Face came out from under the cedar, but he could not look Sun in the face. As Sun looked upon him, he knew that this was a poor, unfortunate boy and took pity on him. The heat then grew less.

Morning Star was out on one of his journeys, and so Sun waited for his return. When Morning Star came into the lodge and sat down in his usual place, his father said to him, "Son, do you wish this young man for a companion?"

"Yes, I do. Very much. I would like to have a companion to go around with me. I am lonely on my journeys."

"Well, you must make a sweat house," replied his father.

So Morning Star went out and prepared a sweat house. When all was ready, Sun went out. At the back of his head, he had a metal disk that looked like brass. He went into the sweat house and began to wipe off the metal disk. Then he asked Morning Star and Scar Face to come into the sweat house. When they were in, the covers were closed down. After a while, the covers were raised and light came in. The two young men looked alike.

When Moon came out to the entrance of the sweat house, Sun asked her, "Which is Morning Star?"

Moon looked at them for a moment and then pointed at one. But she made a mistake; she pointed at Scar Face.

"Oh!" said Sun. "You are a foolish woman. This is the star you mistook for Morning Star. After this, his name shall be The-One-You-Took-for-Morning-Star."

Now Scar Face stayed with his new companion at the lodge of Sun and Moon. Sun told him that he could go anywhere in the sky-land except straight west or straight down. But one morning when Morning Star and Scar Face were out together, Scar Face said, "Let us go that way," pointing to the west.

"No, it is dangerous. My father said that we must not go there."

"Let us go anyway."

Morning Star refused, but at the fourth request, he said, "All right. Let's go."

So the two boys went toward the west and soon came to a place where there were seven large white geese. At once the birds attacked them. Morning Star immediately ran away, calling back to his friend, "Now you see."

But Scar Face did not run. Instead, he killed the seven geese with his club and then went home. When he overtook Morning Star, he said, "There is no danger now. I have killed all of the birds."

When they reached home, Morning Star told his mother what Scar Face had done, but she said, "I will not believe you until you get their heads."

So the boys returned and took the heads of the seven birds.

Some time afterward, when the two went out together as before, Scar Face said, "Let us go that way again." He pointed to the west.

"No, let's not. It will be more dangerous than before."

Scar Face insisted and, after the fourth request, Morning Star consented. As they were going along, they saw seven cranes. When the birds saw them, they started toward the boys angrily. The cranes were terrible-looking birds, and Scar Face was badly frightened. But he took off his robe and held it in front of him. As the cranes came up, they began to peck at the robe. Then Scar Face struck them one by one with his club.

When the young man reached home, Sun asked him where he had been. "While I was walking along, some large cranes took after me, and I killed them with my club."

"I will not believe you until you show me their heads," replied Sun.

So Scar Face returned to the place where he had fought the cranes, and brought back with him the seven heads. Sun not only believed him but was so pleased by the boy's courage that he brought out a bundle.

"Here are some clothes for you," said Sun. "A shirt and leggings. These I give you because you killed some very dangerous and troublesome birds."

The breast and the back of the shirt were decorated with rosettes made of porcupine quills; these represented the sun. The side seams of the leggings and of the sleeves were decorated with strips of quill work and with hair fringes; the fringes represented the scalps of the cranes killed by Scar Face.

On the leggings Sun painted seven black stripes, saying to Scar Face, "I make these here as a sign that you killed seven enemies. All your people shall wear black stripes on their leggings when they kill enemies."

Then Sun taught Scar Face a few songs that were to go with the clothing.

After a time the boy said to Sun, "Now I should like to return to my people. I have been here long enough."

"All right. You may go. And I will give you some messages to take to your people."

Sun gave Scar Face instructions about the sweat house, the Sun Dance, and the making of the Sun Dance lodge. He gave Scar Face a circle of creeping juniper, saying, "The woman that gives the Sun Dance will wear this circle of creeping juniper in her hair."

Sun also handed him a necklace, in the center of which were strung two small shells and a lock of hair. "This necklace," he said, "is to be worn by the husband of the woman who gives the Sun Dance."

"When you return to your people and wish to make an offering to me," continued Sun, "you must first build a sweat house and there make offerings. Then I will hear your prayers and accept them. You may also make offerings to me in the Sun Dance lodge, which some people will call the Medicine Lodge."

He covered the face of Scar Face with red paint, drew a black circle around his face, a black dot on the bridge of his nose, and a black streak around each wrist. "This is the way people must paint themselves when they wish to make offerings to me in the Sun Dance Lodge. For the victory or scalp dance they must paint their faces black."

Then Sun put a hoop or ring of cedar round the head of Scar Face. Immediately the young man found that he could see down to his people. "Now shut your eyes," said Sun.

When Scar Face opened his eyes, he found himself descending to the camp of his people. He saw that some of them were playing the wheel-and-arrow game. One of the players, looking up, saw a black object coming down from the sky. He called out, "Oh, look at that black thing!"

All of the players stopped to look. They watched the object coming closer and saw it touch the ground a little distance from them. It appeared to be a person. Then a good friend of Scar Face recognized him and rushed toward him. But Scar Face called out, "Go back! Go back! Do not touch me! You must first get some willows and make a sweat house out here away from the camp."

His friend went back to the players and explained. All helped him prepare a sweat house. When everything was ready, Scar Face went into the sweat house with a bundle of clothing given him by Sun. When he had taken the sweat bath, he came out, carrying the bundle in his arms. He said to his chum, "My friend Sun gave me these clothes. Now I give them to you."

This is why our people say that the sweat house came from the Sun. The medicine lodge we make at the Sun Dance is the lodge of the

Sun, where Scar Face had been. It faces the east, just as Sun's lodge does. The suit that Scar Face gave to his chum was just like those you see at the Sun Dance today. Scar Face directed that only persons who have done great deeds should be permitted to wear such a suit.

After a while Scar Face went back to the sky world and became a star. We call him Mistaken Morning Star.

For many years after the time of Scar Face, the Blackfeet took scalps to prove that they had killed enemies, and they counted coups at the Sun Dance.

⌘

Two Medicine Creek and Chief Mountain

Two Medicine Valley, in the northeast corner of what is now Glacier National Park, was a favorite camping ground of some bands of Blood Indians. It is a picturesque spot featuring three lakes with creeks connecting them and other creeks flowing into them. Percy Creighton, a member of the Tribal Council on the Blood Reserve, Alberta, heard from his elders, years ago, the following legend about the area and the Sun Lodge. His story has been transcribed from a tape recording made in 1953. By "the Nature," Mr. Creighton referred to the supernatural, the spirit power.

In the long ago time, the Indians were starving. They traveled up and down, all through the country. All they could find was deer, elk, and rabbit, and not enough of them for food for everyone. They couldn't find any buffalo. The women went around picking berries and digging up roots, just anything they could find that could be eaten. But the country was dry. It had not rained for so long that there were few berries, and the roots were small and shriveled.

Finally the Indians came to Two Medicine River. At that time it was not called Two Medicine River. They camped there, and from the camp the young men went out looking for berries and roots. But little food was to be had. The children were hungry. The people grew discouraged.

One night a woman of the camp had a dream. The Dream Person

came to her and said, "You will make a Sun Lodge. Then the Nature will show you where you will find buffalo."

The Dream Person went away. Next morning, when the woman woke up, she told her husband about her dream and about the order of the Dream Person. Immediately her husband said to her, "Cook all the food we have. I will invite the elder men of the camp for a council."

While she cooked, he went out and called on the elder men. They came together in his lodge, and he told them about his wife's dream. They talked over the matter and decided that they must follow the dream. "That is how the Nature will show us how to keep from starving. Before we die, we must follow the order of the Nature. Come, let us build the Sun Lodge."

So they did. They put it up and when it was all finished, they went through the ceremony. "We have no buffalo tongues for the ceremony," the women said, "but we will go through it without them."

So they did. After it was all over—the ceremony takes three or four days—the woman was very tired. She had been fasting and praying all that time, and had had almost no rest. After she was home in her tipi, in bed and asleep, the same Dream Person came to her again. "You must build another Sun Lodge in the same place," the Dream Person told her. "It is the order of the Nature."

Next morning she told her husband what the Dream Person had said to her. Of course her husband gathered all the elder men in his lodge. "Now what shall we do? We've already built one Sun Lodge. But my wife has dreamed that she must build another one."

The elder folks said, "It's the order of the Nature. We'll have to build another one. It won't take long."

So they built another one. The whole encampment got together and built another Sun Lodge, and they went through the ceremonial as usual.

The second night after they had finished the Sun Lodge ceremony, the woman's husband had a dream. The same Dream Person appeared to him. "Get the outstanding young men from your camp," said the Dream Person. "Take a small group of them to the outstanding mountain—that's Chief Mountain. Let the young men stay at the bottom, and you go up on top of the mountain to fast and pray."

So the man did as he was told. He called together certain ones who he knew were very skillful hunters. All went with him to Chief Mountain. At the bottom of the peak he said to them, "You stay here while I go up to fast and pray."

He climbed the mountain and there he stayed all afternoon and all night, fasting and praying. Then he slept up there. In his sleep the Dream Person came to him again. "Now I am going to show you where the buffalo are," said the Dream Person. And he stretched out his left hand toward the Cypress Hills.

As he stretched out his hand, the Dream Person told the man, "You take your group toward Cypress Hill. On your way it will cloud up and it will begin to rain. Before you get to the hill, you will meet buffalo. The rain will bring them along toward you."

The man went down the mountain and told the young men about his dream. As soon as they heard what the Dream Person had said, the young men exclaimed, "Let's go!" And they started to the northeast toward the Cypress Hills. On their way the sky became covered with dark clouds. Before they had gone very far, it began to rain. They kept on going toward the Cypress Hills. Once in a while, one of them would say, "That's just what the Nature told the big man when he was on Chief Mountain." They kept on going, kept traveling one or two days. Then someone pointed toward the northeast and asked, "What's that long black line against the sky?"

"That's buffalo!" the others shouted.

So they met the buffalo right there, just as the Dream Person had said. Some of the young men went on to do the killing. Some went back to the camp to tell the people they had seen the buffalo—plenty of buffalo. The famine was over. They were saved from starvation.

So the people called that river Two Medicine River, because in the long ago days they had built two Sun Lodges on its banks. They knew there was a person up on Chief Mountain. They call it Chief Mountain because it is an outstanding mountain and because the Dream Person lives up there. That is where the big man of their tribe prayed and fasted.

That's the Blood Indians' story, their real story, of Two Medicine River and Chief Mountain. The Medicine Lakes were named by the white people much, much later.

Many years after those two Sun lodges were built there, two lodges were built again along Two Medicine River. The Piegans had gathered there and were just about ready to set up a Sun Lodge. From the north, the Blood Indians were on their way to set up a Sun Lodge there, too. When they reached the Cut Bank River, they sent young men ahead with tobacco for the Piegans and a request. "Ask them to wait for us. Tell them we're on our way. If they will wait, we can set up our lodges together and have the Sun Dance together."

So the young men took the tobacco. The Piegans liked to get their tobacco from the north, for we have stronger tobacco than they have. The messengers gave the tobacco to the Sun priests. "The Bloods are at Cut Bank," they told the priests. "They will be here tomorrow or the next day. They sent us ahead to ask you to wait so that we can all have the ceremony together."

"Tell them we will wait for them," the priests replied.

But after the young Bloods had started back, one priest objected. You know how there is always someone who wants to do the opposite thing. "We've already started our lodge," a certain Sun priest said. "Let's go on with it. When the Bloods get here, they can build their lodge beside ours."

So the Piegans went on with their Sun Lodge, and when the Bloods reached Two Medicine River they built theirs. Soon there were two circles of tipis and two Sun Lodges along the river. One was built by the Piegans and one by the Bloods. The first time, we were all mixed up—the Bloods and Piegans and Blackfeet were all camped there together in the Two Medicine Valley.

❈

Origin of the Medicine Pipe

THE BLOOD INDIANS have had a medicine pipe for a long time. There is one pipe among them that is so old that no one has any recollection of having heard of its being made by anyone. So this pipe must be the real one handed down by the Thunder, for all medicine pipes came from the Thunder.

Once there was a girl who never would marry because her parents could not find anyone good enough for her. One day she heard the Thunder roll. "Well," she said, "I will marry him."

Not long afterward she went out with her mother to gather wood. When they were ready to go home, the girl's pack strap broke. She tied it together and started, but it broke again. Her mother became impatient; and when the pack strap broke the third time, she said, "I will not wait for you."

The girl started after her mother, but the strap broke again. While she was tying it together, a handsome young man in fine dress stepped out of the brush and said, "I want you to go away with me."

"Why do you talk to me like that?" asked the girl. "I have never had anything to do with you."

"You said you would marry me," he answered, "and now I have come for you."

The girl began to cry. "Then you must be the Thunder," she said.

He told the girl to shut her eyes and not to look. She obeyed. When he told her to open her eyes, she found herself upon a high mountain. On it was a lodge. When she went in, she saw many seats around the side but only two people—an old man and an old woman.

When the girl took a seat, the old man said, "That girl smells bad."

"You should not speak in that way about your daughter-in-law," said the old woman.

"I will look at her," he said. When he looked up, the lightning flashed about the girl but did not harm her. So the old man knew that she belonged to the family. At night all the family came in, one by one. The Thunder then made a smudge with sweet-pine needles, one at the door of the lodge and one just back of the fire. He taught his wife how to bring in the bundle that hung outside. This contained the medicine pipe.

After several moons the girl gave birth to a boy. Many moons later she gave birth to a second boy.

One evening the Thunder asked her if she ever thought of her father and mother.

"Yes, I do."

"Would you like to see them?"

"Yes. Very much," she replied.

"Tonight we will go," he said. "You may tell them that I shall send them my medicine pipe, that they may live long."

When night came, he again told her to close her eyes, and soon she was standing near the lodge of her people. It was dark when she went in and sat down by her mother. After a while she said to her mother, "Do you know me?"

"No."

"I am your daughter. I married the Thunder."

At once the mother called in all their relatives. They came and sat around the lodge.

"I cannot stay long," the girl said, "for I must go back to my lodge and my children. The Thunder has promised to give you his medicine pipe. In four days I will return with it."

She left the lodge and disappeared.

In four days, the Thunder came back with the woman, their two boys, and the pipe. Then the ceremony of transferring the pipe took place. When it was finished, the Thunder said, "I am going away, but I will return in the spring. You must save tobacco and berries for me and pray over them."

Then he took the younger boy and left the lodge. A cloud rolled away, and as it went the people heard one loud thunder made by the father and one faint one, made by the little boy.

Now when the Thunder threatens, the people often say, "For the sake of your youngest child," and Thunder heeds their prayers.

When the Thunder left the woman and the older child, he said that if dogs ever attempted to bite them, they would disappear. One day a dog rushed into the lodge and snapped at the boy. After that nothing was ever seen of him or of his mother. To this day the owner of the medicine pipe is afraid of dogs.

❊

Origin of the Beaver Medicine Bundle

THE ELABORATE Beaver Medicine Ceremonial of the Blackfeet is described fully by Walter McClintock in *The Old North Trail*. Owner of the Beaver Medicine Bundle, and also high priest of the Sun Dance, was Chief Mad Wolf; he ceremonially adopted McClintock as his son and gave him a name which means "White Weasel Moccasin."

After the white man observed the Beaver Medicine Ceremonial the first time, Chief Mad Wolf said to him, "When I was a young man, I, too, became interested in the mysteries of the medicine, which have been taught me by old Indians, and what they told me I know to be true. I have never before explained those mysteries to white men, because I have been afraid to trust them. I am now willing to have you repeat these to the white race, because I know you will speak the truth and because I feel toward you as a father to his son. . . .

"What I tell you happened long ago, when our people made all of their tools and weapons from stone, and when they used dogs instead of horses for beasts of burden."

McClintock wrote that it is difficult for a white person to realize "the deep solemnity with which the Indians opened the sacred Bundle. To them it was a moment of deepest reverence and religious feeling."

I N THOSE DAYS, long ago, there were two orphan brothers, Akaiyan and Nopastis. Akaiyan, the younger, lived with Nopastis, who was married to a woman with an evil heart. She disliked Akaiyan, and every day she urged her husband to cast his brother off. One day when Nopastis came home, he found his wife with her clothes torn and her body mangled.

"While you were away," the woman said, "your brother treated me brutally."

Saying nothing to his brother, Nopastis planned how he could get rid of Akaiyan forever. In the middle of the summer, when the ducks and geese were dropping their feathers, he suggested to his younger brother that they go together to an island in a large lake.

"At this time," said Nopastis, "many ducks and geese will be there. We can gather the feathers they have dropped and use them for our arrows."

When they came to the lake, they built a raft by binding logs together with buffalo rawhide. Then they floated on it to an island far out from shore. There Akaiyan wandered off alone. As he was returning to the beach with his arms full of feathers, he was surprised to see his brother out on the lake, going toward the mainland.

"Do not leave me here!" Akaiyan called to his brother. "Do not leave me to perish on this island."

"You deserve no pity," Nopastis called back. "You have treated my wife brutally."

"I have not. I solemnly swear before the Sun that I have never harmed her."

Heartlessly Nopastis replied, "You can live alone on the island all winter. When spring comes, I will return to pick up your bones."

Akaiyan sat down and cried in despair. Then he called upon the animals and the spirits of the water to help him. He also prayed to the Sun, Moon, and Stars:

Behold, O Sun! I cast away whatever of bad I have done.
O Moon! O Stars! Pity me! Give me strength!

After this prayer, Akaiyan felt calmer and stronger. Walking around the island, he found a few branches and built a shelter. He also gathered many feathers, piled them up, and made a bed that fitted his body so well that he slept warm on the coldest nights. Before the ducks and geese started south, he killed many. Some of them he kept for his winter food; others he skinned and made a warm robe for himself by binding the skins together with alder bark.

One day he found a beaver lodge in a spot on the island where he had never been before. For a long time he lay watching it and weeping to himself. At last a little beaver came out of the lodge and said to him, "My father wants you to come into our lodge."

Akaiyan followed the little beaver into the lodge and there saw a big beaver with his wife and family seated around him. The father beaver was white from the snows of many winters, and so large that the man knew he must be the chief of the whole Beaver tribe.

"Be seated," said the Beaver Chief. "Why are you alone on this island?"

"I have been treated unjustly and have been left alone here to die."

The Beaver Chief tried to comfort him. "My son, the time will soon come when we will close up our lodge for the winter. The lake will freeze over, and we will not go out again until the warm winds of spring have broken up the ice. Stay with us here in our lodge. We will teach you many wonderful things. When you return home, you can take with you knowledge that will be of great value to your people."

The beavers were so kind that Akaiyan decided to stay with them. He took into the lodge with him many ducks and geese for food and his bird skin robe to keep him warm. Before the weather turned cold, the beavers closed their lodge, leaving at the top a hole for air. During the coldest days and nights the beavers lay close to Akaiyan and placed their tails across his body to keep him warm. He made friends with the whole family, but he liked best the smallest and youngest beaver. Little Beaver was the favorite also of Beaver Chief.

The family taught Akaiyan the names of herbs and roots which the Blackfeet still use to cure our people when they are sick. They showed him, also, different paints and explained their use, saying, "If you should use these, they will bring your people good luck and will keep sickness and death away." They gave him the seeds of tobacco and taught him how to plant them with songs and prayers. He saw many dances belonging to their medicines, and he listened carefully to their songs and prayers. Beaver Chief and his wife taught Akaiyan the prayers and songs and dances of their own medicine, saying to him, "If you will give this Beaver Medicine Ceremonial when any of your people are sick or dying, they will be restored to health."

Akaiyan noticed that the beavers never ate during their ceremonial, that they beat time with their tails, and that they always stopped when they heard any suspicious noise, just as they do when they are working. They made scratches on the wall of the lodge to mark the days and then marked the moons with a stick. "We count seven moons," they said, "between the time when the leaves fall and the time when we open the lodge in the spring. When we hear the ice breaking in the lake, we know it will soon be time for us to leave our winter home."

One day Little Beaver said to Akaiyan, "Before you leave us, my father will offer you a gift and allow you to choose anything within the lodge. When he asks you for your choice, you say that you will take your little brother. He will ask you four times to choose something else, but you must take me with you because I have more power to help you than any of the others have."

When the ducks and geese were flying north, the beavers opened their lodge for the summer. Then Beaver Chief said to Akaiyan, "You will soon be leaving us, because it is time for your older brother to return to the island. Before you start, I want you to choose something, anything, from my lodge to take with you."

Remembering the advice of Little Beaver, Akaiyan replied, "I would like to have your youngest child."

Four times the Beaver Chief tried to persuade him to take something else, and four times Akaiyan asked only for Little Beaver. After the fourth reply, Beaver Chief said, "My son, you show great wisdom in your choice. I am sorry to see him go, for he is my best worker and the wisest of my children. But because of my promise, I will let you take him."

"When you return to your people," Beaver Chief continued, "make a sacred Bundle like the one you saw us using in our ceremonial. We will teach you the songs and prayers and dances that belong to that Bundle. When any of your people are sick or dying, if a relative will make a vow to the Beaver Medicine, the sick person will be restored to health."

One evening, when Beaver Chief returned from his cutting, he said to Akaiyan, "My son, stay in the lodge tomorrow and do not show yourself. Today when I was among the trees on the shore of the mainland, I saw your brother's camp."

The next day, watching from the lodge, Akaiyan and Little Beaver saw Nopastis coming to the island on the raft. They saw him land and walk along the shore, looking for his brother's bones. Then Akaiyan, with Little Beaver under his arm, ran to the shore and got on the raft. They were far out on the lake before Nopastis saw them. The older brother then realized that Akaiyan had power stronger than his own and had become a great medicine man.

When Akaiyan reached the tribal camp, he went at once to the head chief's lodge and told his story. All the people received him with honor when they learned of the wisdom and power that had been given him by the Beavers. He gathered together a Beaver Bundle just as the Beaver Chief had directed. All winter he and Little Beaver taught the people the songs, prayers, and dances given him by the Beaver family.

When spring came, Akaiyan invited all the animal people to add their power to the Beaver Bundle. Many animals and birds of the prairies and of the mountains offered their skins and taught him their songs, prayers, and dances to accompany the skins, just as the Beavers had done. Elk and his wife each gave him a song and a dance, as did also Moose and his wife. Woodpecker gave three songs with his dance. Of all the animal people, only Frog could neither dance nor sing, and therefore is not represented in the Bundle. Turtle could not dance and had no song, but he borrowed from Lizard, who owned two songs.

The following spring Akaiyan returned to the island with Little Beaver. He saw his older brother's bones on the shore and knew that the Beavers had not helped him. The Beaver Chief gave him a warm welcome. And when he gave Little Beaver back to his father, the Chief was so grateful that he presented Akaiyan with a sacred pipe and taught him the songs, prayers, and dances that belonged with it. When he reached home, Akaiyan added the sacred pipe to the Beaver Bundle.

Every spring Akaiyan went across to the island to visit his friends the Beavers, and each time the Beaver Chief gave him something to add to the Beaver Bundle. Akaiyan led the Beaver Medicine Ceremonial as long as he lived, and he was known as a great medicine man. When he died, the ceremonial was continued by his son, and it has been handed down ever since.

✖

Origin of the Sacred Buffalo Horn

FOR MANY YEARS the Sacred Buffalo Horn was the most treasured possession of the clan of Water Busters among the Gros Ventres. In 1938 it was given to the Museum of the American Indian in New York City. At that time, an old Gros Ventre named Foolish Bear told about this experience his grandfather had had when a boy.

WHEN MY GRANDFATHER was about twelve years of age, his uncle returned one day from a buffalo hunt. It was winter, and snow was falling.

"You may water the horses," the uncle said to the boy.

On the way to the river and on the way back, the boy was scared, for he was very timid. Seeing a buffalo's carcass along the path, he crawled into it, between the ribs, and slept there that night.

The next morning when he returned home, his uncle asked him why he had not come back right after watering the horses.

"I just didn't come home," he answered. "That's all."

The boy himself did not know what had taken place during the night he spent in the buffalo's carcass, but later he realized that the spirit of the buffalo had entered his own body. After a while, the boy smelled incense from a mossy weed at the base of a nearby pine tree. Then the spirit of the buffalo within him moved, and something came up from his system and out of his mouth.

It was a buffalo horn. By a sign, it indicated what kind of herb should be used as incense. When the plant was brought and the incense was burned, the boy inhaled it and the horn went back into his body.

When the uncle saw what had happened, he rebuked the boy. "You are very foolish. You must put a stop to this nonsense."

Then the boy asked that more incense be burned. Again he inhaled it. This time the tip of the nose of the buffalo was expelled from his mouth. Then the feet. Then the tail. Each came out separately. The entire buffalo was not expelled.

That night when the boy was asleep, he dreamed that he was inside a tipi and that he heard the barking of dogs and the tread of a buffalo's feet coming closer and closer. After a while the sounds reached his tipi, and the buffalo opened the door with the tip of his nose.

"I am doing all this for your benefit, my son," said the buffalo. "Look at me."

The boy did not want to look at it, but he did. He saw that it had been wounded. It had been pierced with arrows and with bullets, and blood was flowing down both sides. As the animal moved toward the boy, arrows and bullets dropped from its flesh.

"If you will take care of my wounds now," said the buffalo, "I will make you able to heal yourself whenever you are wounded."

So the boy bound up the wounds of his visitor.

When years had passed and he took part in battles and was injured, he was able to heal himself. A buffalo horn became his sacred possession.

He lived to be an old man, my grandfather did. Before he died, he gave the horn to his son, my father, whose name was Sittingbird. It was a token of sacredness. When I became twenty-four years of age, my father passed the horn on to me. I have had it in my possession for sixty years, for I am now eighty-four years old.

✼

The Legend of the Snow Tipi

DURING A TEN-DAY STORM of wind and snow, Walter McClintock heard his Blackfeet companions tell "many thrilling stories of war and adventure, also of strange and unearthly experiences with disembodied spirits. The storytelling generally began in the evening, continuing far into the night. . . . They are superstitiously opposed to relating legends in daylight and insist that they should be told after dark and in the winter time."

One night, after a long silence around the lodge fire, Chief Mad Wolf told the following legend.

WE BLACKFEET HAVE a Snow Tipi that was given us by the Maker of Storms and Blizzards. It has such great spirit power that whenever it is pitched, cold weather and winds are sure to come. What I am about to tell you happened many years ago, after the moon of the colored leaves.

The ducks and geese had flown south, the last of their flocks having disappeared many days before. It was past the time of the beginning of winter, but the air at noon was warm and the sky was cloudless.

One morning, a band of hunters were running buffalo on a broad plain. Sacred Otter and his young son, Morning Plume, had been successful and had begun at once to skin their buffalo. The men were so busy that they did not notice an approaching storm.

When they had finished skinning a large buffalo bull, Sacred Otter saw a heavy black cloud hanging low in the northern horizon and extending high into the sky. As he and his son watched, the cloud began spreading out and rolling over and over. Soon they saw a low, flying mass of clouds advancing rapidly over the plain.

"It is a blizzard!" exclaimed the father. "And there is no chance for escape!"

They lay on the ground beside the dead buffalo bull, but the cloud became so intense that Sacred Otter knew they would soon be frozen. He took the fresh buffalo hide and made a low shelter behind the carcass. Then both men crawled inside. Soon the frozen hide was covered with deep snow, and the men inside the shelter lay warm and comfortable.

When Sacred Otter fell asleep, he dreamed that he was traveling alone on the plains. In the distance stood a large tipi—a decorated tipi, he discovered as he came nearer. Its top was yellow like the sunlight. On each side, clusters of seven stars had been painted to represent the north, from which the blizzards come. At the back of the tipi was a red disk, representing the sun; to its center was attached the tail of the sacred buffalo.

At the bottom of the tipi, the rolling ridges of the prairie had been painted with their rounded tops. There was also a broad yellow band decorated with green disks to represent the color of holes in ice. Beneath the yellow top, where the four main lodge poles stood, four green claws with yellow legs had been painted. They represented Thunderbird. Above the door, which was made of spotted buffalo calfskin, was a buffalo head painted red, with black horns and ice-green eyes. Horsetails were tied over the door, on both sides. Fastened to the ends of both ear poles of the tipi were bunches of grass attached to small bells that tinkled whenever the wind blew.

While Sacred Otter was studying these picture paintings, he heard a voice. It asked, "Who is that walking around my tipi? Why do you not enter?"

So, lifting the door flap, Sacred Otter entered. Seated at the back of the lodge, and smoking alone, was a large, handsome man crowned with white hair and dressed in a long, white robe. Sacred Otter sat near the door and looked around the lodge anxiously while the white-robed man smoked in silence. In front of him was an altar of fresh earth with juniper branches laid on top. Smoke was rising like incense from a hot coal close to the altar.

Sacred Otter noticed that the man's face was painted yellow except for a red line across his mouth and another across his eyes to his ears. In one hand he held a yellow medicine stick. In his back hair he wore a black feather, and around his waist were strips of otter skin with small bells attached. Beside him lay a tobacco sack which also was made of minkskin. He smoked a black stone pipe, the stem of which had been blackened with fire.

After smoking a long time in silence, the man behind the altar began a long speech to Sacred Otter.

"I am the Maker of Cold Weather, and this is the Snow Tipi or Yellow Paint Lodge. I bring the cold storms, the whirling snow, and the biting winds from the north. And I control them at my will.

"I have called you to my lodge because I have taken pity on you. I am going to help you for the sake of your son Morning Plume, who was caught in the blizzard with you. I now give you the Snow Tipi with its decorations and its medicines.

"With it I give you also the minkskin tobacco pouch, the black stone pipe, and my supernatural power. You and your son will not die in the storm. Your lives will be spared. When you return to your camp, make a tipi just like the one you are in now."

Then the Cold Maker explained to Sacred Otter the decorations to be used in the painting and advised him to remember them carefully. He also taught the man the songs and the ceremonial to be used when transferring the tipi to anyone else.

"Always wear the minkskin as a charm whenever you go to war," continued the white-robed man. "The horsetails which hang over the door will bring you good luck, both in keeping your own horses and in getting others from the enemy."

Then Sacred Otter awoke from his sleep. He saw that the storm was abating—that the Cold Maker was already keeping his promise. After a while he and his son returned to their people.

At their winter camp he made a model of the Snow Tipi, painted it just as the Cold Maker had directed, and gathered together the medicines necessary for the ceremonial. In the spring, the time when the Blackfeet make their new lodges, Sacred Otter made and painted the Snow Tipi.

During the following winter, the Blackfeet found that the supernatural power which Sacred Otter had received from the Cold Maker was very great. When the snows were deep, they were camped near the mouth of the Cutback Canyon. When meat became scarce, a band of hunters and their families crossed the high plateau to hunt on the North Fork of Milk River. They killed a few buffalo and, while skinning them, were caught in a blizzard. All around them was an exposed plain. No shelter was in sight. They did find a few small willows with which they built a fire to thaw out the frozen hides.

Part of the band started back toward their village, but they soon lost their way. After wandering around in a circle, they came back to the place they had started from. As the small fire of willows burned low, the men held a council. It was useless, they decided, to try to cross the high plateau in such a storm. But if they should stay where they were, they knew that all would be frozen to death.

Morning Plume, remembering the previous experience with his father, said to Sacred Otter, "Will you not try the power given you by the Cold Maker? If his medicine is strong, now is the time to use it."

"I did not come from the Sun," replied Sacred Otter. "How can I drive back the blizzard?"

"Try your power," urged Morning Plume. "For the sake of our women and children, I call upon you for help."

Sacred Otter had with him the minkskin tobacco pouch and the black pipe given him by the Cold Maker. When he was ready to open the medicine bundle, he gave directions to the men.

"Wrap up the women and children as warmly as possible, and place them on the travois. You men go in advance and break a trail for the horses through the deep snow."

When all were ready to start, Sacred Otter called out to them, "As soon as I begin to pray for power to break this storm, start at once. Travel toward camp as fast as you can, for I can hold back the storm only a short time. When it starts again, it will blow more fiercely than before."

He filled the black pipe, and as he began smoking he gave the signal for all to start. First he blew the smoke from his pipe toward the northeast, the direction the storm was coming from. Then he held up the sacred pipe and prayed.

"Maker of Storms, listen and have pity! Maker of Storms, hear us and take pity on our women and children as you once took pity on my son and me. Pity us now and hold back this storm. Let us survive! Listen, O Maker of Storms!"

When Sacred Otter blew the pipe smoke toward the southeast, the sun shone through a rift in the clouds.

"Hurry!" Sacred Otter called after his people. "Hurry as fast as you can across the high ridge. The storm will soon come upon you again."

Then he smoked and prayed toward the southwest, and the clouds began to break up. When he made his final smoke and prayed toward the northwest, the clouds drew back and he saw blue sky in all directions. Then he himself hurried after his people. He knew that the Cold Maker was only holding the blizzard back.

All crossed the plateau safely and began the descent toward the river. Suddenly the blizzard came upon them again, enveloped them, and blinded them so that they could not see their way. But their camp was not far distant, and they finally reached their lodges in safety.

Since that time, the Blackfeet have believed in Sacred Otter's dream. But he could never again be persuaded to try his supernatural power. He believed very strongly that power to control the storms would not be given to him a second time.

The Yellow Buffalo Tipi and Father De Smet

THE FOLLOWING STORY is a good example of legend combined with fact. It also illustrates the tolerance and the tact of Father De Smet, qualities which helped to make him a successful missionary among the Indians of the northern Rockies. In 1841, Father De Smet persuaded thirty brave Kalispel Indians to go with him through the country of the Blackfeet, known for their hostility toward white people. Later, while living with the Blackfeet in 1846, he wrote that they equaled other tribes in their hospitality.

A LARGE BAND of Blackfeet, out hunting buffalo, were once camped on the Okoan River, in the moon when the leaves were falling. One of the chiefs, named Mastopeta, brought down a large buffalo with his spear. While he was skinning it, the bull surprised him by rising to its feet. It caught the man upon its horns and tossed him into the air many times.

The other hunters, hearing the bellow of the bull and seeing it run with its hide hanging loose, hurried to aid Mastopeta. They found him lying as if dead and carried him back to his lodge. While they were doctoring his wounds, he opened his eyes and spoke to them:

"It is useless, my children, for you to try to cure these wounds. While I was lying on the ground, the buffalo bull stood over me and said, 'My son, I have done this because you showed me no pity. Also, I want to prove to you my supernatural power. You must die from these injuries, but I will give you my power. Through my power your spirit will return to your body if you will follow my directions.

" 'You must be painted all over with yellow paint, for yellow paint is sacred to me. Your body must be wrapped with your pipe in a buffalo robe, colored with yellow paint. Then it must be thrown into the river, where the water is deep and the current is swift. In this way you will recover from these injuries, and you will come forth unharmed from the river.' "

At the time of the setting sun, Mastopeta's spirit left his body. His people carefully followed all the directions of the buffalo bull. After painting the chief's body, they wrapped him with his pipe in a buffalo robe painted yellow. Four of the best warriors carried him to a place where the banks of the river are steep. They swung the bundle three times, then a fourth time. After the fourth swing they tossed it far out into the stream where the water was deep and the current was swift.

The banks of the river were crowded with Blackfeet. When they saw the bundle sink beneath the water, many people supposed that they would never see Mastopeta again. But some of them ran to the top of the ridge to look down the stream and see if he might appear. To their surprise, they saw him come up from the river unharmed.

After this experience, Mastopeta continued to have dreams in which Buffalo Bull appeared to tell him how to paint the Yellow Buffalo Tipi and to instruct him in the ceremonial. You can still see his Yellow Buffalo Tipi in our big camps. Around the middle of it are two buffalo painted yellow. A yellow buffalo calfskin is used for a door flap. The top is painted black to represent a night sky, and the many small discs represent stars. Around the bottom is a black band with a single row of dusty stars. It is the tipi Mastopeta painted.

Many years later, in the moon when the grass is green, the chief, then an old man, was very sick. Realizing that he would die soon, he asked for his relatives and friends, and bade them farewell.

"My children, I know that I will not recover from this illness. My spirit has left my body three times during my life, but it has always returned. This time I must go away forever."

Soon after the sun rose, Mastopeta died. His wives made a death lodge to receive his body, pitching the lodge in a dense thicket where it would not be disturbed by heavy winds. Using new poles, they fastened the bottom securely to the ground and tightly laced the front with rawhide so that no wild animals could enter. They dressed the old chief in war clothes decorated with porcupine quills, placed his spear and his bow and arrows beside him, and tied his pipe to the lodge poles over his head.

As proof of their sorrow, his wives gave his relatives almost everything they had. They kept only the clothing they wore, one robe, and a travois. Because his youngest wife had a baby, she was permitted to keep also a rawhide bag of buffalo meat for food.

Not long afterward, when the tribe was preparing to move camp, Mastopeta's favorite wife, Akaniki, and her daughter visited the death-lodge. They found the door securely fastened, just as they had left it; but when they looked inside, the body was gone. Mastopeta's pipe still hung from the pole; his spear, bow, and quiver full of arrows were where his wives had left them.

Akaniki and her daughter aroused the camp, and everyone joined them in the search. "Perhaps he has come back to life and has wandered away," said someone. His people searched the thicket around the lodge carefully, but they could find no sign of Mastopeta. Some of them rode far out on the plains and looked from the high buttes. But still they saw no sign of their old chief.

His relatives remained behind to go on with their search, after the tribe had moved camp. But no trace of him was ever found. His wife and daughter continued their mourning. During the day they walked through the camp, whipping themselves and cutting their bodies with sharp arrow heads. At night, they went to the top of a lonely ridge to cry and wail.

Next spring Akaniki and her daughter were camped with the clan of Small Robes. One day when they were alone in the Yellow Buffalo Tipi, they were startled by a deep and long sigh, which seemed to come from someone with a heavy heart. They sat in silence and then, to their surprise, they heard the voice of Mastopeta. It seemed to come from overhead, down through the top of the lodge.

"Alas! my poor children," the voice said, "I pity you. I do not wish to come back to your life, for I would soon long to return to the spirit world. There will always be trouble on the earth, because the people who live there must suffer from famine and pain. Here is a beautiful country. It is neither too hot nor too cold. There is plenty of game here, and the people are never hungry. They never suffer.

"Only your unhappiness troubles me. My heart is heavy when I see you cutting your bodies and when I hear you wailing. I have now come to tell you that I am happy in the spirit world and to ask you not to mourn for me any longer. If you lead straight lives and keep your heart good toward all people, when you die you, too, will come to this country where I now live.

"My children, this is the last time I will come near you. This is the last time you will hear my voice. Farewell."

Akaniki and her daughter told everyone in the camp what the spirit of Mastopeta had said to them. So no one again mourned for the old chief.

It happened that, at that very time, the Black Robe was living among our people. When the two women told him what they had heard, he said to them, "What the spirit of Mastopeta has told you is true. There is a beautiful country where people who have lived good lives will go when they die and where they will be happy. Your husband and father is there now, and you, too, will go there if you lead good lives just as he did."

Akaniki and her children, and many of the clan of Small Robes, were baptized by the Black Robe. They and their children have ever since attended his church and have believed in the white man's heaven after death.

❋

The Bunched Stars—The Pleiades

MANY INDIAN TRIBES related myths about the Pleiades, which were usually spoken of as seven stars, occasionally six, occasionally twelve. In Iroquois tradition, their name means "There They Dwell in Peace." In other Indian traditions, they are known as "the Seven Sisters in the Sky," "the Seven Dancers," "They Sit Apart from

Others," and in the far north as a herd of caribou being chased by three hunters transformed into stars.

The following myth is from the Blackfeet. They showed great interest in the sky and had considerable knowledge of astronomy.

I N A CAMP of our people there once lived a family of six boys, the sons of very poor parents.

Every spring, people went out to hunt for buffalo. At this time of the year, buffalo calves are red, and their skins were much desired as robes for children. But the parents of the six brothers were so poor that they could do little hunting. Their sons had to wear brown robes or those made of old buffalo skins, and so were teased by the other children. The brothers felt that they were made fun of because they were not dressed like the other boys.

One day one of the six said to his brothers, "Why do we never get any red robes? If we do not get any next spring, let us leave the camp and go up into the sky."

Then they went out to a lonely place to talk the matter over. Finally they agreed that, if they did not get robes the following spring, they would go up into the sky country.

The next spring, when the buffalo hunting season had passed, the boys still had no red robes. So the oldest brother said to the others, "Now I will take you all up to the sky."

"Let us take all the water away from the people," said the fourth brother, "because they have been bad to us."

The oldest brother found some weasel hair and placed a little on the backs of the other boys. He took another bunch of hair, put it first into his mouth, and then rubbed it on his palm.

"Now shut your eyes," he said.

He blew the weasel hair upward and soon told his brothers to open their eyes. When they did, they found themselves in the house of the Sun and the Moon. The Sun, an old man, and his wife, the Moon, asked them, "Why have you come?"

"We left the earth because the people never gave us red robes," the oldest brother replied. "All the other children have nice red robes made from buffalo calves, but we have always had brown ones. So we have come to you for help."

"What do you want me to do?" asked Sun.

The fourth brother replied, "We want all the water to be taken away from the people for seven days."

The Sun made no answer, but the Moon had pity and said, "I will help you, but you must stay in the sky."

The Moon felt so sorry for the boys that she cried. When she asked the Sun to help her in taking away the water from the people, he at first made no answer. Seven times Moon asked him, and at last he promised to help her.

The next day it was very hot on the earth. The water in the streams and lakes boiled, and in a short time it all evaporated. The next night was hot and the moon was very bright. When they found that the water was gone, the people in the camp said to each other, "Let us take two dogs with us out to the river bed."

When they reached the river, the two dogs began to dig a hole in the bank. After they had dug a long time, water came out of the hole like a spring. In this way the first springs were made.

The days continued to be hot, so that the people had to dig holes in the hillsides and crawl into them. They would have died if they had stayed on top of the ground.

When the water in the first springs gave out, the dogs made other springs.

The leader of the dogs was a medicine dog. He had strong spirit power and was old and white. On the sixth day of the intense heat, the dogs began to look at the sky and to howl. The medicine dog was praying to the Sun and Moon and was explaining why the six brothers had had no red robes. "Take pity on the dogs here below," he begged.

On the eighth day, the Sun and Moon sent rain upon the earth. It was a big rain and it rained a long time.

Ever since that time the people have had great respect for their dogs. Ever since then, dogs have sometimes howled at the moon.

The six brothers remained in the sky, where they may be seen every clear night. They are the Bunched Stars, which white people call the Pleiades.

❈

The Sleeping Gros Ventres

SOMETIME IN THE 1920's, a big landslide down one of the mountains in the Jackson Hole country of Wyoming dammed the Gros Ventre River. Shown pictures of the sliding hillside, a Gros Ventre man on the Fort Hall Reservation told the following legend which his people had handed down for generations.

LONG AGO, there was a large cave which was entered from the side of this mountain in the picture. Inside the cave was a large valley covered with rich grass. A stream flowed through the valley, and there was plenty of wood for fires. Few people ever went into the cave because it was so very large and because its far interior was dark. Only during times of danger would the Indians use it as their retreat.

Once when a large party of hunters were killing buffalo, the sun became covered with something. Darkness came in the middle of the day.

People were very much frightened. They thought that the great ball of fire (*Coona*) had gone out. So they went into the cave, driving before them a herd of buffalo. Almost immediately, the entrance fell in and completely closed the cave. As the day was very dark anyway, when they entered, the people did not know they were shut in. They felt safe in their retreat.

As there was no other opening to the cave, they are still there. They are now a large tribe. The buffalo also have increased, and are now an immense herd. When the Indians within the cave gather to hunt and kill buffalo, they have a great roundup. Many horses and buffalo run through the valley inside the mountain. Then the ground shakes and trembles. The mountain is made to quiver and great landslides occur.

When the mountain is quiet, the Indians are sleeping.

271

Chief Mountain

CHIEF MOUNTAIN (9,056 feet in altitude) is a conspicuous landmark in the northeast corner of Glacier National Park. Tribes on both sides of the international boundary told legends about it. The one that follows is from the Piegans.

MANY YEARS AGO, a young Piegan warrior was noted for his bravery. When he grew older and more experienced in war, he became war-chief of a big band of Piegan fighters.

Shortly after he became war-chief, he fell in love with a girl of his tribe, and they were married. He was so fond of her that he took no other wife, and he did not go out on war parties. He and his wife were unusually happy together, and when in course of time a baby boy joined them, they were happier still.

Some moons later, a war party that went out from his village was almost destroyed by the enemy. Only four men came back to tell the story. The war-chief was greatly troubled. He saw that if the enemy was not punished, they would raid the Piegan camp. So he gave a big war feast and asked all the young men of his band to come to it.

After they had eaten, the war-chief arose and addressed them in solemn tones: "Friends and Brothers, you have heard the story our four young friends have told us. All the others who went out from our camp were killed by the enemy. Only these four have come back to our campfires. Those who were killed were our friends and relatives.

"We who live must go on the warpath to avenge their deaths. If we do not, the enemy will think that we are women and will attack us again. Let us not permit them to attack us here in the camp.

"I will lead a party on the warpath. Who will go with me against the enemy who have killed our friends and brothers?"

A party of brave warriors gathered round him, willing to follow their leader. His wife also said that she would go with him, but he forbade her.

"If you go without me," she replied, "you will find an empty lodge when you return."

The Chief talked with her, calmed her, and finally won her consent to remain with the women and children and old men in the camp at the foot of a high mountain.

Leading a big war party, the Chief rode out of the village. The Piegans met the enemy and defeated them. But their war-chief was killed. Sadly, his followers brought his body back to the camp.

His wife was crazed with grief. With vacant eyes she wandered everywhere, looking for her husband and calling his name. Her friends took care of her, hoping that in time her mind would become clear again. One day they could not find her in the camp. Searching for her, they saw her far up on the side of the mountain, the tall mountain above the camp. She was carrying her baby in her arms. The head man of the village sent runners after her, but from the top of the mountain she signaled that they should not try to reach her. All watched in horror as she threw her baby out over the cliff. Then she herself jumped from the mountain to the rocks far, far below.

Her people buried the woman and her baby there among the rocks. They carried the body of the Chief to the place and buried him beside them. From that time on, the mountain that towers above the graves was known as *Minnow Stahkoo*, "the Mountain of the Chief," or "Chief Mountain."

If you look closely, even today, you can see on the face of the mountain the figure of a woman with a baby in her arms, the wife and child of the Chief.

✾

The Legend of Writing Stone

WRITING STONE IS a cliff near Shelby, Montana. The picture-writing on it includes many pictures of tipis, said now to predict the numerous oil derricks in the region. The following legend about the stone was told many years ago by a woman who was then about ninety-five years of age.

M Y FATHER, Old Man Mandan, told me about the cliff. When he was a boy, he went there and slept at the foot of it, hoping to have his dream-vision. For two nights he did not dream anything or see anything.

The third night, a man came to him in his dream and said to him, "My boy, why are you here?"

"I am staying here," the boy answered, "because I hope that some spirit will give me power. I want a spirit to give me power so that I may become a brave warrior some day."

"That is good," the man answered. "I am the spirit of this place. You shall get your wish, if you will stay here one more night. In the morning you will see all of my children. They are the ones that make the pictures on the Writing Stone. We know what is going to happen ahead of time, and my children draw the pictures that tell what is going to happen."

So my father slept at the bottom of the cliff another night. When he woke up early in the morning, he looked at the stone. At first he did not see anything. The second time he looked, he saw many little birds of every color fly from above and light on the cliff. Some of them were blue, some red, some yellow. They were pretty birds of all colors.

My father sat there and watched them for a long time, as they were doing something on the rock. After they had finished, the whole flock darted up at once and flew away. He did not see the birds again during the day, but when he looked at the cliff, he found new pictures.

Then my father knew that the man who had spoken to him was a bird. The boy stayed there all day and slept there a fourth night.

That night the man came to him again and said, "My boy, I have come to give you my power to become a brave warrior. In the days to come, you will be a great warrior and a chief. You will also have the power to heal the sick, and the power to know ahead of time what is going to happen.

"You have seen my children, the birds. In the days to come, you will have as many horses as there are birds in that flock. Your horses will be many colors. Remember that I like to help people and that you are the kind of person I like to help. Whenever you need anything, call on me. I give you many powers."

Then Old Man Mandan woke up and went home. Not long after, he went out on a warpath and had success. Each time he went, he had good luck against the enemy. He took their horses, and soon had many horses of different colors. He killed many people and took their scalps.

After a while he became chief of his band, Chief Old Man Mandan. He was able to cure the sick, and he was able to prophesy the future. He was the most powerful person in his tribe.

The pictures on the rock tell the future. In the old days, before a war party started on a raid, the men went to the cliff and looked at the pictures. If anyone saw his own picture there, he knew that he would be killed.

That is the true story of Writing Stone. We tell white people that angels did the drawing. We do not tell them that the drawings were made by birds of different colors.

✖

The First Buffalo Stone

THE SACRED BUFFALO STONE, or *Iniskim*, is the most common medicine object of the Blackfeet. It is usually a fossil shell, picked up on the prairie, and highly prized by its owner. Some of these stones bear remarkable resemblance to animals. . . . In the old days the buffalo stone was used in a ritual for calling buffalo."

It was said to call attention to itself, on the prairie, by making a faint chirp such as a bird might make.

ONE TIME LONG AGO, before we had horses, the buffalo suddenly disappeared. So the hunters killed elk, deer, and smaller game along the river bottoms. When all of them were either killed or driven away, the people began to starve. They were camped in a circle near a buffalo drive.

Among them was a very poor woman, the second wife of her husband. Her buffalo robe was old and full of holes; her moccasins were old and ripped.

While gathering wood for the fire one day, she thought she heard someone singing. The song seemed close, but when she looked around she could see no one. Following the sound and looking closely, she found a small rock that was singing, "Take me! I am of great power. Take me! I am of great power."

When the woman picked up the rock, it told her what to do and taught her a special song. She told her husband her experience and then said, "Call all the men together and ask them to sing this song that will call the buffalo back."

"Are you in earnest?" asked her husband.

"Yes, I am. First get me a small piece of the back of a buffalo from the Bear-Medicine man."

Then she told her husband how to arrange the inside of the lodge in a kind of square box with some sagebrush and buffalo chips. "Now tell the men to come and ask them for the four rattles they use."

It is a custom for the first wife to sit close to her husband in their lodge. But this time, the husband told the second wife to put on the first wife's dress and sit beside him.

After all the men were seated in the lodge, the buffalo stone began to sing, "The buffalo will all drift back. The buffalo will all drift back."

Then the woman said to one of the younger men, "Go beyond the drive and put a lot of buffalo chips in line. Then all of you are to wave at the chips with a buffalo robe, four times, while you shout in a singsong. The fourth time you shout, all the chips will turn into buffalo and will go over the cliff."

The men followed her directions, and the woman led the singing in the lodge. She knew just what the young man was doing all the time, and she knew that the cow-buffalo would take the lead. While the woman was singing a song about the leader that would take her followers over the cliff, all the buffalo went over the drive and were killed.

Then the woman sang a different song: "I have made more than a hundred buffalo fall over the cliff, and the man above hears me."

Ever after that time, the people took good care of a buffalo stone and prayed to it, for they knew that it was very powerful.

✖

How the Piegans Got Their First Horses

AN OLD PIEGAN WOMAN who died about 1880 at the age of approximately 116 related this legend many times to a pioneer family in Montana. She was called *Sikey-kio*, Black Bear, in memory of her father, a

Piegan chief. She had seen men of the Lewis and Clark Expedition on the Missouri River, near the present city of Great Falls. Variants of the first part of the story, usually recorded under the title "Star Husbands," have been found among many tribes from the North Atlantic coast to the Pacific.

LISTEN, AND I will tell you how the Great Chief of the Sky World gave horses to the Indians.

One evening, long ago, when the Piegans were camping on a large flat, the two daughters of the chief lay looking at the stars. One star was so bright that it attracted the attention of the younger daughter. As she looked, a strange feeling came over her, and she murmured, half to herself, "If that star were a young man, I should marry him."

And she looked long at the star, marveling at its brightness. The next day, the chief gave orders to hitch the dogs to the travois and move camp. On the trail, the younger daughter, who had charge of one of the travois, fell behind on account of a broken strap. The rest of her people passed out of sight. As she was about to start again, she looked up and saw, standing in front of her, a young man, beautiful in form and features. Frightened, the girl knelt before him.

"Do not be alarmed," he said. "I am the star you wished to marry. Close your eyes, and I will take you up to the Star World where I live."

The girl did as she was told, and when she opened her eyes, she was in her husband's lodge, far above the stars. His father was the great chief of many lodges. Everyone was kind to her and looked after her every need and wish, so that she was really happy in that distant land.

In the wide fields of the Star World grew many roots which the girl liked very much. One root she was told she must never eat.

"All the roots except this one you may dig and eat," her Star Husband said to her. "Only this root you must neither dig nor eat."

For a long time she had no wish to eat the forbidden root, but one day while digging, she felt a great curiosity about it. The more she thought about it, the greater her curiosity and her desire became. Being alone in the field, she took her sharpened stick and began to dig. The root, she soon learned, was a very long one. She dug so deep that she made a big hole in the ground of the Sky World. Stooping low, she looked through the hole and saw the Earth World, and she saw her father and her sister and her friends coming and going in the village far below. As she watched, she became sad. Her heart so ached with homesickness that she wept.

She was still weeping when her husband and his father found her. Both were sad at heart, for they knew that she would leave them. The next morning they made a long rope of buffalo hides and gently lowered her through the hole in the Sky World to her old home on the Earth World.

All her people were happy and made great rejoicing because the long-lost daughter of their chief had come back to them. Soon after her return, she gave birth to a son. Five years later, the young mother died from a plague that swept away many of the tribe. Her little boy was left in the care of an uncle, now the chief. All the people were very poor. Hunger stalked through the camp, the lodges were without food, there was no one to make moccasins or to dress buffalo hides for them, and there were no dogs for the travois.

Up in the Sky World, the child's father, his grandmother, and his grandfather the Great Chief saw the suffering of the people. Their hearts were so sad that they thought and thought about what they could do. At last the Great Chief and his wife came to the Earth World and, finding the boy alone, told him why they had come. The grandparents and the little boy wept together.

"Now then, my son," said the Great Chief as he seated himself on the grass, "bring me some wet clay."

When the little boy brought it, the Great Chief molded it in his hands. As he did so, he muttered strange words to make strong medicine. When he had finished, he put on the grass the thing he had made from the wet clay. As the little boy looked at it, it grew and grew, and at a word from the Great Chief it began to move.

The Great Chief was so pleased with his work that he called a council of all the trees of the forest, the birds of the air, and the beasts that roamed the plains. All came as he called, for he was ruler over them.

When they had gathered for the great council, he said to them, "I have made a horse for my grandson, an animal for him to ride. And it will also carry his burdens. Now each of you will give me of your wisdom, so that this horse may be perfect."

Pine Tree answered, "Great Chief, your work is good, but the horse has no tail. It needs a tail in order to be perfect. From my plenty I gladly give it."

So the Pine Tree gave the horse a tail. And the Great Chief murmured, "It is good."

Then Fir Tree said, "Great Chief, your work is good, but the horse has no mane. It needs a mane also in order to be perfect. From my plenty I give it."

So the Fir Tree gave the horse a mane. And the Great Chief murmured, "That is good."

Then Turtle said, "Great Chief, your work is good, but the horse has no hoofs. Out of my plenty I will give them."

So Turtle gave hoofs to the horse. And the Great Chief murmured, "That too is good."

Then Elk said, "Great Chief, your work is good, but the horse is too small. I am too large. Of my plenty I will give what it needs."

So Elk made the horse larger. And again the Great Chief murmured, "That is good."

Then Cottonwood said, "Great Chief, your work is good, but the horse has no saddle. Out of my plenty I will give it a saddle."

And it was so, and the Great Chief murmured, "That, too, is good."

Then Buffalo said, "Great Chief, your work is good, but the saddle Cottonwood has given is bare. Out of my plenty I give a cover for the saddle. And there is no hair rope with which to lead the horse. Out of my plenty I give it also."

And it was so. Again the Great Chief murmured, "That is good, very good."

Then Snake, raising his head from his coil, said, "Great Chief, your work is good, but the saddle has no straps. Out of my plenty I will give a strap."

So Snake gave a strap, and the Great Chief murmured, "That, too, is good."

Then Wolf said: "Great Chief, your work is good, but the saddle needs a soft cover. Out of my plenty I will give."

So Wolf gave a fur robe.

And the Great Chief murmured, "It is good. The horse is now complete. Take it, my son. The council is ended."

The grandmother then turned to the boy and gave him a sack of pemmican, saying, "My son, treasure this carefully. It is a magic sack of pemmican. It will never become empty, though you eat from it all the time."

After giving the horse and the pemmican to the boy, the Great Chief and his wife returned to the Sky World. The boy was left wondering. Then he mounted his mare and rode to his people. The strange animal surprised them, and all marveled at him. Soon the mare had a colt, and then another. In a short time there were enough horses to carry his uncle's lodge-skins and lodge-poles from camp to camp. Then the other people became envious.

So the young man said to the chief, his uncle, "If you will take the tribe to the great lake tomorrow, I will make strong medicine there and perform a miracle."

Next morning the chief did as his nephew wished. Near the edge of the great lake the people dug holes, hid in them, and waited. Soon the young man came down from the hills on his mare, with her many colts following behind.

Calling his uncle, the young man said to him, "I am going to leave you. You will never see me again. Here is the magic sack of pemmican. I have made strong medicine, and before I go I will make every fish in the lake turn into a horse, so that there will be plenty for your people. Tell them to watch. Tell them that when they see the horses coming from the lake, they should catch as many as they can.

"But you, uncle, are to catch none until my old mare comes from the water. Then you are to catch her and her alone. If you and your people do as I tell you, all will be well."

With these words the young man mounted his mare, rode into the lake, and was soon lost to view in the deep water. Soon the surface of the lake began to bubble and foam. The Indians were frightened and would have run away if the old chief had not ordered them back to their posts. In a little while, horses' heads appeared above the water, and the animals came swimming toward the shore. Hundreds and hundreds of horses dashed up the bank. The Indians sprang up and captured many of them, but many others escaped and formed the bands of wild horses that even today are found on the plains. The chief obeyed his nephew and caught none of them until the old mare came out of the lake. She was the last to come.

The people laughed while he caught her, for she was old and feeble. Having faith in his nephew, the uncle paid no attention to their jeers. That night he picketed the mare near his lodge. Just as the moon came up over the distant hills, the old mare neighed three times, and out of the thick brush thousands of colts came running. Soon the chief's lodge was surrounded, and the chief had hundreds and hundreds of horses. His people never again jeered at him, for he was richer than any of them.

That is how the Great Chief gave horses to the Piegans.

❈

The Prophecy of the Old Blackfoot

SOMETIME AFTER 1700, the Blackfeet were camped in Prickly Pear Valley, a few miles north of where the city of Helena now stands. They had about seven hundred tipis all together, each clan having its own section of the camp.

One morning the people were wakened by the shouts of an old man who was greatly respected, not only for his bravery in battle, but also for his kind deeds. He was known then as Moving-Another-Place. On this morning he was going from clan to clan and calling out all the minor chiefs. "I want to tell you a strange vision I have had," he said. On his arm he carried the robe he had slept on, and on his face were signs of emotion and excitement.

To the chiefs he related what had been said to him in his vision: "Our way of living, our customs, and our freedom will die with this generation. After all who now live have died, another generation will come that will wear clothing different from ours. Half of their clothing will be buckskin, and half will be made from the hair of sheep and goats. The men's fingers will explode, and all our wild game will be killed.

"That generation of people will die. Then there will come a new group of our people who will have no chiefs. All the men will want to be chiefs, but there will be no one with authority. Our people will think strange things, the old will wander away, and our tipis will be destroyed. Our children will live in square-like structures and will sit on the branches of trees.

"That generation also will die. Other people will come who will do even stranger things. In time, they will no longer need our horses, for large black beetles will carry them rapidly wherever they wish to go. They will wear buckskin clothing, and they will cut the earth into small pieces for each one. The people will become more and more skillful. They will remember the good times of their fathers, but they will have more knowledge. They will be able to watch the chief geese flying across the sky."

The prophecy of this old leader has come true. The early traders and trappers changed the style of clothing. Our manner of living changed from tipis to houses. The firearms brought by the white man killed off the buffaloes and the smaller game animals. Soon the Indians' form of government broke down. The black beetles are the automobiles, and the chief geese flying across the sky are the airplanes.

VII. Siouan Tribes: The Crows, thn Sioux and the Assiniboines

⬥

THE CROWS AND THE ASSINIBOINES, next to the Blackfeet, were the most powerful tribes in Montana during much of the nineteenth century. Lewis and Clark, in November, 1804, and in July, 1806, reported that great numbers of Crow Indians were roving over the extensive Big Horn valley; from there they would journey across the plains, into the Black Hills and into the Rockies, to hunt the plentiful buffalo, elk, deer, and antelope.

Maximilian described the Crow men as picturesque "mounted warriors, with their diversely painted faces, feathers in their long hair, bows and arrows slung across their backs. . . . The haughty Crows rode on beautiful panther skins, with red cloth under them, a whip of elk's horn in their hand." They had between nine and ten thousand horses. Ferris described the Crows as "tall, active, intelligent, brave, and haughty and hospitable. . . . [They] are supplied with horses, which they steal from other nations, with whom they are constantly at war." He said that they were good hunters, accomplished horsemen, and "masters of theft."

But the American artist George Catlin, who painted portraits of members of many tribes in the 1830's, heard a different opinion of their integrity. Sublette and Campbell, who had traded with the Crows for several years, told Catlin that "they are one of the most honourable, honest, and high-minded races of people on earth." Catlin himself was much impressed by the handsome, well-formed Crow men, most of them six feet tall, who had "a sort of ease and grace added to their dignity." The hair of the men was "incredibly long";

"some of them have cultivated their hair so that it sweeps the ground as they walk."

The Crows were "the most beautifully clad of all the Indians" in the region, wrote Catlin. The skins of which their clothing was made were dressed until they were "as white as linen" and then were picturesquely decorated. They had the most beautiful lodges, also. These, too, were made of white skins, decorated with porcupine quills, painted and ornamented "in such a variety of ways as renders them exceedingly picturesque and agreeable to the eye." He obtained such a lodge, "large enough for forty men to dine under."

The Crow bands, from the time of Lewis and Clark until they were assigned to a reservation, lived along the Yellowstone River and its tributaries from the south. Their reservation is in southern Montana, near the center of their former territory. The name for the Crow Indians is thought to be a faulty translation of their name for themselves: *Apsaruke* or *Absaroke*. To Professor Lowie it was explained "as the name of a bird no longer to be seen in the country"; to an earlier observer, Lieutenant Bradley, the impression was given that it is "the name of some kind of bird known to the Crows when they dwelt to the southeast but forgotten after they migrated to a country where the bird is not known."

The Crow Sun Dance, although outwardly similar to that ceremony among other Plains tribes, had a different motivation and function: it was pledged by some mourner who wanted to avenge the killing of a close relative by an enemy tribe and thus was a prayer for revenge. Although the Sun was mentioned, most of the ceremony was not connected with him.

The Sun, however, was "the great Crow deity." To the Sun they offered all their sacrifices. These were chiefly blankets, scarlet cloth (in historic times), and skins of animals placed in a tree or on a pole erected for that purpose and left until destroyed by winds and rains. When they sat down to smoke, someone in the circle pointed the stem of the pipe toward the sun and toward the earth, as an offering; many others reverently bowed their heads.

More important as a religious ceremony than the Sun Dance was the annual Tobacco Ceremony. It was performed according to the vision of some member of the Tobacco Society, one of the most highly respected of the Crow secret orders. A myth about the origin of the sacred tobacco was recorded by both Bradley and Curtis. Another about its origin and also the origin of the Tobacco Society was recorded by Lowie: When the Creator, or Transformer, was walking over the newly formed earth, he saw a human being and said to his companions, "That person is one of the Stars. Let us look at him." Drawing near, they found that the star-being had transformed himself into a tobacco plant, the first plant on the new earth. The Creator announced that the Crow should plant it in the spring, according to ritual, and should dance with it. Then the Sun adopted a poor boy who was fasting, and with him started the Tobacco Society. Only the men of that society could plant the sacred seed and harvest it. Planting this supernatural gift was necessary to make sure that the Crow people would have good health and would prosper the following year.

In Crow mythology, the tales about Old Man or Old Man Coyote resemble the culture-hero-trickster cycle related by many other tribes. In one episode, seemingly unique, his wife is the culture-heroine, who made the first moccasins, tanned the first hides, and prepared the first pemmican. Old Man Coyote was sometimes identified as the Sun, sometimes as a separate individual—by the same narrator.

In the collection of Crow tales recorded by S. C. Simms in the summer of 1902, almost all are about Old Man Coyote. In a larger collection, "not complete but representative," published by Lowie after repeated visits, nineteen episodes in the creator-trickster cycle are followed by four groups of stories; hero tales, tales of supernatural patrons, miscellaneous tales ("Adventures with Buffalo," "The Dipper," etc.), and historical traditions (chiefly of warfare and of peace-making).

Next to the Old Man Coyote cycle in popularity was the hero tale of the gruesome adventures of Old Woman's Grandchild. A long story (twenty-two pages in Lowie's partly condensed version, forty-four pages in Linderman's), it begins with an episode found in the mythology of other Plains tribes: a girl was lured to the sky by a porcupine in a tree that grew higher and higher. In the Crow narrative, Old Man Coyote took her to the lodge of the Sun, who wanted her for his wife. After the birth of their son, the mother became homesick and with her child descended by means of a rope which Old Man Coyote made of buffalo sinew. The mother was killed on the way down; the son found a home with an old woman whose patch of corn and pumpkins he had enjoyed.

With the four supernatural arrows given him by the Sun, the boy, soon known as Old Woman's Grandchild, killed some of the monsters on earth and made others less harmful. His encounters with these evil beings form the major part of the story. Finally, deciding that he did not like the earth, he shot his last arrow at a white cloud, grabbed the feathers of the arrow, and went up with it. In the sky, according to one version, he became the Morning Star; in another version, he became the North Star and the Old Woman became the Moon.

A favorite of the tales about supernatural patrons concerned the child who fell from a travois and was cared for by the Little People, who made the stone arrow points found near Pryor Canyon. They lived in caves and, although very small, were so strong that they could carry buffalo on their backs. The boy stayed with them until he became a man of superhuman strength. As commanded in the story, the Crows, through the years, built hundreds of piles of rocks in Pryor Canyon. The big stone which was the home of the Little People is called Medicine Rock. Each year men would shoot arrows into its crevices and pray that their strength might be as great as the Little People's and their aim with their bows and arrows be as true. The women would leave offerings of beadwork and other ornaments.

The Crows, the Sioux or Dakotas, and the Assiniboines are members of the Siouan language family, the largest family north of Mexico except the Algonquian. Sioux is an abbreviation of *Nadowessioux*, a French corruption of the name given them by the Chippewa Indians (of the Great Lakes area); the word means "snake" or "adder" and, by metaphor, "enemy."

The largest division of the Siouan family, called Dakota by themselves and by anthropologists, are popularly called Sioux. Their hunting and war parties often entered Montana and Wyoming, but until the reservation period of historic times, they had no permanent settlements there. Most of the Sioux now live in South Dakota; several hundreds of them live on the Fort Peck Reservation, Montana. They are mentioned here briefly because of their legends about landscape features in Montana and Wyoming.

The Assiniboines are a branch of the Sioux, one of whose dialects they speak. They "are a fine and noble looking race," wrote Catlin, with less enthusiasm than he showed in his description of the Crows. "They are good hunters, tolerably supplied with horses ... and in a country abounding with buffalo ... live well. Their dances, frequent and varied, were generally exactly the same as those of the Sioux."

The name *Assiniboine* comes from a Chippewa Indian term that signifies "one who cooks by the use of stones." Hence the Assiniboines are often called Stoney Indians or Stoneys, especially in Canada. After separating from the Sioux in prehistoric times, the Assiniboines moved northward, allied themselves with the Crees, and soon adopted Cree dress, tents, and customs.

With these new allies, they were almost constantly at war with the Sioux. A wandering Plains people, moving from place to place in search of food, they roamed from the Saskatchewan and Assiniboine rivers of Canada south to the Milk and Missouri rivers in Montana. About half of the tribe now live on reserves in Alberta (some of them between Calgary and Banff), about half of them on the Fort Belknap and Fort Peck Reservations in Montana.

In former days, the most important event of the year among the Assiniboines of Montana was the Medicine Lodge Dance, now mistakenly called the Sun Dance. It was held about the middle of June, after being carefully prepared for throughout the spring. During the two nights and nearly two days of the ceremony, everyone fasted. Each day the people prayed and made their offerings to Thunderbird, who might be considered the god of rain. Some gave thanks for past favors; some asked help for the future—for a safe journey, for instance, or for success in war. Sometimes sick people were brought to be treated by the Master of the ceremony. Just before the singing of the last group of songs on the last day, the Master prayed aloud for a rainy, productive season and offered to Thunderbird all the sacrifices which the people had brought or made. If rain and thunder came soon after the end of the Medicine Lodge Dance, people whispered to each other, "The Thunderbird and his helpers are coming for our sacrifices."

In later years, the Horse Dance was of similar importance with the Medicine Lodge Dance. It was the property of one of the men's social organizations, of which the Assiniboines had several. According to tradition, a member of the tribe was told, in a dream, that if he would perform the Horse Dance ceremony in a certain way he would obtain horses. During prayer for the welfare of the tribe and for plenty of horses, the pipe was offered to the Sun, to the Earth, and to Thunderbird. Then followed ritualistic songs, a feast, and a dance in which women joined their husbands. In the twentieth century, the Grass Dance, obtained from the Sioux but greatly altered, has been the principal ceremony among the Assiniboines. They carefully follow all rules and regulations in an elaborate ceremony; they wear elaborate costumes, for they consider the Grass Dance the appropriate occasion for exhibiting their most skillful handiwork.

The mythology of the Assiniboines shows much influence from that of the Crees and also of the Blackfeet and the Arapaho–Gros Ventres, all of them Algonquian tribes. The Assiniboine culture-hero instructs mankind, steals summer, kills giants. As a trickster, he persuades ducks to dance around with their eyes shut and then kills most of them, just as the Cree trickster does; he learns an eye-juggling trick from some birds, throws both his eyes on a tree, and when they remain there, he has to make new eyes. A similar episode is found in the Coyote cycle of the Shoshonis.

The Assiniboines related tales about witches, giants, orphan children, and supernatural experiences of people with animals. They told a variation of the widespread story of two girls who married stars, a theme found in this volume in the first part of "How the Piegans Got Their First Horses." Only a few themes suggest the historic connection of the Assiniboines with the other Siouan tribes.

Repetitiousness and length are characteristics of the tales of both the Assiniboines and the Crows. And they had the same storytelling custom: the narrator expected his listeners to exclaim "*E!*" ("Yes!") after every few sentences. When he no longer heard this response, he knew that all his audience had gone to sleep. Then he, too, slept or returned to his own lodge, perhaps expecting to continue the tale the next evening.

✖

The Creation of the Crow World

FROM THE SEVERAL versions of the Crow creation myth that have been recorded, this one has been selected because it is the most revealing of the material culture of the tribe and because it has less similarity with creation myths of other tribes. "The people of the old times referred to the Sun as the Old Man; he was the Supreme Being," wrote Lowie. Old Man was "identical with Old Man Coyote."

LONG BEFORE there was any land and before there was any living thing except four little ducks, the Creator, whom we call Old Man, came and said to the ducks, "Which one of you is brave?"

"I am the bravest," replied one duck.

"Dive into the water," Old Man said to the duck, "and get some dirt from the bottom. I will see what I can do with it."

The brave duck went down and was gone a long time. It came up again carrying on its beak some dirt that it gave to Old Man. He held it in his hand until it became dry. Then he blew the dirt in all directions and thus made the land and the mountains and the rivers.

Old Man, who was all-powerful, was asked by the ducks to make other living things. So he took more dirt in his hand and, after it had dried, he blew it off. And there stood a man and a woman, the first Crow Indians. Old Man explained to them how to increase their number. At first they were blind; when their eyes were opened and they saw their nakedness, they asked for something with which to clothe themselves.

So that they might have food and clothing, Old Man took the rest of the dirt brought up by Duck and made animals and plants. Then he killed one of the buffalo he had made, broke a rock, and with one of the pieces cut up the animal. Then he explained its parts and told the man and woman how to use them.

"To carry water," he said, "take the pouch from the inside of the buffalo and make a bucket. Make drinking cups from its horns and also from the horns of the mountain sheep. Use the best pieces of buffalo for food. When you have had enough to eat, make a robe from the hide."

Then he showed the woman how to dress the skin. He showed the man how to make arrowheads, axes, knives, and cooking vessels from hard stone. "To make a fire," said Old Man, "take two sticks and place a little sand on one of them and also some of the driest buffalo chips. Then take the other stick and roll it between your hands until fire comes."

Old Man told them to take a large stone and fasten to it a handle made from hide. "With it you can break animal bones to get the marrow for making soup," he said to the woman. He also showed her how to scrape skins with a bone from the foreleg of an animal, to remove the hair.

At first, Old Man gave the man and woman no horses; they had only dogs for carrying their things. Later he told them how to get horses. "When you go over that hill there, do not look back, no matter what you hear." For three days they walked without looking back, but on the third day they heard animals coming behind them. They turned around and saw horses, but the horses vanished.

Old Man told them how to build a sweat lodge and also explained its purpose. And he told the man how to get dreams and visions. "Go up in the mountains," he said, "cut a piece of flesh from yourself, and give it to me. Do not eat while you are there. Then you will have visions that will tell you what to do.

"This land is the best of the lands I have made," Old Man said to them. "Upon it you will find everything you need—pure water, vegetation, timber, game animals. I have put you in the center of it, and I have put people around you as your enemies. If I had made you in large numbers, you would be too powerful and would kill the other people I have created. You are few in number, but you are brave."

❋

How Elder Brother Helped the Assiniboines

IN THE ORIGIN MYTH of the Assiniboines, which begins with a vast expanse of water (like many origin myths), Muskrat is the creature that brings up dirt from the bottom of the sea. From this dirt the culture-hero made the earth, people, and horses. He told the Assiniboines that they were always to steal horses from other tribes. After a quarrel with Frog about the length of winter, the culture-hero agreed that seven months would be long enough.

Because *Inkton'mi*, the name of the culture-hero and trickster in Assiniboine myths, is difficult to pronounce, and because in the myth about the theft of summer he calls Rabbit "Younger Brother" and the other animals "Brethren," Elder Brother is here substituted for Inkton'mi. Episodes in the Inkton'mi cycle are similar to those in the Cree tales about Wisakedjak, who is sometimes referred to as "Elder Brother."

E LDER BROTHER was living with the Assiniboines. One day he went to the top of a hill and cried out, "Let everyone get ready for the buffalo hunt!"

All the men got their horses ready, and when they saw the buffalo running across the hills, they made a rush and killed them. Elder Brother went among them, teaching the Indians how to skin the animals. They had no knives, and so he picked up a bone and made a knife. Then he showed them how to cut off the legs and ribs, how to clean the entrails, and what parts could be eaten uncooked.

He broke a leg of a buffalo and showed the people the marrow. After the entrails had been removed, he told a man to take the paunch with the liver and kidneys to the river, wash them, and eat them raw.

"From now on," said Elder Brother, "your people will live on such food. The buffalo will live as long as your people live. There will be no end of them until the end of time. You will have a son who will chase buffalo and provide meat for you until you are gray-headed and ready to die."

Later, when Elder Brother was living in the forest, he made up a great many songs. He packed them on his back and set out traveling. After a few days, the load got so heavy that he could walk but very slowly. So he set the bag of songs down and considered what he should do next. At last he decided to summon the birds and the beasts.

He called out to the buffalo, the crane, the crow, the cock, the fox, the wolf, the horse, the owl, and the coyote, and asked them to gather before him. "I am going to divide my songs among you," he said.

The first song and powers that go with it he gave to the buffalo, saying, "People will dream of you; then you will give them your song and tell them about the dance and the costume that should go with it."

To the cock he gave a song and also the grass-dance. "Your crest," said Elder Brother, "will represent the porcupine headdress that will be used in the grass-dance."

To each of the other birds and animals he gave a song and told them what ceremony and what costume should go with it. Then he told them to go in different directions.

"Wherever people live," he said, "appear to them in dreams and give them your dances."

So they separated, each with his own song, and they spread over the whole world. The songs that Elder Brother kept for himself were those connected with the women's dance and with the practices of the medicine men.

Then Elder Brother went to the sky and told the sky people to keep it open, so that the earth people could get there easily.

"When people come up here from the earth," said Elder Brother, "no one shall go down again."

❋

Old Man Coyote and the Theft of Summer

THE FOLLOWING CROW MYTH on a familiar theme in folklore is very similar to an Assiniboine myth. The relay race is common in North American mythology, especially in stories about the theft of fire.

ALONG TIME AGO, it was always winter here. Toward the south it was always summer, and all the beautiful birds lived there.

The Maker of all things appeared on the earth in the form of Coyote, who was all-powerful. And yet at times he got into troubles that a child could have got out of, so silly and weak he was.

One time Old Man Coyote came up to a boy who was blowing on his hands to keep warm. "What is the matter with you?" he asked. Then he pointed to the south. "Down that way, all is summer, and boys like you run after buffalo calves. When the birds have their young ones in the spring, the boys have a good time. What are you doing here, where it is always cold?"

The boy was made sad by Old Man Coyote's words. He wanted to see the land of summer and to run after the buffalo calves.

Old Man Coyote spoke again. "I can help you get there, for I am going after Summer. Summer and Winter are owned by a woman with a strong heart living in a large tipi. To get Summer, I have to have four animals."

So he called the male Deer, the male Coyote, the male Jack Rabbit, and the male Wolf, and asked them how far they could run. Each told Old Man his greatest distance.

"I am going to turn myself into an elk," Old Man said to them. "You, Coyote, are noted for being sly. So I will give you a medicine paint to rub on the face of the woman who keeps the summer, if you find her in her tipi. I will go along through the woods. When the people of Summer Land come to kill me, I will draw them out of their tipis.

"You watch your chance, Coyote. When the woman comes out to see if her children are going to kill me, you slip into her tipi. There you will find two bags. The dark one contains Summer; the white one contains Winter. Be sure not to take the white bag. Be sure to take the dark bag."

So Old Man in the form of Elk went down south. As soon as the people of Summer Land saw him, they ran out to kill him. Hearing the shouts, the woman who owned the two bags rushed out, and sly Coyote slipped into her tipi. As she turned back, she thought that her door had been moved. Hurrying inside, she met Coyote in the doorway. When he rubbed the medicine paint on her face, she lost her voice. So she was unable to call her children, in spite of all her efforts to attract their attention.

Carrying the bag, Coyote rushed to the woods and found Elk, who told his four helpers what to do next. Coyote ran with the bag until he was tired out, and then he gave it to Jack Rabbit. Jack Rabbit carried it a long way, always keeping ahead of the people of Summer Land who were chasing him. When he was tired out, he gave it to Deer, who ran until he was tired. Deer gave the bag to Wolf, but by the time Wolf reached the place where the boy was waiting for them, the people chasing him were very close. Wolf quickly tore open the bag and gave Summer to the boy.

But the people of Summer Land would not give up entirely. "You may have summer only half of the year," they said to the boy.

That is why birds come north in the spring and fly away before winter.

Old Man made a gift for the boy—the Prairie Chicken. Its body he made from the muscles of the buffalo, its head from the snake, its bill from the wolf's claw, its tail from the rattle of the rattlesnake, its wings from the claws of the black bear, its legs from the caterpillar.

Old Man said to Prairie Chicken, "You are a bird. When you rise to fly, you will scare people with your whirring noise."

So the boy had summer part of the time, and he had the buffalo calves to chase, as did the boys in the Summer Land.

✻

The Seven Stars

LONG AGO there were seven boys in the world, one of whom was red-haired. They did not know whether they had parents or not, and they were having a hard time.

"What shall we turn into?" they asked one another.

"Let us change into the earth," said one.

"No, the earth is mortal," said the boy named the Wise-one. "The earth gets caved in."

"Let us become rocks," suggested a second boy.

"No," said the Wise-one. "They are destructible; they break to pieces."

"Let us change into big trees," suggested a third boy—"into very big ones."

"No," said the Wise-one, "they are perishable. When there is a big storm, they are blown down."

"Let us change into water," suggested a fourth boy.

"No," said the Wise-one. "It is destructible. It dries up."

"Let us change into the night," said the fifth boy.

"No," said the Wise-one, "the night is fleeting. Soon the light appears again."

"Let us be the day," suggested the sixth boy.

"No, it, too, is fleeting. When the sun disappears, darkness comes again. But the blue sky is never dead," said the Wise-one. "It is always in existence. Shining things live up there. Let us change into the shining things. Let us live in the sky world forever."

And so they do. The smallest of the boys took them up, hoisting them by means of his spider web. He set three on one side of him and three on the other, and then seated himself in the middle. When the last boy had reached the sky, the smallest one tore the web in the middle, threw it down, and gave it to the spider.

✳

The Great Serpent in the Missouri River

THIS LEGEND, one of the first recorded in the region, was told to Prince Maximilian to explain the robes and colored blankets attached to poles at different places in the Missouri River. They were offerings made by Minnetarees (or Hidatsa), a tribe closely related to the Crows in language; according to traditions of both tribes, they separated in prehistoric times. They once claimed territory in southeastern Montana, but they now live in North Dakota.

ONCE A WAR PARTY was on its way to the Upper Missouri to meet an enemy tribe. Two young men, after traveling a considerable distance with the war party, turned back. At a certain spot they found a serpent, coiled up. After looking at it for a while, one of the men built a fire and burned the serpent. When the fire had burned down, he picked up a piece of the charred remains and smelled it. It smelled so good that, in spite of the warnings of his companion, he ate a small part.

As he took off his moccasins that night, he was amazed to see that his feet were striped like the serpent he had roasted. He said to his companion, "This is wonderful! When I get home, I will take off my moccasins and everybody will look at my feet."

Next day he found that his legs were striped as far as his knees. He laughed with delight. "No longer will I have to mark my adventures with stripes," he said. "Nature has given them to me."

The third day his legs were striped all the way to his hips. On the fourth morning he was completely changed into a serpent.

"Do not be afraid of me," he said to his companion. "I have neither arms nor legs and so can not move from this spot. Carry me to the river."

Finding him too heavy and too long to be carried, his friend dragged him to the river and there pushed him in. The new serpent swam out, dived to the bottom, and then came back to the surface to comfort his companion. "Do not weep, my friend. Go home in peace. Four things, however, I do ask of you: a white wolf, a skunk, another skunk painted red, and a black pipe."

Then he dived into the water again. His friend went home and after some time returned to the spot along the river, carrying the four things the serpent had asked for. All day he waited on the river bank, weeping and lamenting. At last the serpent appeared and spoke to him: "It is good that you have kept your word. You will go to war and will kill as many enemies as the objects you have brought to me.

"My head will be at the old Mandan village, and my tail will reach the mouth of the Yellowstone River. I will be able to hear all that happens a two days' journey north of me and a two days' journey south of me. Always before you go to war, come here and see me, for I will give you supernatural power."

Four times the man went to war, and four times he killed an

enemy. He told his companions, and they, too, went to the serpent in the river for special fighting power.

The Indians still go to the river and make offerings to the serpent.

❊

The Man Who Turned into a Monster

THE FOLLOWING STORY was recorded more than a century ago from an old Assiniboine priest, but the only people named in it are Gros Ventres. The first episode in his story, a creation myth, is here omitted because of its similarity to other creation myths.

AFTER THE EARTH had been formed from the mud brought up from the bottom of the ocean by Muskrat, the seven Gros Ventres who had been saved from the flood by being on a raft longed for spring. They thought the earth damp and cold and barren, and they longed to see something grow. So they sent two brothers, very brave and venturesome, to travel eastward in quest of spring.

After six moons they reached warm weather, where they found Spring bundled up, on a scaffold, with packages of flowers, seeds, turnips, and roots. Two large Cranes stood beneath the scaffold. The brothers ordered the Cranes to fly back to their people with Spring and her packages. The birds started and in another moon arrived with their cargo safe.

The two brothers then started westward to explore the new country. After a long time they came to the Rocky Mountains. In one of the valleys they saw a movement in the earth at a certain spot, as if it was boiling or as if some animal was trying to get out.

"Let's shoot an arrow into it," said one brother.

"I think we had better let it alone," said the other.

But the first brother, who was very reckless and would never listen to advice, shot an arrow into the spot. Immediately, a whirlwind gushed out and rose up into the air in a black column, bearing the two men up with it. Higher and higher they rose until they were so far above the earth that they could not see it. Then the wind carried them eastward for several days.

When at last they descended to the earth, they were on the other side of the sea. Here they rambled about for some time until they found an old woman working in a cornfield. They begged her for something to eat, and she gave them some corn and potatoes. After eating, they asked the old woman if she would tell them how to get back to their family.

"I will tell you," she replied, "if you will promise to obey my instructions. If you do not follow them, some harm will befall you."

After they had made the promises she required, she took them to the seashore, made a sacrifice of some corn to the water, and asked for Wau-wau-kah to appear. Immediately they saw, far in the distance, an object moving over the surface of the ocean, spouting the water high into the air. Approaching very rapidly, it soon arrived where the two brothers stood. The creature had the head of a man, though it was of monstrous size; out of it projected two horns as large as the largest trees. The body was that of a beast covered with long, black hair, its tail was like that of a large fish covered with scales, and it was endowed with a spirit.

To this monster the woman gave directions. Then in each of its horns she made a seat, like a bird's nest, and in each seat she placed a man. To one she gave a sack of corn, to the other a sack of potatoes. When she had spread out her hands and invoked the sun, the monster departed with its cargo, and after a great many suns arrived safely on the opposite shore.

The old woman had told the brothers that immediately upon landing they should make a sacrifice to the water by throwing into it a little corn. One of the men did so, but the reckless and stubborn one did not. When the monster reproached him for not obeying the old woman, he shot an arrow into it and was instantly swallowed by the beast.

The good brother was in great distress. Remembering what the old woman had done, he made a sacrifice of some corn, stretched out his hands, and prayed to the Sun for help. Immediately, a dark round spot appeared in the west. It came toward him with terrible speed and a whistling sound, increasing in size and speed as it approached. This was a thunder stone. With an awful report and a bright flash, it struck the monster on the back, cut it in two, and thus set the man free. Then a terrible storm arose, the sea rolled, and the monster disappeared.

The two brothers traveled westward and after many days came to a lodge where lived an old man and his family. When they asked for something to eat, the old man showed them immense herds of buffalo. Apparently all of them were tame, and all were black except two, which were snow white.

"Kill whichever buffalo you wish," he said, "but do not destroy more than you need for food and clothing."

The good brother killed a fat cow; because it was more than he needed, he took the rest of the meat to the old man's lodge. The other brother remained behind and shot arrows into a great many buffalo. The old man reproved him for killing the animals uselessly. After they had feasted together and were about to depart, the old man showed them a great number of ducks and geese. "These, with the buffalo, are our life," he said. "Treat them well."

But when the old man had left, the bad brother started killing the birds with a club and made great havoc. The old man returned and said, "You have done wrong; you are a bad man. Evil will befall you; the Wau-wau-kah will bar your way home. But your brother is good, and for his sake some of my buffalo will follow him home to his people. The white buffalo skin shall be his talisman to remember me by."

Continuing their journey, the brothers camped that night on the prairie at the foot of what they supposed was a mountain. But it was really the Wau-wau-kah, lying across their path. In the morning they started to go around it, but whatever way they turned, the monster turned with them. They spent the whole day trying to go forward, but made no headway.

"Let us try to appease the monster by sacrificing some corn," said the good brother.

But the other became angry and would not listen to any peaceful measures. Instead, he collected great piles of buffalo dung all around the monster and set it on fire. The Wau-wau-kah was roasted alive.

The smell of the meat being very appetizing, the bad brother cut a slice and ate it. He offered some to the other man, but he would not taste it.

The next morning when they got up, the one who had eaten the flesh of the monster said, "Look, my brother. See what handsome black hair is growing from my body."

The other looked and saw on his brother the hair of the beast. The next morning the bad brother said, "Look at my head, my brother. Horns are coming out of it." And so they were. On the third morning he said, "Look at my legs, my brother. Fish scales are growing there." And so they were.

Every morning when they arose, the man had more and more the appearance of the monster whose flesh he had eaten. They now had to travel slowly because of his difficulty in walking while the lower part of his body was changing into the form of a fish.

After a while they reached the mouth of the Yellowstone River and camped together for the last time. The bad brother's change was now nearly completed. When he arose the next morning, he looked exactly like Wau-wau-kah.

He said to the other one, "Depart from me. I am no longer your brother. I am no more a man. I am either your friend or your enemy, according to the way you treat me. Leave me now. You will find your people several days' travel down on the banks of the Missouri River. Take them the corn. The buffalo will continue to follow you home.

"Your people will become a powerful nation if they will sacrifice some corn to me every year by throwing it into the river. If they do not do this, the wind will blow, too much rain will fall, the water of the river will rise and destroy their crops.

"As for me," he continued, "I shall be separated here. My head will go up into the clouds and govern the wind; my tail will go into the water and become a monstrous fish to disturb it. My body will rove through the Rocky Mountains; my bones will be found there, but my spirit will never die. Depart. You have a good heart."

At the end of this speech, the winds blew, the thunder rolled, and the lightning flashed. During a terrible storm, the monster disappeared. The good brother returned to his people and told them the story of his travels.

To this day the Gros Ventres sacrifice corn to the Missouri River, to appease the spirit of the Wau-wau-kah.

❋

The Monster in the Missouri River

LONG AGO, the Sioux noticed a strange thing in the Missouri River. At night something red and shining like fire pushed itself against the current. As it passed upstream, it made the water roar. If anyone saw the strange object in the middle of the day, he soon became crazy. He twisted as if in pain and then died.

One man saw it and lived. It had red hair all over its body, he said, and its body was shaped like that of a buffalo. It had one eye, and in the middle of its forehead was one horn. Its backbone was just like a crosscut saw; it was flat and notched like a saw or cogwheel.

When a person sees it, the man said, he gets confused, and his eyes close at once. When he gets home, he is crazy for a day. Then he usually dies.

The Sioux called this strange creature a sea monster. They believed that it caused the ice on the river to break up in the spring of the year.

❋

The Spirits of the Rivers

IN ALL THE RIVERS in the Crow country, from the earliest times, there have lived strange animals or spirits. They are always hungry and ready to devour human beings. When we are about to cross a stream, we always throw food into the water first, to feed these creatures so that they will spare us. We paint our bodies with spots and stripes in bright colors, to frighten them so that they will allow us to cross over the water safely.

The last times they were seen, they were in the Tongue River, the Rosebud, and the Little Big Horn. They have the form of human beings except that they are very fat and have arms and legs of unusual size. In the Tongue River, the creature was dead and its face was partly gone; its hair was like wool. In the Rosebud River, one was seen swimming and making a big disturbance as it moved. One of the three men who saw it raised his gun to shoot, but it suddenly raised itself in the water and looked so horrible that the man dropped his gun in his fright. All three men ran from the spot as fast as they could.

In the Little Big Horn River, three creatures were seen together, playing in the water like children. In fact, the man who saw them first thought that they were children, but when he looked at them closely he found that they were spirits.

As he sat on his horse gazing at them in wonder, there came a flash across the water like a flash of lightning. It lashed the water into foam, dazzled the man, and so frightened his horse that the animal reared and threw him. When the man had picked himself up, the spirits were gone, but his eyes could follow the track of the flash by a muddy line in the water. The spirits of the river had been in the lake at the head of Little Big Horn.

⌘

Legends of Lake De Smet

LAKE DE SMET, in northern Wyoming, is said to have strange noises at night. Pioneers in the area have reported that horses and dogs are afraid of it and that a monster occasionally appeared in the mist that rises above the water. Many weird tales were told about it.

ONCE, WHEN A BAND of Crow Indians were camped beside the lake, a young warrior named Little Moon asked his sweetheart, Star Dust, to meet him at the edge of the water when their people had gone to sleep. Little Moon arrived at the spot before Star Dust did. As he stood waiting for her, he saw, in the mist that hung over the lake, the beautiful face of a girl. She was more beautiful than any girl he had ever seen, and she beckoned to him with a smile.

While the face in the mist smiled as if to charm him, Star Dust came to him and tried to put her arms around his neck. Spellbound by the strange beauty, Little Moon pushed the girl aside angrily. But when he turned his eyes back upon the lake, the face in the mist had gone.

Next morning someone found the drowned body of Star Dust

wound around the bluff north of the lake. Her father, demanding revenge, bound Little Moon to the rock, and his people left him there to watch for the mysterious maiden.

Now when the wind moans over the lake, Indians say that the faithless lover is calling. The wind is the voice of the disloyal sweetheart.

❧ ONE TIME A BAND of Indians were camped beside the lake that is now called Lake De Smet, named in honor of the first white man known to have seen it. The Indians found the water too bitter for drinking and for cooking, and they decided that the bitterness was caused by evil spirits in the lake.

That night they heard weird noises. All day they had seen great hordes of large birds flying about and had seen them on the lake at dusk. At the time, the Indians did not know the name of the birds; now they think that they were seagulls. The people thought the noise hideous, and they were frightened as the birds rose and then swooped down in great numbers.

All night long the gulls soared and droned and swarmed. At the break of day the birds rose at one time and flew out of sight.

That morning the people had a terrifying experience. After breakfast their best swimmer ran to the edge of the lake and plunged in, giving a happy whoop as he started to swim. The people watching him saw him turn around as if to swim back to the shore, open his mouth as if to call out, widen his eyes as if in horror, and then disappear below the surface of the water.

Panic-stricken, the Indians circled around the lake, waiting for the swimmer to reappear, but he did not come to the surface again. When they thought they had waited long enough, they hurriedly seized their belongings and fled in terror.

No Indian ever went to the lake again.

✳

Red Plume and the Medicine Wheel

THE MEDICINE WHEEL in the Big Horn Mountains west of Sheridan,

Wyoming, is a structure of mysterious origin built at an altitude of 9,956 feet. Hundreds of slabs of limestone and boulders are laid in the form of a wheel 245 feet in circumference; the spokes are twenty-eight or twenty-nine lines of stone extending from the center. On some projecting slabs, the bleached skull of a buffalo lies looking toward the rising sun.

The Indians have no legends explaining the origin of the Wheel. When asked about it, they may reply, "It was built before the light came."

They believed that it was intended for worship. That it has been visited by multitudes of people in comparatively modern times is evident from the worn trails of travois still visible for two or three miles around it.

Revering the Wheel, the Crow Indians visited it when they wished to communicate with the spirits of nature or with the spirits of the dead. They stopped there on their travels to and from the hunting grounds in the Wind River country. On their return they held thanksgiving ceremonies at the Medicine Wheel and left offerings of the best game they had killed. The women left offerings of beads.

The Crows believed that in the rock shelters near the Wheel lived some of the Little People. Many men fasted there, in solitude, in order to have visions and to hear the message of a spirit.

R ED PLUME WAS a great chief of the Crow Indians at the time of Lewis and Clark.

When he was a young man seeking his mystery power and his guardian spirit, he climbed the mountains to the Medicine Wheel. He wanted strong spirit power, the strong mystery power given by the Little People. He wanted to become a great warrior and a great leader.

For four days and four nights he stayed beside the Wheel, without food or water or clothing. On the fourth night, four Little People came to him, three little men and one woman. They live in an underground passage connected with the Wheel. They guided the young man to their home and kept him there for three days and three nights.

For three days and three nights they taught him how to wage war and how to be a good leader in times of peace.

"The Red Eagle will be your protector, your guardian spirit," they told him. "He will give you mystery power. He will guide you and protect you through life. You must always wear the soft feather that grows just above the tail of Red Eagle. It will be the symbol of your mystery power. Never go without it."

This soft red feather gave him his name—Red Plume. He became a great warrior and a great leader of his people. When he lay dying, an old man, he said to his people, "My spirit will remain near the Medicine Wheel. It will be in a shrine that is not connected with the rim except by an extended spoke. There you may come to me and commune with my spirit any time you need me."

This is the story of Red Plume and the Medicine Wheel.

❦

The Origin of the Devils Tower

THE DEVILS TOWER is the chief feature in Devils Tower National Monument, which is located in the northeast corner of Wyoming. The Tower rises 1,280 feet above the bed of the Belle Fourche River and about 865 feet above its apparent base.

Considered "a geological mystery," it looks like a "huge, fluted monumental shaft set upon a mound." At its base are fragments of fallen columns.

The Sioux Indians used to say that the Thunderbird takes his gigantic drums to the top of the Tower, beats them, and thus causes the noise of thunder and the storms that follow.

Chief Sitting Bull is said to have gone near it for supernatural power and to have received assurance from the spirits there that he would be victorious in one of his biggest campaigns.

The Sioux called the Tower *Mateo Tipi*, meaning "Grizzly Bear's Lodge," and related the following legend about it. The Kiowa Indians, who, according to their traditions, once lived along the Montana-Wyoming border, also had a legend about the Tower: the seven little girls who climbed the rock became the stars we know as the Pleiades. The Cheyennes related a very different story about the Tower.

ONE DAY in early summer, three girls went out on the prairie to pick flowers. Just as they were starting home, they were frightened by three bears. They ran to the top of the nearest rock, which at that time was only a few feet above the ground. The bears also started to climb the rock.

Frightened still more, the girls called on the spirits for help, and the spirits caused the rock to grow. Higher and higher it rose. Again and again the bears tried to reach the top where the girls were, but the surface was so smooth and the rock so steep that they could make no headway. At last the three bears were so tired that they could try no longer. They fell down the giant rock and were killed on the broken rocks at its base.

The three girls, safe at the top of the column, had watched all the actions of the bears. When they saw that the bodies moved no more, the girls took the flowers they had gathered and braided them into a rope. This they fastened to the top of the rock and then, one by one, they climbed down the rope and reached the ground.

This happened a long time ago, but on the sides of the Grizzly Bear's lodge you can still see the marks of the bear's claws. They were made while the three bears were struggling to reach the three girls on the top of the rock.

�֎

Traditions of the Black Hills

THE BLACK HILLS of western South Dakota and of northeastern Wyoming were the sacred land of the Sioux, the home of many spirits. The Sioux often hunted in the foothills of those mountains and came there for lodge-poles. Each year their bands traveled long distances to cure their illnesses in the warm springs of the region. But according to one pioneer, they "rarely ventured very far into the interior."

The following traditions were recorded by pioneers, an explorer, and a missionary among the Sioux.

IN THE DARK of night, the rocks in the Black Hills turn into spirits that sing strange songs. Then water that will heal the sick flows from holes in the rock walls. People fill their cups of buffalo horn with this water, drink it, and become pure.

Beside the tall needles of rock that touch the sky are places of prayer and vision for the medicine men. There they pray to the spirits, so that their powers may be strengthened. Nearby on the rock walls are picture-paintings made long before the Sioux came to this land. From these paintings the medicine men learned how their people should live.

Hidden beneath the ground are crystal caves which have great mystery. The glistening rocks of the region should be used only as sacred objects, to protect the wearers and to bring them good fortune.

On Bear Butte in the Black Hills, the father of Crazy Horse performed the ceremonies of a medicine man. A spirit in the form of a bear appeared to him there and gave him strong supernatural power.

In the past, the Sioux never climbed the mountain now called Harney Peak because Thunderbird often stops there. Whenever he does, he causes much thunder and lightning around him. When angry, he shoots forth tongues of lightning, hurls thunderbolts, and causes violent winds to blow. When very angry, he causes trees to be torn up by their roots and their trunks to be splintered.

WE OFTEN HEAR, in the Black Hills, rumbling noises like the sound of thunder. That high peak there is the Hill of Thunder. When my father was a young man, the peak was on fire. A large volume of smoke poured forth from it, day after day. The smoke was the breathing of the giant white man that is buried beneath the mountain.

The rumbling noises are the moans of that white giant, when he is pressed by the rocks. He was buried there as punishment for being the first white man to come into the sacred land of the Sioux, and the pressing of the rocks is further punishment. We know that he occasionally comes forth from the mountain, for in the snow we have seen his tracks, twenty feet in length.

He will be imprisoned there forever as a warning to all white men to leave the Indians in possession of their hunting grounds and the dwelling places of the spirits.[1]

An Evil Spirit lived in the dark ravines and gorges of the hills, where the sun never shines. One time he became angry at the people and caused the mountains to spew forth sand and gravel and fire. He wanted to terrify and to destroy all the Indians in the area.

But the Good Spirit had pity on them, put out the fire, and drove the Evil Spirit away. The people returned to their wicked ways, however, and the Evil Spirit came back. Again he spewed forth rocks and fire. When the people repented of their wickedness and made sacrifices, the Good Spirit again took pity on them and drove the Evil Spirit back to his home. For forty snows the Good Spirit has not allowed the Evil Spirit to return.

Once, the daughter of a Sioux chief was so beautiful that she was envied by all the other girls of her band. With her people she often came to the Black Hills to bathe in the wondrous waters there.

She was deeply in love with a young warrior who was below her in rank. Her father, however, had selected for her a young man who was descended from generations of medicine men and was of high rank. Unfeeling and ambitious, he insisted that his daughter marry the young man of his choice.

The girl determined not to obey her father. The next time that her family visited the spring, she slipped away by herself and climbed to the top of a towering cliff. She threw herself from it and was dashed to fragments on the rocks below.

The name of the girl became the name of the spring.

✖

The Origin of the Badlands

The Badlands National Monument is in southwestern Dakota; less extensive and less spectacular badlands are in southeastern Montana and in northeastern Wyoming. They are rugged areas without water,

[1] This legend was recorded in 1859.

and all have strange formations of clay and stone. Windblown sand and rain have carved the soft rock into unusual shapes, some beautiful, some weird. In the rocks, scientists have found evidences of prehistoric animals. The Sioux Indians called the area *Mako Sica,* "Land Bad," meaning that it was difficult to travel through.

The following Sioux legend explaining the origin of the badlands seems to be of fairly recent creation (or revision), because of the mention of horses. It was told by Red Bird, a very old historian of his people.

Long ago, the Badlands did not exist. Instead, there was a high plain covered with grass or with trees. Much game could be found there—deer and elk and buffalo. So each autumn many tribes camped there to hunt and make ready their winter supply of meat. Tribes that were at war with each other at other times of the year met peacefully on the plains in the autumn and enjoyed friendly powwows. Quarrels were forbidden.

But after many snows, a fierce tribe from the mountains toward the setting sun came and disturbed the peace of the plains. Wanting the high tableland for themselves only, they drove off the other people. They claimed all the grass for their own horses, killed the best of the game, and refused to allow other tribes to set up camp as in the old days.

Again and again the Sioux and their friends from the north and the east fought for their ancient hunting ground, but the mountain tribe from the west defeated them. Many of their warriors died in battle. At last the men of the plains held a great council of all the tribes. To appease the spirits, people fasted for many days. Some tortured themselves. The medicine men did everything they could to win the favor of the spirits, but they received no answer. Their people were in despair.

At last the spirits sent their answer. The midday sky became as black as a midnight sky. Lightning flashed, seeming to come from the ground, and thunder rolled. Strange fires lighted the entire country with their flames. The earth shook. Where the western tribe had their camp, waves of land like waves of a great water rolled back and forth. In the troughs of these gigantic waves, the whole warring tribe with their tipis and their horses sank and were engulfed by the next waves. With them went the grass, the trees, the streams, the game animals— everything that had been on the high plain.

As the frightened people from the north and the east watched from a distance, the great commotion suddenly stopped. The fires burned themselves out. When dawn came, the peaceloving tribes saw that the rolling waves of earth had become fixed, bare rocks. Their beautiful plain was now a wasteland on which nothing could ever grow.

The spirits, in their wrath, had taken away the cause of the quarreling and the killing. To the people who lived, the Badlands were left as a reminder of the anger and the power of the spirits.

⌘

The Sun, the Wolf, and the Buffalo

LIEUTENANT JAMES A. BRADLEY, while stationed among the Crows from 1871 to 1877, recorded many traditions and facts about them learned from those who were his scouts. The next four myths and legends were related to Bradley by Little Face, one of his scouts, then about sixty years old.

MANY YEARS AGO the Crow nation was very large, and our people were the favorites of the Sun. One time the Sun came down among them and took a Crow woman as his wife. They had a handsome lodge, where the woman lived, greatly respected by the tribe. Occasionally the Sun came down and lived with her for a while. Because of his love for his wife, the Sun blessed her people with an abundance of food, corn, and buffalo, and also with success over their enemies in war.

But there was a fool-dog among the Crows, a man with an evil spirit. He roamed about the village, doing harm to anyone he could harm. No one punished him, because he was a fool-dog and could not help it. Once when the Sun was away from his lodge on earth, the fool-dog visited it and abused his wife. She bore her shame in silence, but prepared herself for death. When the Sun came to see her, she told him what the fool-dog had done and then put herself to death before her husband's eyes.

The Sun was so angry that he determined to destroy the entire Crow nation. He caused their corn to fail, prevented buffalo from coming to their country, and gave their enemies power over them. The Crows were forced to become wanderers over the earth, to seek a new home where they might have food and rest.

A long time they wandered, suffering greatly from hunger. When they were in danger of total destruction from starvation, White Wolf, a servant of the Sun, took pity on them and made up his mind to save them.

"Make a pile of rice stalks and other fuel," White Wolf told them. "Make little pellets of meat and corn meal and throw them upon the pile, one by one, until the pile bursts into flames. Ten buffalo will rise from the midst of the flames. You must kill all of them. If one should escape, he would be sure to go to the Sun and tell what you have done. Then there would be no hope for you."

The people were distressed by these orders. Although they could find enough meat for the sacrifice, they thought there was not so much as a kernel of corn among them. But at last they learned that an old woman had preserved a small amount of corn for seed. She gladly contributed it to save her people from starvation.

They made ten pellets of meat and corn meal; they made a pile of rice stalks and other fuel. The best hunters stood by with their bows drawn while the pellets were thrown upon the pile, one by one. There was no flame after the first pellet, none after the second, none after the third or even the ninth. The Crows were almost in despair. But when the tenth pellet was thrown into the pile, a bright flame burst forth and ten fat buffalo galloped out of the midst of the flames.

The hunters let fly a shower of arrows, and the ten buffalo fell dead. The women prepared a big feast amid rejoicing throughout the camp. At the suggestion of White Wolf, the people repeated the charm. The next flames produced twenty buffalo, the next thirty, and so on until the number reached ninety. The hunters killed all of them and all the people had an abundance of food.

In those days there were no firearms and no horses. It was difficult for the men on foot, using bows and arrows, to kill so many animals. The number troubled all the people; they feared that one might escape and would cause the Sun to show his anger against them again. When the number of buffalo galloping out of the flames reached one hundred, one animal did escape. He ran directly to the Sun and told the whole story.

The Sun was very angry—with White Wolf more than with the Crows, who had showed themselves to be brave in a time of trouble.

"Go to the Crow people," the Sun said to White Wolf, "and tell them that I shall no longer work to destroy them. You yourself will forevermore be a vagabond, an outcast among the animals of the world."

Wolf has been a vagabond to this day. And Sun has never again taken a wife among the Crow women.

❈

How the Crows Got Their First Horses

ACCORDING TO ONE of the traditions Bradley heard from his scouts, the first white men and the first horses they had ever seen came out of the big water they had once lived beside.

WHEN MY GRANDFATHER was a young man, the Crows had no horses and did not know what they were except through a vague tribal tradition. Dogs and women carried their packs. When they traveled, women walked with heavy burdens on their backs. Dogs carried the lodges. These were as large as they are now, too heavy a load for a single dog. So each lodge was divided and carried by two dogs.

After the Crows reached the Yellowstone country, they were visited by a party of Nez Percés, who offered to trade them some horses. Horses are larger than dogs, the Nez Percés told them, and strong enough to carry heavier burdens. So a party of Crows visited the Nez Percé camp and there saw, for the first time, the large animals which our elders said had once come out of the big water far to the southeast. The Crows purchased a few and set out with them to return to their own camp.

On the way, my grandfather had a strange and wonderful experience. As he stood near the stream, a man clothed in black from head to foot rose suddenly from the water and stood before him.

"What are you doing in this place?" the man asked my grandfather.

"I have come after horses and am returning home."

Thereupon the strange man gave a loud call, and at once from the woods nearby pranced a hundred horses of all colors. Most of them were fine animals.

"Take your choice," said the man in black.

My grandfather chose a handsome, coal-black horse, his favorite of the whole group.

"Now mount him," ordered the stranger. "He is strong and can carry all you wish to put on him. Make haste home, but do not look back. Never under any circumstances look behind you until you have reached your village. If you do not obey my warning, you will have ill luck."

Although my grandfather had never ridden a horse, he obeyed the command at once. He galloped away, enjoying the motion and the sense of power, knowing that he was traveling faster than any Crow had ever traveled before. As he rode, he heard the constant clatter of hoofs close behind him. He seemed to be followed by a herd of animals like the one he was riding. Was the man in black so generous? The pounding of hoofs continued, but the creatures did not come into view and he dared not look back.

When night came, he dismounted and lay down to sleep, being careful to lie on his face with his head pointed toward his village. He wanted to be sure that if he should awaken suddenly he would not look behind him. After two more days of travel, my grandfather reached home. The clatter of hoofs had followed him all the way. To his great joy and to the amazement of his people, he had brought home all one hundred of the large and beautiful horses he had seen near the stream. Not only would they take the place of dogs as beasts of burden, but they would carry on their backs the Crow warriors and hunters in all their future travels.

From that time on, the people continued to obtain horses by trading, until they were abundantly supplied. Never since then have the Crows been without them.

"And we put heavy loads upon them," said Little Face, "because the man in black told my grandfather that they were strong and powerful."

Thunder Medicine's Adventure in Yellowstone River

According to Little Face, there was a place in the Yellowstone River below the mouth of the Big Horn River where a horse lived under water but occasionally came forth. Both he and other Crow Indians had seen the animal; it was "of a blue-earth color, with black stripes running around its legs and body," and it had a black nose. Little Face, relating the story to Lieutenant Bradley in 1876, said that the incident had occurred about twenty-two years earlier.

At the time of this story, a band of Crows were camped along Big Horn River, and a band of Piegans along a stream north of the Yellowstone. One day, about sixty Crow warriors went to attack the Piegans. They crossed the Yellowstone, went up through the pass of Fleischman's Creek, and down to the Piegan camp. There they seized a number of horses and managed to slip away without being pursued.

On their return, all the warriors crossed the Yellowstone without difficulty, except one man called Slender Woman. He rode the finest horse of all. Strangely, although the horse had never before been afraid of water, this time he showed terror whenever he approached the stream. Several times he turned back from it in spite of his rider's efforts to force him in. At last he did plunge in; but in the middle of the river, he reared wildly, threw his rider, and returned to the shore.

Slender Woman, determined not to lose so fine an animal, also made his way back to the shore. Once more he forced the horse into the stream. But at the midway point, the horse again reared wildly and threw his rider. This time the animal went on to the opposite shore, leaving his rider struggling in the water.

Although the current was very swift at the place, Slender Woman did not float with it. And although the river was very deep, he soon rose until only the lower part of his body was under water. But he seemed unable to get to shore.

"Why don't you come on?" shouted his friends.

"I can't," he replied. "Something under the water has seized me and holds me fast."

Warm Horse, a brave young man, drew his knife and plunged into the water to aid his friend. But just as he reached the spot, Slender Woman sank from view. Warm Horse and his companions watched the river for a long time, but they caught no glimpse of Slender Woman. Mourning him as dead, they returned to the Crow village and told the story of his disappearance.

When the period of mourning had ended, a warrior named Thunder Medicine offered to go to the river and recover the body of the lost man. Thunder Medicine was a relative of Slender Woman, and he had strong spirit power—from Thunder. His friends begged him not to go, not to undertake so dangerous a journey. But Thunder Medicine was determined. He persuaded Long Horse, who had been one of the war party, to go with him and show him the place where Slender Woman had disappeared.

When they reached the spot, the Yellowstone River was at full flood, and swift and powerful. Long Horse was afraid for his friend.

"Let us turn back," he said to Thunder Medicine. "You will lose your own life in that raging water."

Thunder Medicine was certain that his special power was strong enough to protect him. He stripped off his clothes, but before entering the water, he gave directions to Long Horse.

"Go away from the shore for some distance. Do not look back at the river, lest you break the charm and put my life in danger."

When Long Horse was out of sight, Thunder Medicine slipped into the water. He had expected to sink beyond his depth at once, but he found himself supported at waist depth by a soft, yielding bottom, like a carpet of grass. Without any difficulty he walked to the spot where Slender Woman had drowned. Here the soft bottom supported him no longer, and he sank suddenly. Swiftly he was carried along by the rushing water, which was all that he could see. How far he was taken he did not know. Suddenly he fell over a wrecked boat and found himself in a dry spot at the bottom of the river.

This spot, about forty feet across, was hemmed in on all sides by rocky walls. Overhead, the muddy water leaped from one side of the enclosed space to the other and then rolled on, without a drop reaching the place where Thunder Medicine stood. To his amazement he saw, in the center of the dry area, a dilapidated lodge, the roof of which almost touched the water raging above it. As Thunder Medicine walked toward it, a little girl opened the door, and he walked in. Inside the lodge he saw an old man and an old woman sitting with bowed heads. When he entered and sat down opposite them, they did not raise their heads or speak to him. He saw that they were wrinkled and ragged, that they seemed to be very old and very poor. Probably they are man and wife, he thought to himself, and the little girl is their daughter.

Then he heard the woman speak to her husband, without moving or lifting her head. "My child has traveled a long way to the country of his enemies, to find the body of the man you drowned. I begged you not to eat his body. I knew that his friends would come for it. Have you not enough to eat? Must you cause human beings to drown, and then devour their bodies?"

"He may have what is left of his friend," said the old man solemnly. "He will find it near the door."

Thunder Medicine found beside the door all the bones of Slender Woman except the skull. Some of the flesh still clung to the bones. He also found Slender Woman's necklace of white beads and his earrings of precious shells. These he gathered together and prepared to carry them away with him.

Then he saw the old man coming toward him leading a horse. The horse was like the ones used by human beings except that its hair had the fine texture and the sleek appearance of animals that live in the water.

"You may take this horse with you," the old man said to Thunder Medicine.

When he started to take the halter, the old woman cried out, "Do not take it, my child! Do not take it!"

"Why not?" he asked, surprised by her earnestness.

"I do not want harm to come to you, my child," she replied. "You please me greatly. That horse is not like the horses of your country. It will be an enemy of those horses and have the power to destroy them. This horse will bite the others, and every one that it bites will die. Take my advice and refuse the gift."

While the old woman was talking, her husband said nothing. His head remained bowed in sullen silence. Feeling certain that the old woman had spoken the truth, Thunder Medicine thanked the old man but left the horse with him. Pleased with the stranger's answer and seemingly afraid that some new danger might befall him, she spoke to her husband again.

"My child's friend stands on the bank of the river crying for him, thinking that he has perished like Slender Woman. Let my child go, therefore, so that he may comfort his friend. Let him return to his people with the bones of Slender Woman."

"Very well," said the old man, in the same stern, sullen manner. "Let him stand upon the palms of my hands and shut his eyes."

And he placed the backs of his hand on the ground so that Thunder Medicine could slip into them.

Thunder Medicine did as he was told. Suddenly he felt himself whizzing through the water, and soon he was standing on dry land, on the bank of the river. On the opposite bank was Long Horse, walking up and down, beating himself and mourning for his friend as one who had perished. Great was his surprise and great his joy when Thunder Medicine called out that he was alive.

Thunder Medicine was almost afraid to venture into the water again, to cross to the other bank. But Long Horse encouraged him and he plunged in, still carrying the bones and the ornaments of Slender Woman. To his surprise, he found himself buoyed up by the same soft, grass-like bottom that had supported him earlier. In water that was fathoms deep, he walked across without sinking deeper than his waist.

Long Horse met him at the edge of the stream and heard with wonder the story of his adventure in the strange lodge under the water. Together they returned to their village. They and their friends buried the bones of Slender Woman, but the necklace and earrings Thunder Medicine kept as a symbol of his mysterious power. Because of this experience he was revered as one of the most powerful medicine men of his day.

❈

Long Hair, Great Medicine Man of the Crows

CHIEF LONG HAIR was the first to sign the Crows' first treaty with the United States—in 1825. When the fur trader and trapper Zenas Leonard met him in 1834, he was "quite a venerable old man of 75 or 80 years of age," who "worships nothing but his hair, which is regularly combed and carefully folded up every morning into a roll about three feet long by the principal warriors of his tribe."

Leonard and Prince Maximilian estimated the length of his hair at about ten feet. Catlin recorded that two traders, Sublette and Campbell, who had lived in the chief's "hospitable lodge for months . . . had measured his hair by correct means and found it to be 10 feet and 7 inches in length."

"This cumbersome bunch of hair," wrote the fur trader Denig, "he rolled into two large balls and carried them in front of his saddle while riding. When on foot, the balls were attached to his girdle."

"On any great parade or similar occasion," recorded Catlin, "his pride is to unfold it, oil it with bear's grease and let it drag behind him; some three or four feet of it spread out upon the grass, and black and shiny like a raven's wing."

Chief Long Hair was an old man when the narrator of the following story, Little Face, was young.

N OT MANY YEARS AGO, there lived in the Crow nation a boy who was always boasting about what he would do when he became a man. He seemed to have no more ability than other boys of his age, but he was always saying that he would some day be a great chief and a great medicine man. His people laughed at him and called him Fool-boy. They ridiculed him also because his hair was very short, so short that, among the Crows, he seemed to have almost no hair at all.

As Fool-boy approached manhood, he spent long periods in the mountains alone, longer than most boys did. He was eager to learn, from his dreams and visions, what would be his special power and what would be his medicine. After a while he told his people that a spirit had given him a perfect medicine and at the same time had informed him that it would guide him to victory in battle and to wisdom in council.

"In time," he continued, "I will be the most important man in the tribe. As proof, the spirit will send a sign that all of you will see. Then you will know that what I have spoken is true."

Again the people laughed at him. "If what you say is true," they taunted, "why don't you take the pipe and lead a party to war? If your power is as strong as you say it is, why don't you bring home scalps and horses and captives? These are signs of bravery and of great power."

"I shall go to war," replied Fool-boy. "But I was told in my dreams to think of only the Sioux and the Blackfeet as enemies. All other tribes are to be my friends. I go now against the Sioux, and when I return I shall bring something with me to prove that my medicine is strong."

Then he made up a war party and left the village. A few days later, on the banks of the North Platte River, he surprised several lodges of Sioux and killed all the people except a boy and a girl. He and his party returned in triumph, bringing many scalps and the two captives. Soon he made a second expedition and brought another boy as his captive and slave.

Great was the wonder in the village that Fool-boy had done so well. While they were marveling and were praising him, a sign appeared, the sign that the spirit had promised him in his dreams: Fool-boy's hair suddenly began to grow! Before long, it hung round his shoulders in a heavy brown cloud.

"This is the sign I told you of," he explained. "But it has only begun to grow, as you will see."

"Surely he has spoken the truth," the people began to say. "Truly he was given a strong medicine."

Soon his hair was waist length. In a short time it almost reached his feet. Then the people no longer called him by scornful names. They had called him Fool-boy, First-born Calf, and Feather-on-the-side-of-the-Head. But now they named him *Is-she-u-huts-ki-tu*, meaning "Long Hair." And Long Hair he was for the rest of his life.

When his hair began to touch the ground, he did it up in a bundle. But still it grew, and every little while he had to roll it again. When it stopped growing, it was one hundred and one hand-breadths long, and this length it remained for the rest of his life.

Long Hair continued to be successful in battle. After a battle with the Piegans, he brought back many scalps and also a captive girl. Now he had two captive boys to herd his horses and his father's horses; he had two captive girls to help his mother with her work. Again and again he was foremost in battle. Never had such a warrior been seen among the Crows.

As a medicine man, he was equally famous. He would not tell his people what his medicine was, but it was so strong that whatever he prophesied came true and whatever he attempted he accomplished.

One time a party of unknown Indians drove off some of the Crows' horses. Then Long Hair gathered some of the earth from a mole hill and with it formed a circle on the ground. In the circle he made a pile of buffalo chips and set them on fire. Placing his pipe in his mouth, he swept the bowl around in a circle, lighted it at the fire, and took several whiffs.

"Now go in that direction," he said to his warriors. "You will find your enemies sitting down. I have stopped them with my power, and they can go no farther until we have taken our horses from them."

Going where he pointed, his men found the Piegans sitting down, as he had said. The Crows secured all their horses and killed two men before their enemies escaped.

Many such deeds Long Hair performed. If he could get some article dropped by the enemy, he could place a charm upon it so that they could not possibly escape from the Crow warriors.

One time, Long Hair made the largest lodge the Crows had ever seen. The upper half was painted red, and the lower half in red and white stripes two feet wide. The two poles that held the smoke wings were painted red except the part that touched the wings. At the bottom of each of these poles was placed a large bundle of sweet grass, and the whole lodge was scented with beaver bait.

The first time that it was pitched, many people gathered around it, all amazed at its great size.

"Watch the lodge," said Long Hair, when everything was ready. "Watch closely, and you will see something worth seeing."

He then went into the lodge. Soon after, the people saw smoke coming from the bottom of each of the poles that held the smoke wings. The smoke rose in two long spiral lines till the top of it reached the clouds, the lower end still resting upon the lodge. At the same time the two bunches of sweet grass rose into the air and ascended slowly until they were lost in the clouds. All the people watched in wonder.

By many such signs did Long Hair make his people realize his power as a medicine man.

When he became an old man and knew that he would soon die, he made a prophecy to his people.

"There are three things," he said, "that will come to pass. First, a darkness will come that is longer than ever was known on the earth before. Next, the wolves will become so numerous that they will fill the villages of the Crows and will devour horses before the eyes of the owners. Last, the white men, whom you have seen in small numbers, will swarm over the land of the Crows in such numbers as you can not imagine. Afterward, the Crows will decay and will never again be as powerful as they have been in the past."

After Long Hair died and was buried, only a few people remembered the prophecy he had made. But one morning when the women were cooking breakfast, when the boys were loosening the horses and driving them out to graze, the sun began to disappear in the sky. Before long, even though it was yet morning, darkness was thick upon the land. Many people were terrified and began to cry out, "The end of the world is at hand. All of us will perish."

But someone remembered the great medicine man's prophecy. "This is the long darkness that Long Hair told us would come," he said. "We shall not die. Now we know that his words were true. We know that two other things will come to pass, which we are to see before we perish from the earth."

After a while the sun appeared again, and all was as it had been before.

Many snows later, the Crows were camped in several villages on Tongue River, Big Horn, and Bitter Grass. It was a severe winter, and soon the Crows saw more wolves around them than they had ever seen before. The hungry animals covered the land and soon began to attack and eat the horses grazing on the prairie. When the Crows went out of their lodges in the morning, they found wolves lying beside their doors. At other places in the villages were wolves as tame as dogs. The Indians were forced to keep their horses tied near at hand and then stand nearby with clubs. But in spite of all they could do, the wolves were so numerous that they devoured almost all of the horses in every village. When spring came, only a few horses were left. Thus the second prophecy of Long Hair came to pass.

After many years, the Crows one day saw a long train of wagons coming across the plains, along the eastern slope of the mountains. Sitting in the wagons and walking beside them were white people—men, women, and children. Soon afterward, another band of Crows found similar trains coming from the southeast of the mountains. Then they saw steamboats loaded with white people come up the Missouri River, and in the country north of them white people soon outnumbered the Crows.

All that Long Hair had prophesied had now come true. In death, as well as in life, he had given proof of his wonderful powers. The Crow people now reverence him as the greatest man of their nation, for he was great in war and great in spirit power.

✾

Defiance at Yellowstone Falls

THE FOLLOWING INCIDENT is said to have occurred at some time during the struggles between the Crows and the United States Army over what the Crows considered their territory. The lower cascade in the Yellowstone River, 308 feet high, seems to fall directly out of the forest that grows down to the brink on each side of the canyon.

THE INDIANS WERE AFRAID of the geyser area of what is now Yellowstone Park; they believed that in the spouting water and the hissing steam they heard the voices of evil spirits. But the mountains at the head of Yellowstone River they considered to be the crest of the world, from which they could see into the next world. They loved this high country in which their fathers and grandfathers had hunted. And so, when they were driven back from the white settlements, a band of Crow warriors took refuge along the upper Yellowstone.

But even there the soldiers pursued them, determined to avenge the deeds of the Indian warriors. When only a few of the Crow band remained alive, when only a few had escaped the bullets of the white warriors, they gathered at the head of the Grand Canyon of the Yellowstone River. There they decided to seek death in their own way rather than be shot or be taken captive.

From the trees beside the river they built a raft and placed it at the foot of the upper falls. For a few days they enjoyed the peace their fathers had enjoyed there in earlier times. But one morning they again heard the crack of the white warriors' rifles. The time had come for them to go to death as they had planned.

Taking their places on the raft, they pushed it toward the middle of the stream. If they had any thought of crossing to the opposite side, the rapid current changed it. The few Indians who had guns shot them, but they had little effect on the white men standing on the shore. Too amazed or awed to shoot again, the soldiers watched the swiftly moving raft. It turned and pitched and whirled, and then whirled on faster and faster down the river.

Chanting their death songs, the Indians turned their faces toward their enemy and looked upon them with defiance. The triumphant death chant, the rush of the rapids, and the distant booming of the cascade below made a combination of blood-chilling sounds. The white soldiers, hardened though they were, shuddered.

Soon the raft was between the walls of the narrow canyon, its colors brilliant in the noonday sun. There was no escape now from the death the men had decided upon. Like a race horse, the raft galloped through the white foam. As it tipped for the final descent, the Indians shouted a cry of triumph.

Then foam and mist blotted out all signs of life in the river. The Crow warriors had met death without the help of the white warriors.

Source Notes

The source notes for the introductions to the seven main sections follow, as closely as possible, the order in which the materials are used. Complete data are given in the Bibliography.

I. How These Indians Lived: Driver, 15–16; Spinden (a); Turney-High (b) and (c); Teit (a); Haines (b), 13; Museum of the Plains Indians, Browning, Mont.; Linderman (b), 252, 311; Lowie (f) and (g); Ferris, 233, 245; Maximilian, XXIII, 102–11; Dorsey (b); Wissler (a); Brooks, 146; Culin (b); Dodge, 325, 336–37; Stuart, II, 51; Denig (a), 607; Belden, 269; Clark (e), 43–44; Wilson, 22–38; Alexander, 85–87; Ewers (b), 162–65.

II. The Nez Percés: Lewis and Clark, III, 77–106, and V, 13ff.; Bakeless, 313–33; Swanton, 400–403; Henshaw in Hodge, II, 65–67; McBeth, 19, 24–28; Josephy; Haines (b), 17–24, 292–99; Idaho, 41–48; Joseph; Spinden (a), (b), and (c); Curtis, VIII, 52–69; Fletcher in McBeth, 10; Clark (b), 91–96, 118–20, 193–95; Phinney, 282–85, 454–56.

"Coyote and the Monster of the Clearwater"—Variants: Armstrong, 186–89; Clark (b), 117–18, 172–75; Farrand, 148–51; Phinney, 18–129; Stuart, II, 53–56.

"The Beginning of Summer and Winter"—Williams MSS (a). Headnote: Clark (b), 169–71.

"Coyote Arranges the Seasons"—Variants: Spinden (a), 186–87, and (c), 16.

"Origin of the Sweat House"—Williams MSS (b) and (c). Headnote: Hodge, II, 660–66; Lowie (g), 168–69. Variant: Clark (b), 182–83.

"The Great Flood"—Story 2: McWhorter MSS, Folder 5. Story 3: McBeth, 260. Variants: Clark (b), 11–12, 14–15, 31–32, 42–43, 44–45.

"Origin of Fire"—Wood, 47–50.

"Preparing for the New People"—Variant: Spinden (c), 13–14.

"Origin of the Lolo Trail"—McWhorter MSS (a).

"The Guardian of Lolo Hot Springs"—McWhorter MSS (b).

"The Strange Creatures in Wallowa Lake"—Story 1: Nelson, 17. Story 2: McWhorter MSS (c). Story 3: *History of Union and Wallowa Counties*, 527. Story 4: *Wallowa County Chieftain*, n.p. Variant of story 4: Clark (b), 75–78.

III. The Flatheads, the Kalispels, and the Coeur d'Alênes: Lewis and Clark, III, 52–53; Thompson, 218–20; Cox, 102, 121; Ferris, 73; Swanton, 393–95, 399–400, 411–12; De Smet; Turney-High (b); Teit (a), 184–86, 387; Teit (c), 122; Mengarini; Clark (b), 117–18; McDermott.

"In the Beginning"—Mengarini.

"Origin of the Moon and the Sun"—Curtis, VII, 97–99. Variant: Teit (c), 123–24.

"Creation of the Red and the White Races"—Whealdon MSS. Headnote: Lewis and Clark, VII, 148.

"Origin of Death"—Curtis, VII, 95–97.

"Medicine Tree Hill"—Irvine. Headnote: Stuart, II, 41.

"The Ram's Horn Tree"—Headnote: Ross, II, 18–19; Weisel.

"How Missoula Got Its Name"—Stone (a), (b), 181–86, and (c), 9. Variants of the first part: McDermott, 240–42; Teit (c), 115–16.

"Why There Are No Salmon in Lolo Creek"—Variant: Wheeler, II, 79–80.

"Coyote's Prophecy Concerning Yellowstone Park"—Complete tale: Clark (g). Headnote: Ferris, 205–206.

"The Great Flood in the Flathead Country"—McWhorter MSS (c).

"Sheep Face Mountain"—Whealdon MSS.

"The Mystery People of Flathead Lake"—Whealdon MSS. Footnote: Turney-High (b), 18–21, 11–12.

"Burning Star Jumps into the Lake"—Whealdon MSS and personal letter.

"The Bluejay Ceremonial Dance"—Whealdon MSS. Headnote: Turney-High (a), 103, and (b), 39–41.

"Bluejay Brings the Chinook Wind"—This and the next five stories are from the Whealdon MSS. Harry Burland and Thomas Eulopson were Whealdon's interpreters. His informants included the following Kalispel-Flatheads: Alex Beaverhead, Eneas Conko, John Delaware, Louise Finley, David Finley, Joseph and Tom MacDonald, Chief Moses Michell, Blind Michell, Charley Michell, Domicie Michell, Antoine Morigeau, Philip Pierre, Quequesah, Lassau Redhorn, Francois Skyema, and Mrs. Allen Sloan.

"Star Myths"—Teit (a), 178–79.

"Water Mysteries"—Stories 1 and 2: Teit (a), 181–83, and (c), 127–28; Story 3: *Idaho Lore*, 145.

"A Legend of Spirit Lake"—Baltimore. Headnote and variant: *Idaho Lore*, 145–46.

"Giants and Tree Men"—Teit (a), 180–81.

"The Little People"—Story 1: Turney-High (b), 13. Story 2: Teit (a), 180.

"Spirit Power from the Little People"—Turney-High (b), 33–34. Headnote: Clark (b), 109–10.

"The Vision before the Battle"—MacDonald.

"Lewis and Clark Among the Flatheads"—Story 2: Wheeler, II, 65–68. Headnote: Lewis and Clark, VII, 149–50.

IV. THE KUTENAIS: Cox, 263–64; De Smet, 765, 796–97; Swanton, 392–96; Chamberlain (b); Turney-High (c); Mason; Curtis, VII, 117–55; Boas (b) and (c); Stevens, XII, 150; Linderman (a).

"The Animals and the Sun"—Boas (b), 67–69.

"The Great Flood in the Kutenai Country"—Curtis, VII, 146–47.

"A Visit to the Sky World"—Boas (b), 73–83, 288–90. Variants: Clark (b), 151–52, 158–60, 189–92; (e), 32–33.

"The Mysteries in Flathead Lake"—Headnote: Nez Percé legend, Otis Halfmoon; Sarcee, Clark (e), 92–93; Blackfeet, Cecile Blackboy MSS.

"Origin of Flathead River"—Chapman MS.

"Blacktail Deer Dance"—Curtis, VII, 143–46; Wissler and Duvall, 157–58.

V. THE SHOSHONIS AND THE BANNOCKS: Lewis and Clark, I, 287; II, 329; and III, 47–48; Trenholm and Carley; Swanton, 398–99, 403–12; Henshaw in Hodge, I, 129–30; and II, 556–57; Haines (a); Liljeblad and Madsen, personal letters; Madsen; Nash MS and personal interview; Olden, 37–41; St. Clair, 272–73; Lowie (a); Overholt MSS (a); Rees MSS; Dixey, personal interview; *Idaho*, 243; Harrington, personal interview and letter.

"The Fire, the Flood, and the Creation of the World"—Liljeblad MS. Variants: Clark (e), 1–3, 7–9.

"The Theft of Fire"—Lowie (a), 244–46.

"Rabbit and the Sun"—Overholt MSS (c), 1–2.

"The Little People"—Story 1: Landmichl MSS, 3; Olden, 8, 33–34; Culin (a), 17; Lowie (a), 234–35; Overholt MSS (a), 19; Mamie Tyler, personal interview. Story 2: Stuart, II, 56–58.

"The Shoshoni Sun Dance"—St. Clair MS. Part of headnote: Lowie (d).

"Legend of the Old Indian Hunter"—Harrington MSS (a).

"The Indian Spirit at Mesa Falls"—Harrington MSS (a).

"The Great Medicine Man and the Spring"—Harrington MSS (b) and personal interview.

"Craters of the Moon"—Harrington MSS (a). Headnote: *Idaho*, 267.

"The Lava Beds of the Snake River"—Jones. Headnote: *Idaho*, 210–11.

"The Mysteries in Bull Lake"—Story 1. Van Derveer MS. Stories 2 and 3: Overholt MSS (d), 22–24.

"Origin of the Big Horn River"—Johnson MS.

"Origin of Big Horn Hot Springs"—Johnson MS. Headnote: Walker, 191.

"Legend of the Sweet and Bitter Springs"—Ruxton, 243–47.

"Lewis and Clark among the Shoshonis"—Ferris, 75–78.

"The Story of Sacajawea"—Overholt MSS (b); David, 307–13; Rees. Headnote: Roberts; Eastman MS; Hebard; Letters, 638–39. (Parallels in the Lewis and Clark journals: De Voto, 63, 80, 92–93, 109–10, 135–52, 171, 202–29, 249–50, 256–57, 301, 367, 448–49.)

VI. The Arapahos, the Gros Ventres, and the Blackfeet: Swanton, 384–86, 389–90, 395–98; Curtis, VI, 137–50; Mooney (a), 953–58, (b) and (c); Mooney and Thomas; Scott, 558–59; Ferris, 252; Maximilian, XXIII, 91; Bakeless, 337–42; De Smet, 233, 318; Stanley, 449; Ewers (a) and (b); McClintock.

"Creation of the World"—Kroeber (b), 59–61.

"Origin of the Flat-Pipe"—Olden, 41–42; Ziegler, 61–62. Headnote: Curtis, VI, 140–41; Kroeber (a), 309–10; Olden, 45.

"Origin of the Arapaho Sun Dance"—Dorsey (a).

"The Beginning of Many Things"—Dorsey and Kroeber, 7–8.

"The Little People"—Olden, 8–12; Culin (a), 17–18.

"Old Man and the Beginning of the World"—Grinnell (a), 137–43, 257–58.

"Old Man and Old Woman"—Wissler and Duvall, 19–21.

"Old Man and the Roasted Squirrels"—McClintock, 338–40; Wissler and Duvall, 25–27.

"Scar Face and the Sun Dance"—Wissler and Duvall, 61–65; Wissler (b), 269–70. Variant: McClintock, 490–500; Clark (e), 63–67. The ceremony: Ewers (b), 174–84.

"Origin of the Medicine Pipe"—Wissler and Duvall, 89–90.

"Origin of the Beaver Medicine Bundle"—McClintock, 76–124. Variant: Wissler and Duvall, 74–78.

"Origin of the Sacred Buffalo Horn"—*Indians at Work*, 35–36.

"Legend of the Snow Tipi"—McClintock, 132–38.

"The Yellow Tipi and Father De Smet"—McClintock, 162–66.

"The Bunched Stars"—Wissler and Duvall, 71–72. Variant: McClintock, 490. Headnote: Clark (b), 155–56; (e), 71–76; Wissler and Duvall, 12.

"Sleeping Gros Ventres"—Harrington MS (b) and personal letter.

"Chief Mountain"—Holz and Bemis, 194–96.

"Legend of Writing Stone"—Blackboy MS C–137.

"First Buffalo Stone"—Michelson, 246–47; Grinnell (a), 124–26. Headnote: Museum of the Plains Indians, Browning, Mont.

"How the Piegans Got Their First Horses"—Vaughn, 359–401.

"Prophecy of the Old Blackfoot"—Sanderville, BAE MS 4076.

VII. The Crows, the Sioux, and the Assiniboines: Lewis and Clark, I, 130, and V, 297; Maximilian, XXII, 346–51; Ferris, 244–45; Catlin, I, 50–57; Thomas and Swanton in Hodge, II, 579; Swanton, 387–88, 390–91; Bradley (b), 210–22; Lowie (b), (c), (e), (f), and (g), 172–78; Curtis, IV, 61–67; Linderman (b), 35–51, 207–54; Simms; Long; Clark (e), 10–13.

"Creation of the Crow World"—Simms, 281–82. Variants: Lowie (e), 14–19, and (f), 122–32.

"How Elder Brother Helped the Assiniboines"—Lowie (b), 129–30.

"Old Man Coyote and the Theft of Summer"—Simms, 282–84. Variants: Lowie (b); Long, 3–7.

"The Seven Stars"—Lowie (b), 177.

"Great Serpent in the Missouri"—Maximilian, XXIII, 380–82.

"Man Who Turned into a Monster"—Denig (a), 613–17.

"Monster in Missouri River"—Dorsey MS.

"The Spirits of the Rivers"—Bradley (c), 296–97.

"Legends of Lake De Smet"—McPherren MSS. Headnote: *Wyoming*, 272–73.

"Red Plume and the Medicine Wheel"—Mokler, 204–206. Headnote: Grinnell (b); Wilmesmeier MS; *Wyoming*, 51–52, 380–81.

"The Origin of the Devils Tower"—Mokler, 202–204. Headnote: *Devils Tower National Monument*.

"Traditions of the Black Hills"—Story 1: Tallent, 113–14; *Legends of the Mighty Sioux*, 109–10. Story 2: Rosen, 264. Story 3: Rosen, 250. Story 4: Tallent, 645.

"Origin of the Badlands"—*Indian School Journal*. Headnote: *Montana*, 365.

"The Sun, the Wolf, and the Buffaloes"—Bradley (b), 213–15.

"How the Crows Got Their First Horses"—Bradley (c), 298–99.

"Thunder Medicine's Adventure in Yellowstone River"—Bradley (b), 232–36.

"Long Hair, Great Medicine Man of the Crows"—Bradley (b), 224–28. Headnote: Denig (b), 63; Catlin, I, 56–57.

"Defiance at Yellowstone Falls"—Skinner, II, 204–206.

Bibliography

To avoid excessive repetition, the following abbreviations have been used:

APAMNH   *Anthropological Papers*, American Museum of Natural History

BAE   Bureau of American Ethnology, Smithsonian Institution

FCMAS   Field Columbian Museum Anthropological Series

JAFL   *Journal of American Folklore*

MAAA   *Memoirs* of the American Anthropological Association

MAFS   *Memoirs* of the American Folklore Society

Wyo. State   Manuscript File, Wyoming State Archives and Historical Department, Cheyenne, Wyo.

I. ORAL SOURCES

<table>
<tr><td></td><td>Pat Shea, of the United States Forest Service, Flathead Reservation, Mont.</td></tr>
<tr><td>The Blackfeet:</td><td>Percy Creighton
Chewing Blackbones (interpreted by Mary Chief Coward)</td></tr>
<tr><td>The Coeur d'Alênes:</td><td>Julia Nicodemus
Stanislaus Aripa</td></tr>
<tr><td>The Flatheads:</td><td>Pierre Pichette
Sophie Moiese (interpreted by Louis Pierre)</td></tr>
<tr><td>The Kalispels:</td><td>Nick Lassah
Eneas Conko</td></tr>
</table>

The Kutenais: William Gingrass

        Madeline Lefthand (interpreted by Adeline Matthias)

        Mary Susan Finley

The Nez Percés: Otis Halfmoon

        Lucy Armstrong Isaac

        Elizabeth Wilson

        Lizzie Lowery (interpreted by Oliver Frank)

        Sam Slickpoo

The Shoshonis: Ralph Dixey

        Mamie Tyler (interpreted by Viola Hill)

2. MANUSCRIPT MATERIALS

Blackboy, Cecile. "Blackfeet Tales." Collected for the Work Projects Administration. Used by permission of Claude Schaeffer, curator (1953) of the Museum of the Plains Indians, Browning, Mont.

Chapman, Robert H. "Flathead Lake and Beaver." (Kutenai or Salish, 1900.) BAE MS 3777.

Dorsey, George. "Monster in the Missouri River." BAE MS 3163, p. 37½.

Eastman, Charles. "Selected Documents Relating to the Burial of Sacajawea." Records of the Bureau of Indian Affairs, 34836–22–034 Shoshoni, The National Archives, Washington, D. C.

Harrington, J. A. (a) Legends dictated by Harrington and written by Edna Harrington and Gretta Northey (1927), Public Library, Idaho Falls, Idaho.

―――. (b) Personal collection, Boise, Idaho.

Johnson, Orville. "The Big Horn Basin Legends." Wyo. State.

Landmichl, L. S. "Ancient History of the North American Indians." Wyo. State.

Liljeblad, Sven. Bannock Creation Myth. Personal collection.

McPherren, Ida. "Indian Legends of Lake De Smet." Wyo. State.

McWhorter, Lucullus. L. V. McWhorter Manuscript Collection, Washington State University Library Archives: (a) "Legendary Origin of the Lolo Trail (Nez Percé)." 1516, No. 27.

————. (b) "Legend of Wallowa Lake. Peo-peo Tholekt." 1516, No. 28.

————. (c) "The Rattlesnake as Guardian of Good Water Springs." 1516, No. 29.

————. (d) "Nez Percé Legend of the Lolo Hot Spring. Horse Blanket. 1926." 1516, No. 30.

————. (e) "Flathead Tradition of a Flood." 1515, No. 17.

————. (f) "Nez Percé Tradition of a Flood." Folder 5.

Nash, Alice B. "Old Indian Traditions: the Shoshones." Personal collection of a former missionary on the Wind River Reservation.

Overholt, Helen (teacher and editor, Wind River Community Day School, Fort Washakie, Wyo.) (a) "The Warm Valley Folk." (1937)

————. (b) "The Shoshones." (n.d.)

————. (c) "Legends and Near Legends." (n.d.)

————. (d) "Some Wyoming Place Names." (n.d.)

Rees, John. Manuscript collection, Idaho Historical Society, Boise, Idaho: (a) "Origin of Bannocks, told by Old Chief Tihee."

————. (b) "Sacajawea."

St. Clair, Lynn. "The So-Called Sun Dance, which the Shoshones Call: Da-g-oo Wi-no-de." L. L. Newton Collection, Acc. 17, University of Wyoming Archives and Western History Department, Laramie, Wyo.

Sanderville, Richard (Chief Bull). "Old Indian Prophecy Fulfilled." (Blackfoot, 1934). BAE MS 4076.

Van Derveer, Nellie H. "Bull Lake." Wyo. State.

Whealdon, Bon. Personal collection. Hot Springs, Mont.

Williams, Lewis. (a) "Summer versus Winter." (Nez Percé, 1896). BAE MS 683a, Legend 3; and MS 683b.

————. (b) "All the People Scatter—Origin of the Sweat House." BAE MS 683a, Legend 8.

————. (c) "Sweat Houses." BAE MS 685.

Wilmesmeier, Robert. "The Medicine Wheel." Wyo. State.

3. PRINTED MATERIALS

Alexander, Hartley B. *North American.* Ed. by L. H. Gray. Vol. X of *The Mythology of All Races.* Boston, Marshall Jones Co., 1916.

Armstrong, Ralph. "Some Nez Percé Traditions Told by Chief Armstrong," ed. by Ella E. Clark for the *Oregon Historical Quarterly,* Vol. LIII (1952), 181–91.

Bakeless, John. *Lewis and Clark: Partners in Discovery.* New York, William Morrow & Co., 1947.

Baker, Paul E. *The Forgotten Kutenai.* Boise, Mountain States Press, 1955.

Baltimore, J. M. "Legend of Spirit Lake," *The State,* Vol. III (March 20, 1899), 74–75.

Belden, George P. *The White Chief.* Ed. by James S. Brisbin. Cincinnati, C. F. Vent, 1872.

Boas, Franz, ed. (a) *Folk-Tales of Salishan and Sahaptin Tribes.* MAFS, Vol. XI (1917).

———. (b) *Kutenai Tales,* together with texts collected by Alexander Chamberlain, BAE Bulletin 59 (1918).

Bradley, James A. (a) "The Journal of James A. Bradley," *Contributions to the Historical Society of Montana,* Vol. III (1896), 140–228.

———. (b) "Bradley Manuscript -F," *ibid.,* Vol. VIII (1917), 197–250.

———. (c) "Indian Traditions," *ibid.,* Vol. IX (1923), 288–99.

Brooks, Elbridge S. *The Story of the American Indian.* Boston, Lothrop, 1887.

Catlin, George. *North American Indians: Being Letters and Notes on Their Manners, Customs, and Conditions Written during Eight Years' Travel amongst the Wildest Tribes of Indians in North America, 1832–1839.* 2 vols. Edinburgh, John Grant, 1926.

Chamberlain, Alexander. (a) *The Kootenay Indians.* Annual Archeological Report, Ontario (1905), 177–87.

———. (b) "Kutenai," in Hodge, I, 740–42.

Clark, Ella E. (a) "Watkuese and Lewis and Clark," *Western Folklore,* Vol. XII (July, 1953), 175–78.

――――. (b) *Indian Legends of the Pacific Northwest*. Berkeley, University of California Press, 1953. (Paperback, 1958)

――――. (c) "Sesquicentennial Remembrances: The Lewis and Clark Expedition as Seen through the Eyes of the Indians of the Northern Rocky Mountains," *Montana, the Magazine of Western History* (Spring, 1955), 31–39.

――――. (d) "Mission in the Wilderness," *ibid.*, Vol. V (Winter, 1955), 51–57.

――――. (e) *Indian Legends of Canada*. Toronto, McClelland and Stewart, 1960.

――――. (f) "Sacajawea Loyally Served Lewis and Clark," *Inland Empire Magazine, the Spokesman Review* (October 23, 1955), 8–9.

――――. (g) "How Coyote Became a Sachem," *Northwest Review*, No. 6 (Summer, 1963), 21–26.

Cox, Ross. *The Columbia River, or Scenes and Adventures during a Residence of Six Years on the Western Side of the Rocky Mountains*. Ed. by Edgar and Jane Stewart. Norman, University of Oklahoma Press, 1957.

Culin, Stewart. (a) "A Summer Trip among the Western Indians," *Bulletin of the Free Museum of Science and Art*, Vol. III (Philadelphia, University of Pennsylvania, 1901), 1–22.

――――. (b) *Games of the North American Indians. BAE Twenty-fourth Annual Report* (1902–1903). Washington, 1907.

Curtis, Edward S. *The North American Indian*. 20 vols. Cambridge, Mass., University Press, 1907–30. Vols. IV, VI, VII, VIII.

David, Robert. *Finn Burnett: Frontiersman*. Glendale, Calif., The Arthur H. Clark Co., 1937.

Denig, Edwin T. (a) "Indian Tribes of the Upper Missouri," ed. by J. N. B. Hewitt. *BAE Forty-sixth Annual Report* (1928–29), 375–628.

――――. (b) "Of the Crow Nation," ed. by J. C. Ewers. *BAE Anthropological Paper No. 33, Bulletin 151*. Washington, 1907.

De Smet, Pierre Jean. *Life, Letters, and Travels of Father Pierre Jean de Smet, S. J., 1801–1873*. Ed. by H. M. Chittenden and A. T. Richardson. 4 vols. New York, Harper, 1905.

Devils Tower National Monument. Washington, D. C., National Park Service, United States Department of the Interior, n.d.

De Voto, Bernard, ed. *The Journals of Lewis and Clark.* Boston, Houghton Mifflin, 1953.

Dodge, Richard Irving. *Our Wild Indians: Thirty-Three Years of Personal Experiences among the Red Men of the Great West.* Hartford, Conn., A. D. Worthington & Co., 1883.

Dorsey, George. (a) *The Arapaho Sun Dance; the Ceremony of the Offerings Lodge.* FCMAS, IV (Chicago, 1903).

———. (b) "The Sun Dance," in Hodge, II, 649–52.

Dorsey, George, and A. L. Kroeber. *Traditions of the Arapaho.* FCMAS, Vol. V (Chicago, 1903), 1–475.

Driver, Harold E. *Indians of North America.* Chicago, University of Chicago Press, 1961.

Ewers, John C. (a) *The Story of the Blackfeet. Indian Life and Customs* Pamphlet-6, Bureau of Indian Affairs, Department of the Interior, 1952.

———. (b) *The Blackfeet: Raiders on the Northwestern Plains.* Norman, University of Oklahoma Press, 1958.

Farrand, Livingston. "Sahaptin Tales," in Boas (a), 135–79.

Ferris, Warren Angus. *Life in the Rocky Mountains, 1830–1835.* Ed. by H. S. Auerbach and J. C. Alter. Salt Lake City, Rocky Mountain Bookshop, 1940.

Gibbs, George. "George Gibbs' Account of Indian Mythology in Oregon and Washington Territories, ed. by Ella E. Clark for the *Oregon Historical Quarterly*, Part I, Vol. LVI (December, 1955), 293–325; and Part II, Vol. LVII (June, 1956), 125–67.

Grinnell, George B. (a) *Blackfoot Lodge Tales: The Story of a Prairie People.* New York, Scribner's, 1892 and 1920.

———. (b) "The Medicine Wheel," *American Anthropologist* (n.s.), Vol. XXIV (1922), 299–310.

Haines, Francis. (a) "The Northward Spread of Horses to the Plains Indians," *American Anthropologist*, Vol. XL (1938), 429–37.

———. (b) *The Nez Percés.* Norman, University of Oklahoma Press, 1955.

Haywood, Charles. *A Bibliography of North American Folklore and Folksong.* New York, Greenberg Publisher, 1951.

Hebard, Grace. *Sacajawea, a Guide and Interpreter of the Lewis and Clark Expedition.* Glendale, Calif., The Arthur H. Clark Co., 1933.

Henshaw, H. W. (a) "Shoshoni," in Hodge, I, 556–57.

———. (b) "Sweating and Sweat Houses," *ibid.*, 660–62.

———, and Cyrus Thomas. "Bannock," in Hodge, Vol. I, 129–30.

———, and Livingston Farrand, "Nez Percés," in Hodge, Vol. II, 65–67.

History of Union and Wallowa Counties (Oregon). Spokane, Wash., Western Historical Publishing Company, 1902.

Hodge, Frederick W., ed. *Handbook of American Indians North of Mexico.* 2 vols. *BAE Bulletin 30.* Washington, Government Printing Office, 1907–10.

Holtz, Mathilde, and Kathering Bemis. *Glacier National Park: Its Trails and Treasures.* New York, George H. Doran, 1917.

Idaho: A Guide in Word and Picture. American Guide Series. Compiled by the Federal Writers' Project of the Works Progress Administration. Caldwell, Idaho, Caxton Printers, 1937.

Idaho Lore. American Guide Series. Prepared by the Federal Writers' Project of the Works Progress Administration. Caldwell, Caxton Printers, 1937.

Indians at Work, Bureau of Indian Affairs, Department of Interior, Vol. V (March 1, 1938), 35–36.

Indian School Journal, Chilocco Indian School, Chilocco, Oklahoma (February 26, 1937), 8 (reprinted from *American Indian Bulletin,* n.d.).

Irvine, Caleb. "Medicine Tree-Hill," *Contributions to the Historical Society of Montana*, VI (1907), 472–73.

Jones, E. W. "Lava Beds of the Snake River in Indian Tradition," *West Shore*, Vol. XII (April, 1886), 116–17.

Joseph, Chief. "The Retreat of the Nez Percés," reprinted in *Cry of the Thunderbird: The American Indian's Own Story.* Ed. by Charles Hamilton. New York, Macmillan, 1951.

Josephy, Alvin M. "The Naming of the Nez Percés," *Montana Magazine of Western History*, Vol. V (October, 1955), 1–8.

Kroeber, Alfred. (a) *The Arapaho, Bulletin*, American Museum of Natural History. New York, Vol. XVIII, 1902–1904.

———. (b) "Gros Ventres Myths and Tales," *APAMNH*, Vol. I (1907), 55–139.

La Farge, Oliver. "Popular Misconceptions," in *American Indians* (pp. 22–27), ed. by Walter M. Daniels. New York, H. W. Wilson Co., 1957.

Leach, Maria, ed. *Standard Dictionary of Folklore, Mythology, and Legend*. 2 vols. New York, Funk and Wagnalls, 1949.

Legends of the Mighty Sioux. Comp. by workers of the South Dakota Writers' Project of the Work Projects Administration. Chicago, Albert Whitney Co., 1941.

Letters of the Lewis and Clark Expedition with Related Documents, 1783–1854. Ed. by Donald Jackson. Urbana, University of Illinois Press, 1962.

Lewis, Meriwether, and William Clark. *Original Journals of the Lewis and Clark Expedition, 1804–1806*. Ed. by R. G. Thwaites. 8 vols. New York, Dodd, Mead & Co., 1904–1905.

———. *Journals*. See De Voto.

Liljeblad, Sven. *Indian Peoples in Idaho*. Pocatello, Idaho State College, 1957.

Linderman, Frank. (a) *Kootenai Why Stories*. New York, Scribner, 1926.

———. (b) *American: The Life Story of a Great Indian, Plenty-Coups, Chief of the Crows*. New York, The John Day Co., 1930.

———. (c). *Old Man Coyote*. New York, John Day, Co., 1931.

Long, James Larpenteur. *The Assiniboines: From the Accounts of the Old Ones to First Boy (James Larpenteur Long)*. Ed. by Michael Stephen Kennedy. Norman, University of Oklahoma Press, 1961.

Lowie, Robert H. (a) "The Northern Shoshone," *APAMNH*, Vol. II (1908–1909), 163–306.

———. (b) "The Assiniboine," *ibid.*, Vol. IV (1909–10), 1–270.

———. (c) "The Sun Dance of the Crow Indians," *ibid.*, Vol. XVI (1915), 1–50.

———. (d) "Wind River Shoshone Dance," *ibid.*, Vol. XVI (1919), 393–94.

———. (e) "Myths and Traditions of the Crow Indians," *ibid.*, Vol. XXV (1918), 1–308.

———. (f) *The Crow Indians.* New York, Farrar and Rinehart, 1935. (Paperback, 1956)

———. (g) *Indians of the Plains. (Anthropological Handbook No. 1,* published for the American Museum of Natural History.) New York, McGraw-Hill Book Co., 1954.

McBeth, Kate. *The Nez Percés since Lewis and Clark.* New York and Chicago, F. H. Revell Co., 1908.

McClintock, Walter. *The Old North Trail; or Life, Legends, and Religion of the Blackfeet Indians.* London, Macmillan, 1910.

McDermott, Louisa. "Folklore of the Flathead Indians of Idaho," *JAFL*, Vol. XIV (1901), 240–51.

MacDonald, Angus. "The Vision before the Battle," *New Northwest* (May 24, 1878). (In Montana State Historical Archives, Helena.)

McLean, John. (a) "Blackfoot Indian Legends," *JAFL*, Vol. III (1890), 296–98.

———. (b) *Canadian Savage Folk: The Native Tribes of Canada.* Toronto, W. Briggs, 1896.

Madsen, Brigham. *The Bannocks of Idaho.* Caldwell, Caxton, 1958.

Mason, Otis. "Pointed Bark Canoes of the Kutenai and Amur," United States National Museum *Annual Report* (for 1899), 1901.

Mattison, Ray H. "Devils Tower National Monument—a History," *Annals of Wyoming*, Vol. XXVIII (April, 1956), 3–20.

Maximilian, Prince of Wied. *Travels in the Interior of North America, 1832–1834.* Vols. XXII, XXIII, XXIV in Thwaites' *Early Western Travels, q.v.*

Mengarini, Gregory. In Gibbs, Vol. I, 301–304.

Michelson, Truman. "Piegan Tales," *JAFL*, Vols. XXIV (1911), 238–48; and XXIX (1916), 408–409.

Mokler, Alfred. *Transition of the West.* Chicago, R. R. Donnelly & Sons, 1927.

Montana: A State Guide Book. American Guide Series. Comp. by the Federal Writers' Project of the Work Projects Administration. New York, Hastings House, 1939.

Mooney, James. (a) "The Ghost-Dance Religion," *BAE Fourteenth Annual Report* (for 1892–93), Part 2, 653–828.

———. (b) "Arapaho," in Hodge, I, 72–74.

———. (c) "Siksika," in Hodge, II, 570–71.

Mooney, James, and Cyrus Thomas. "Assiniboin," in Hodge, I, 102–104.

Murphy, Robert F. and Yolanda, "Shoshoni-Bannock Subsistence and Society," *University of California Anthropological Records,* Vol. XVI, No. 7 (1955–61), 293–338.

Nelson, A. W. *Those Who Came First.* La Grande, Oregon, 1934.

Olden, Sarah E. *Shoshone Folklore, as Discovered from the Rev. John Roberts, on the Wind River Reservation in Wyoming.* Milwaukee, Milwaukee Publishing Company, 1923.

Pacific Railroad Report of Exploration and Surveys to Ascertain the Most Practicable and Economical Route for a Railroad from the Mississippi River to the Pacific Ocean, 1853–1855. 12 vols. Washington, Government Printing Office, 1855–60. Vols. I and XII.

Packard, R. L. "Notes on the Mythology and Religion of the Nez Percés," *JAFL,* Vol. IV (1891), 327–30.

Phinney, Archie. *Nez Percé Texts.* Columbia University *Contributions to Anthropology,* Vol. XXV (1934).

Rees, John. "The Shoshoni Contribution to Lewis and Clark," *Idaho Yesterdays,* Vol. II, No. 2 (Summer Issue, 1958), 2–13.

Reichard, Gladys. *An Analysis of Coeur d'Alêne Myths.* MAFS, Vol. 47 (1947).

Roberts, John. "The Death of Sacajawea," *Indians at Work,* Vol. II (April 1, 1935), 7–10.

Rosen, Peter. *Pa-ha-sa-ah, or the Black Hills of South Dakota.* St. Louis, Nixon Jones Printing Co., 1895.

Ross, Alexander. *The Fur Hunters of the Far West: A Narrative of*

Adventures in the Oregon and Rocky Mountains. 2 vols. London, Smith, Elder & Co., 1855. Vol. I.

Ruxton, George F. *Adventures in Mexico and the Rocky Mountains.* New York, Harper and Brothers, 1848.

St. Clair, H. H., and R. H. Lowie, "Shoshone and Comanche Tales," *JAFL,* Vol. XXII (1909), 265–82.

Schultz, James Willard. *My Life as an Indian.* New York, Doubleday, 1907.

Scott, Hugh L. "The Early History and Names of the Arapaho," *American Anthropologist* (n.s.), Vol. IX (1907), 545–60.

Simms. S. C. *Traditions of the Crows.* FCMAS, Vol. II, No. 6 (1903).

Skinner, Charles M. *Myths and Legends of Our Land.* 2 vols. Philadelphia and London, Lippincott, 1896. Vol. II.

Spinden, Herbert B. (a) *The Nez Percé Indians.* MAAA, Vol. II (1908).

———. (b) "Myths of the Nez Percé Indians," *JAFL,* Vol. XXI (1908), 13–23, 149–58.

———. (c) "Nez Percé Tales," in Boas, *Folk-Tales of Salishan and Sahaptin Tribes (q.v.),* 180–201.

Stanley, John M. "Report of John M. Stanley's Visit to the Piegan Camp at the Cypress Mountain," *Pacific Railroad Report,* Vol. I, Book I, 447–49.

Stevens, Issac I. "Isaac I. Stevens' Narrative of 1853–1855," *ibid.,* Vol. XII, Book I, 150.

Stone, Arthur. (a) "The Dragon of the Selish," *Sunday Missoulian,* Missoula, Montana (December 16, 1911).

———. (b) *Following Old Trails.* Missoula, M. J. Elrod, 1913.

———. (c) "Duncan McDonald Tells Indian Tale: Finds Origin of Missoula's Name in Selish Legend," *Tribune,* Great Falls, Montana, July 2, 1944.

Stuart, Granville. *Forty Years on the Frontier, as Seen in the Journals and Reminiscences of Granville Stuart.* Ed. by Paul Phillips. Cleveland, The Arthur H. Clark Co., 1925.

Swanton, John R. *The Indian Tribes of North America. BAE Bulletin 145* (1952).

Tallent, Annie D. *The Black Hills, the Last Hunting Grounds of the Dakotas*. St. Louis, Nixon Jones Printing Co., 1899.

Teit, James. (a) "The Salishan Tribes of the Western Plateaus," *BAE Forty-fifth Annual Report* (for 1927–28), 23–396.

———. (b) "Pend d'Oreille Tales," in Boas, *Folk-Tales of Salishan and Sahaptin Tribes (q.v.)*, 114–18.

———. (c) "Coeur d'Alêne Tales," in Boas, *ibid.*, 119–28.

Thomas, Cyrus, and J. R. Swanton, "The Siouan Family," in Hodge, Vol. I, 577–79.

Thwaites, Reuben G., ed. *Early Western Travels, 1748–1846*. 32 vols. Cleveland, The Arthur H. Clark Co., 1904–1907. Vols. XXII–XXIV and XXIX.

Thompson, David. *David Thompson's Journal Relating to Montana and Adjacent Regions*. Ed. by Catherine White. Missoula, Montana State University Press, 1950.

Trenholm, Virginia C., and Maurine Carley. *The Shoshonis: Sentinels of the Rockies*. Norman, University of Oklahoma Press, 1964.

Turney-High, H. H. (a) "The Bluejay Dance," *American Anthropologist*, Vol. XXXV (1933), 103–107.

———. (b) *The Flathead Indians of Montana*, MAAA, No. 48 (1937).

———. (c) *Ethnography of the Kutenai*, MAAA, No. 56 (1941).

Vaughn, Robert. *Then and Now; or Thirty-Six Years in the Rockies*. Minneapolis, Tribune Printing Co., 1900.

Walker, Tacetta. *Stories of Early Days in Wyoming Big Horn Basin*. Casper, Wyoming, Prairie Publishing Co., 1936.

Wallowa County Chieftain, Enterprise, Oregon, June 28, 1951.

Weisel, George. "The Ram's Horn Tree and Other Medicine Trees of the Flathead Indians," *Montana Magazine of History*, Vol. I (July, 1951), 5–13.

Wheeler, O. D. *The Trail of Lewis and Clark, 1804–1904*. 2 vols. New York and London, G. P. Putnam's Sons, 1926. Vol. II.

Wissler, Clark, and D. C. Duvall. "Mythology of the Blackfoot Indians," *APAMNH*, Vol. II (1908), 5–163.

Wissler, Clark, ed. (a) "General Introduction," *Sun Dance of the Plains Indians, APAMNH*, Vol. XVI (1921).

———. (b) "The Sun Dance of the Blackfoot Indians," *ibid.*, 223–70.

Wood, Charles E. S. *A Book of Tales, Being Some Myths of the North American Indians*. New York, Vanguard Press, 1929.

Wyoming: A Guide to Its History, Highways, and People. American Guide Series. Prepared by the Federal Writers' Projects of the Works Progress Administration. New York, Oxford University Press, 1941.

Ziegler, W. H. *Wyoming Indians*. Laramie, Wyo., 1944.

Index

The text for *Indian Legends from the Northern Rockies* has been set in 11-point Linotype Granjon. Designed by George W. Jones, Granjon draws its basic design from classic sources, but has the refinements made possible by modern methods of punch-cutting.